Making a Difference

Action Research in Middle Level Education

a volume in
The Handbook of Research in Middle Level Education

Series Editor:
Vincent A. Anfara, Jr., *University of Tennessee*

The Handbook of Research in Middle Level Education

Vincent A. Anfara, Jr., Series Editor

The Handbook of Research in Middle Level Education (2001)
edited by Vincent A. Anfara, Jr.

Middle School Curriculum, Instruction, and Assessment (2002)
edited by Vincent A. Anfara, Jr. and Sandra L. Stacki

Leaders for a Movement: Professional Preparation and Development of Middle Level Teachers and Administrators (2003)
edited by P. Gayle Andrews and Vincent A. Anfara, Jr.

Reforming Middle Level Education: Considerations for Policymakers (2004)
edited by Sue. C. Thompson

Making a Difference: Action Research in Middle Level Education (2005)
edited by Micki M. Caskey

Making a Difference

Action Research in Middle Level Education

Edited by

Micki M. Caskey
Portland State University

MIDDLE LEVEL EDUCATION RESEARCH
SPECIAL INTEREST GROUP

INFORMATION AGE
PUBLISHING

Greenwich, Connecticut • www.infoagepub.com

Library of Congress Cataloging-in-Publication Data

Making a difference : action research in middle level education /
edited by
Micki M. Caskey.
       p. cm. -- (Handbook of research in middle level education
series)
 Includes bibliographical references and index.
 ISBN 1-59311-356-0 (pbk.) -- ISBN 1-59311-357-9 (hardcover)
 1. Middle school education--United States. 2. Action research in
education--United States. 3. Educational change--United States. I.
Caskey,
Micki M. II. Series.
 LB1623.5.M24 2005
 373.236'07'2--dc22

                                        2005013192

Printed in the United States of America

MIDDLE LEVEL EDUCATION RESEARCH
SPECIAL INTEREST GROUP

The Handbook of Research in Middle Level Education is endorsed by the Middle Level Education Research Special Interest Group. The purpose of Middle Level Education Research SIG is to improve, promote, and disseminate educational research reflecting early adolescence and middle level education.

The Handbook of Research in Middle Level Education is also endorsed by the Action Research Special Interest Group. The purpose of the Action Research SIG is to encourage and actively assist education practitioners to develop their skills in applied research and professional inquiry in order to improve educational decision-making at all levels.

The Middle Level Education Research SIG and the Action Research SIG are affiliates of the American Educational Research Association.

THE HANDBOOK OF
RESEARCH IN MIDDLE LEVEL EDUCATION

Editorial Advisory Board

CONTENTS

FOREWORD

Sue Swaim

Research conducted over the past few years cites teaching and educational leadership as the two leading school-based factors affecting student learning. Based upon that information, it should not be surprising that action research is a growing segment of research within middle level education. Emily Calhoun (1994) said, "Action research is a fancy way of saying let's study what's happening at our school and decide how to make it a better place" (p. 20). Indeed, highly qualified and highly effective middle level educators are always striving to achieve this.

Action research, often conducted by school-based practitioners in collaboration with university-based colleagues, has the potential to generate genuine and sustained improvements in schools. By its design, it give educators opportunities to reflect on and assess their teaching; to explore and test new ideas, methods, and materials; to reflect with colleagues regarding their work; and to make better informed decisions about their curriculum, instruction, and assessment content and strategies. For these reasons, the *Handbook of Research in Middle Level Education, Making a Difference: Action Research in Middle Level Education*, makes an important contribution to the field. Not only can we can learn from the action research studies and resources shared in this volume, but we can also be inspired to engage in action research with our colleagues.

Making a Difference: Action Research in Middle Level Education, ix–x
Copyright © 2005 by Information Age Publishing
All rights of reproduction in any form reserved.

While there is a promising and expanding body of research regarding the positive academic growth and healthy development of young adolescents when the tenets of the middle school philosophy are implemented fully over time, it remains clear that there is a continued urgent need for more research in this area. Certainly, additional quantitative as well as qualitative studies are needed to enrich our body of knowledge.

Action research makes it possible for classroom teachers to become researchers and to seek in formal ways answers to instructional questions they face in their day-to-day work. Given the nature of education, teacher research can serve as a preliminary step to other research studies that pursue the leads found in action research. Indeed, educational action research is essential.

A strong body of research will assist middle level educators and policymakers in adopting and implementing sound educational policies and practices. Ultimately, research and informed practice will support us in reaching our common goal of implementing successful schools for young adolescents that focus on one thing: the learning and healthy growth of every single student.

Sue Swaim
Executive Director
National Middle School Association

REFERENCE

Calhoun, E. (1994). *How to use action research in the self-renewing school.* Alexandria, VA: Association for Supervision and Curriculum Development.

INTRODUCTION

Taking Action in Middle Grades Education

Micki M. Caskey

Volume V of *The Handbook of Research in Middle Level Education* highlights action research in middle grades education. As a method of inquiry, action research compels educators to take action and think reflectively about those actions in order to effect positive educational change (Mills, 2000). Teachers, administrators, university professors, and other professionals conduct action research in different ways to examine classroom practices and school issues. Educational action researchers initiate their inquiries in various contexts: alone, in small peer teams, or larger faculty groups (Zeichner, 2001). Using individual and collaborative approaches, educators gain insights into teaching and learning processes. As evidenced throughout this volume, action research in the middle grades occurs in a variety configurations.

Increasingly, universities and colleges incorporate action research into preservice teacher and inservice teacher education programs to foster inquiry and reflective practice. Action research is a method of professional development that allows teachers to expand their practice-based knowledge (Cochran-Smith & Lytle, 1999, 2001). Many professional educators engage in systematic inquiry as a central part of school improvement

Making a Difference: Action Research in Middle Level Education, xi–xiv
Copyright © 2005 by Information Age Publishing
All rights of reproduction in any form reserved.

efforts. In addition, faculty researchers are collaborating with teachers and administrators to conduct responsive and rigorous school-based research. Certainly, educational action research continues to flourish in an array of contexts. This volume examines the dynamic ways that preservice and inservice teachers, school administrators, university faculty, and educational consortia use action research.

In Chapter 1, Arhar sets the stage for examining action research in middle level education. After describing research and action, she provides a brief history of action research to reveal how this method of inquiry can align with middle grades philosophy. Next, she proposes a definition action research (Arhar, Holly, & Kasten, 2001) and presents an action research cycle to guide practitioners. Following suggestions for getting started with action research, Arhar shares the experiences of a middle school science teacher who used this framework to investigate an issue.

The next three chapters tender rich descriptions of action research conducted by classroom teachers across the United States. Sanguras explores motivation and her seventh grade language arts students in Chapter 2 as she examines the effects of qualitative teacher praise, grades, and an incentive on her students' achievement on vocabulary tests. In Chapter 3, Shrum investigates how using manipulatives in a seventh grade mathematics class influences students' performance. Using manipulatives also led to changes in classroom practice including cooperative learning and peer tutoring. Then, in Chapter 4, a special education teacher reports about her collaboration with a general education teacher in an eighth grade civics class. Stanton shares this initial experience of inclusive teaching and the outcomes for both special and general education students. Each study highlights the lessons learned and insights gained through systematic examination of an instructional approach by teacher-researchers.

Following these examples of inservice teacher research, the volume shifts to action research practices in preservice programs. In Chapter 5, Stacki describes how six preservice teachers experience action research as a collaborative team. The team examines the perceptions of middle grades teachers in the midst of a very public crisis. Next, Wilder, Combs, and Resor explain the integral nature of action research in an alternative licensure program in Chapter 6. Students develop and complete an action research project across the four terms of their middle level Master of Arts in Teaching (MAT) program. Then, in Chapter 7, Thompson highlights how aspiring middle level administrators integrate theory and practice during their practicum in a middle grades school. She shares three specific examples of action research conducted in a Master's program in educational administration. In each of these instances, preservice educators expanded their understanding and increased their capacity to conduct action research in their future classrooms and schools.

The next selections center on action research in professional development schools (PDS). In Chapter 8, Thornton details how university faculty and teachers used a qualitative participatory research method to develop a process for selecting master teachers. She explains the inquiry and action used to define and select quality teachers to serve as mentors of novice teachers. Next, in Chapter 9, Barker and Basile recount stories of how action research occurred in four middle schools that are professional development schools. They discuss how this model of inquiry became part of the schools' culture and the ways that university-school partnerships can foster action research.

The authors of Chapters 10 and 11 shift the reader's attention to collaborative action research projects in the middle grades. Bishop, Boke, Pflaum, and Kirsh describe an action research project conducted by teachers, the principal, a literacy consultant, university researchers, and students at a suburban middle school in Chapter 10. They explain how this collaborative research team worked as a community to explore how teachers can help students become strategic readers, improve reading instruction, and advance school-wide change. In Chapter 11, Saurino, Saurino, and Crawford report growing interest in collaborative action research and articulate an inquiry model, Collaborative Team Action Research (CTAR), for the middle grades. They share that the team configuration is conducive to determining new actions, guiding the research process, and resolving issues. Similarly, these chapters emphasize the value of collaborative action research for school-based professional development

In the next two chapters, action research broadens. First, Malu uses qualitative action research to analyze a five-year partnership between an urban middle school and university in Chapter 12. She portrays vividly the challenges of the partnership and offers a series of recommendations for consideration. In Chapter 13, Gopalan, West, Montesano, and Hoelscher describe an application of action research to comprehensive school reform. Specifically, they examine the Middle Start comprehensive school improvement model.

The final chapter, "Recommendations and Resources for Action Research," includes information to promote the use of action research in middle grades education. After reviewing some of the findings of the contributing authors, Caskey recommends how practitioners and researchers can advance inquiry and suggests future directions for action research. She provides a list of resources including books, journal, and websites for the novice and experienced action researcher.

REFERENCES

Arhar, J. M., Holly, M. L., & Kasten, W. C. (2001). *Action research for teachers: Traveling the yellow brick road.* Columbus, OH: Merrill Prentice Hall.

Cochran-Smith, M., & Lytle, S. (1999). The teacher research movement: A decade later. *Educational Researcher, 28*(7), 15-25.

Cochran-Smith, M., & Lytle, S. (2001). Beyond certainty: Taking an inquiry stance on practice. In A. Lieberman & L. Miller (Eds.), *Teachers caught in the action: Professional development that matters* (pp. 45-60). New York: Teachers College Press.

Mills, G. E. (2000). *Action research: A guide for teachers.* Upper Saddle River, NJ: Merrill Prentice Hall.

Zeichner, K. (2001). Educational action research. In P. Reason & H. Bradbury (Eds.), *Handbook of action research: Participative inquiry and practice* (pp. 273-283). Thousand Oaks, CA: Sage.

CHAPTER 1

ACTION RESEARCH FOR MIDDLE LEVEL EDUCATIONAL PROFESSIONALS

Joanne M. Arhar

ABSTRACT

The terms *research* and *action* as well as a brief history of action research are explored in an attempt to show the variety of ways action research has come to be understood, some consistent and others inconsistent with middle level philosophy. The potential role of action research in the reform of middle level schools is discussed. A definition of action research is presented that is in line with and supportive of middle level reform initiatives as explored in documents such as *Turning Points 2000: Educating Adolescents in the 21st Century* (Jackson & Davis, 2000). A framework for designing an action research study is presented and illustrated through an example of a middle level teacher using this framework to problematize and deepen her understanding of her students.

RESEARCH ... the word means many things to many people. To some, it strikes terror in the heart as it conjures up dusty libraries, incomprehensible configurations of numbers and statistical formulas, and conclusions that seem far from the daily work of practitioners. To others it means using randomized control groups and quantitative methods to compare the effects of one treatment to another producing the kind of evidence required by the federal government for the funding of school improvement projects. Research is considered a series of steps: do this first (form a hypothesis), this second (test the hypothesis), and so on. And yet to others, research means exploring (through qualitative methods of interviewing, document analysis, and personal inquiry) the meaning of situations from the perspective of insiders.

But for educational professionals, research is less a *method* than a *way of life* characterized by an attitude of scientific inquiry. We inquire into the world of the school and classroom and as we do, we create new knowledge about teaching and learning, use that knowledge to make informed decisions, and develop ethically as professionals. To do our jobs well as professionals we need to inquire well. As I will later show, this attitude of scientific inquiry, in combination with an ethical commitment to improve ourselves and our life with students in ways that make classrooms and schools more democratic places, is the aim of a particular kind of research—action research (Holly, Arhar, & Kasten, 2004).

ACTION.... Action defines the life of the educational professional. Students, parents, the public, the legislature, and the federal government demand our constant attention and action. We make hundreds of decisions resulting in actions each day, often without benefit of time to reflect on the ethical and social consequences of these actions. We respond to demands and in turn make demands on others as if we were *not* colleagues working *with* students to improve teaching and learning. No wonder so many of us go on auto pilot in order to avoid feeling overwhelmed. But, is this what is meant by *action* in action research?

The philosopher Hannah Arendt (1958) offers a view of action that differs from the one presented above. For Arendt, *action* means *initiating* change rather than *reacting* to it. In initiating something new, she believes, we experience freedom. We learn about who we are *through* our actions. In Arendt's view, this type of action is carried out with others who are our equals. Thus, we learn to accommodate the different perspectives of others rather than merely negotiate consensus. John Elliott, a noted British action researcher, commented on Arendt's notion of action:

> If "action" has an aim, it is to enlarge the space in which human beings can relate to each other as unique individuals in the situation. Such an aim is not the intention to produce an outcome or result, but a value built into the process of action itself. (Elliott, 2003)

In this chapter, I argue for a particular view of the terms *action* and *research* that draws on the work of Arendt, Elliott, and others concerned with freedom, developing the human capacity to understand others, and an inquiry stance in the improvement of schools and learning. When teachers and others ask, "How can I improve my practice?" (Whitehead, 1989), and when they systematically pursue ways to address their own questions, they are engaged in action research.

What does action research mean? What is its history? Why the interest in action research at the middle level? How do middle level teachers and administrators (as well as students, parents and community members) do action research? What are the outcomes of such efforts? What does it look like in actual practice? The rest of this chapter will explore these questions as a means of introducing this fifth volume of the *Handbook of Research in Middle Level Education* devoted to action research.

ACTION RESEARCH: A BRIEF HISTORY

Just as the terms research and action hold multiple meanings, so does the meaning of action research. I have heard middle level principals say to teachers, "This is the action research project I'd like you to do this year: look at our student performance data and figure out how to improve test scores." In this era of accountability, it is understandable why school leaders feel compelled to take this authoritative approach to action research and school improvement. But at other schools, I have seen teachers work together on teams to identify areas for study that will improve classroom practice. They do it with principal support for their efforts. These are each two very different approaches to action research that can be understood in terms of differences in the meanings associated with research and action.

Without going into a lengthy history of action research, a brief look at the various traditions in action research illustrates the diverse and sometimes conflicting meanings that underlie these different approaches outlined above. Although Kurt Lewin and U. S. Commissioner of Indian Affairs John Collier first used the term action research in the 1930s and 1940s, the roots of this type of research lie in the work of John Dewey, a progressive educational philosopher who believed that teachers should be reflective practitioners rather than technicians following the mandates of others. He believed that teachers should apply scientific problem solving to education. Rather than jumping uncritically from one innovation to another, he advocated that teachers bring a healthy dose of skepticism to their practice. He also believed that teachers should create democratic classroom communities. He viewed teaching as a cyclical activity involving thought, action, and observation, the very elements that form research practice (Dewey, 1929, 1938).

Lewin, a social psychologist and contemporary of Dewey's, developed guiding principles and methods of action research that could be used in any social organization, including schools. Lewin, an immigrant from Germany, was concerned about the rise of totalitarianism. He conducted experiments to help people become aware of their biases. For example, in one study he helped managers at a new factory examine their beliefs about women and how these beliefs might impede the work of newly hired female trainees. In other studies, Lewin (1946) and Collier (1945) used action research methods to counteract racial prejudice and to promote democratic leadership in the workplace. Lewin also believed that research should remain recursive: each cycle of planning, acting, observing, and reflecting affects future cycles. That is, initial understandings of the nature of the problem might change as situations and understandings change. The work of Dewey and Lewin formed the early basis of action research as a recursive, collaborative, process of problem solving and critical self-reflection on practice, engaged in by practitioners interested in changing their working lives together to make it more socially just. In its application to school settings, however, the meaning of action research changed in subsequent decades. Corey (1953), Dean of Teachers College at Columbia University applied the ideas of Dewey and Lewin (1946) to education and in the process made a long lasting effect on action research in this country. Corey believed that teachers would make better decisions if they conducted research on their own practice. To encourage this, he created institutes linking university faculty and schools. However, he focused on a step-by-step process of hypothesis formation, testing, and data collection, not the cyclical process that characterized the way Dewey and Lewin considered action research processes. Corey intended to help teachers become curriculum developers. However, with the rise of the behavioral objectives movement that centralized control of curriculum development in the hands of bureaucrats, as well as other federal research initiatives, the action research movement died in this country by the early 1960s. Teachers were no longer considered curriculum decision makers, but rather implementers of a curriculum developed by *experts*.

As the action research movement diminished in the U. S. during the 1960s, the teacher as researcher movement in the United Kingdom took off. It evolved as a teacher-driven effort to make curriculum more relevant to increasingly unhappy high school students. University faculty/ researchers such as John Elliott (1976-1977) and John Stenhouse (1968), and others began a series of curriculum development projects supporting teachers as curriculum developers. Stephen Kemmis, one of Elliott's students, and Wilfred Carr, a colleague of Kemmis, took these ideas to Australia. Using the work of critical theorist Jurgen Habermas (1972), Kemmis and Carr (1986) developed a theory of action research as emancipatory practice, that is, practice undertaken by teachers in order to improve the justice of their own practice. They viewed action research for other than emancipatory purposes (e.g. action research to improve student test scores) as conservative research designed to maintain the status quo.

While these British researchers were developing an overtly emancipatory role for action research in Australia, another form of research, called participatory action research emerged in third world countries and focused on adult education and literacy. Its goal is to bring about a more just society. The research process engages participants in actions intended to overcome oppressive situations.

The teacher research movement reemerged in the 1980s in the United States, particularly among writing teachers, in part because of the growing acceptance of qualitative research and in part because of the leadership of teacher researchers. Among the leaders were Nancie Atwell (1987) who created case studies of the teaching of writing. The National Writing Project also played a major role. This research did not necessarily have the emancipatory intention promoted by Kemmis and Carr.

Though the emancipatory and participatory action research traditions have not "taken hold" in the U. S. (Zeichner & Noffke, 2001), researchers such as Patti Lather (1986) have written extensively about the importance of the participation of those effected by action, describing how research participants become involved in developing problem statements, data collection, and interpretation. As teachers, students, and others who have typically been the researched become the researchers, traditional notions of validity are challenged by ideas such as *catalytic* validity, the extent to which the researcher/practitioner actually effects a change leading toward more socially just practice (1986).

As this discussion hopefully makes evident, the tradition of action research is rooted in multiple traditions: experimental research (Lewin), emancipatory research (Kemmis & Carr, 1986), qualitative research (Atwell, 1987, and others), and reflective teaching (Dewey, 1929, 1938). Readers interested in a more detailed history of action research might consult some of the resources used in this review. Chief among them are the work of Zeichner and Noffke (2001), Adelman (1993), Holly, Arhar and Kasten (2004), and McKernan (1996).

A DEFINITION OF ACTION RESEARCH

Drawing on this rich history, Arhar, Holly, and Kasten (2001) framed a definition of action research:

Action research is research undertaken by individuals or groups which is founded on an active ethical commitment to improve the quality of life of others, is critically reflective in nature and outcome, is collaborative with those to be affected by actions undertaken, and is made public. (p. 47)

This definition refers to certain characteristics of action research:

- Action research is above all an *ethical commitment to democratic relationships* with others, and the improvement of ourselves, our practice, and the larger community.
- In response to the question, "How can I improve my own practice?" (Whitehead, 1989) we systematically observe and collect evidence on the consequences of our actions, and then analyze and reflect on the evidence. This is a cycle of reflective practice (see Figure 1.1) in which we *act* to improve our practice, *observe* the social, practical, and ethical consequences of our practice, and *reflect* on the changes in ourselves, others, and our situation.

To understand how natural this cycle is in teaching, try this brief exercise: Describe something you did recently that did not work. Perhaps it worked previously, or it came up for the first time and you had to figure out how to make it work and it took some time trying out different ways. What did you do as a result? In doing this activity, you engaged in an initial cycle of action research.

- Action research necessitates *collaboration* with others, particularly with those affected by the action, in order to develop new insights, to verify our interpretations, and to support improvement in one another's practice.
- Action research is made *public* in order for others to critique and test our ideas. To be considered research, new knowledge must be

The Action Research Cycle

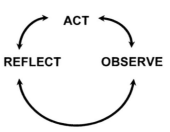

Figure 1.1.   The action research cycle.

open to critique. By sharing what we are learning, we contribute to change.

ACTION RESEARCH AND MIDDLE LEVEL REFORM

Middle grades reform is an on-going process. Its roots are in the progressive educational philosophy of John Dewey whose ideas about learning have evolved into what we now call constructivism and whose ideas about teaching we now call reflective practice. The Vision Statement of the National Forum to Accelerate Middle Grades Reform offers a philosophy of middle level education grounded in Dewey's ideas: successful schools for early adolescents are academically challenging, developmentally responsive, and socially just.

Action research, as defined in this chapter, is a process of change that is consistent with the principles of middle level education. It calls on teachers, students, and administrators to inquire together into ways to make education more just and equitable, challenging for all, and developmentally responsive. While it is important for us to know how action research impacts middle level reform, this will be left to others to document. Importantly, this volume responds to the challenge through its many rich examples of action research in the service of middle level reform.

The following section describes a method for designing an action research study. Holly, Arhar, and Kasten (2004) provide a more complete description in *Action Research for Teachers: Traveling the Yellow Brick Road.*

GETTING STARTED WITH ACTION RESEARCH

Designing an action research study is not a linear process. Like qualitative design projects, it is circuitous: plans change as new knowledge is generated and new situations arise resulting from prior actions. Rather than a method for conducting action research, what is offered below is a series of questions to assist action researchers in getting started:

- What is your research interest? What values motivate your study?
- How will you address your question?
- How will you document the process?
- How will you interpret the data?
- How will you verify your interpretations?
- What will you do next and how will these actions make life better?
- How will you make this public?

In the following section, I elaborate on each of these questions by using an example of a middle level teacher engaged in an action research project with her seventh grade science students.

What is Your Research Interest? What Values Motivate Your Study?

To get started with an action research study, describe an idea or *hitch* in practice that you would like to improve. The focus is not necessarily a problem to be solved, although our every day practice certainly provides many problems. The focus may be something that you heard about at a conference and would like to try out. Or, it might be something that has been nagging at you for a long time and you finally decide it is time to give it your full attention.

Gayle, a middle school science teacher, was concerned about the many misconceptions her students had about the environment (Arhar & Buck, 2000). Environmentalists influenced her values. Her goal as an environmentally-oriented science teacher was to help produce people who were fit to be inhabitants of the planet. But her students' actions were not in line with Gayle's beliefs.

Gayle invited me to be her critical colleague. A critical colleague is a person with whom to share and discuss ideas. It is someone we trust and who will give us honest and respectful feedback. Rather than advice, a critical colleague poses questions to help clarify the situation and to make problematic the things that are taken for granted as natural.

Selecting a critical colleague is an important part of the action research process, not only for the support we need in order to change our practice, but also because of the fresh insights we may gain through honest dialogue in the company of friends. If an entire team initiates an action research study, the team provides a rich context for dialogue and collegiality.

The critical colleague assumes that the person exploring the situation has it within his or her power to figure things out, so open-ended rather than leading questions are best. An example from conversations I had with Gayle will illustrate.

Joanne: What are your feelings about this situation?
  Gayle: This is very frustrating. I felt I was totally prepared to teach environmental education. I had enrolled in workshops and courses and read everything I could to help me prepare my lessons. I was confident that I was making an impact. Much

to my dismay, I learned that the impact I was making was not what I had envisioned.

Joanne: Is this situation in line with your values?

Gayle: Absolutely not. That realization came as I was looking over a set of photographs of the students from my recycling team who volunteered to stay after school and take part in recycling projects for the school and community. I was so proud of that team and the many awards they had won. The photographs pictured my students in front of mounds of plastic jugs, glass jars, and aluminum cans they had collected. Seemingly, the prizes and positive comments I offered paid off. However, I recalled one student's story about dumping soda pop down the drain because she needed that plastic bottle to fill a quota! Was that what I wanted to teach my students? I then began to seriously question my students about what they were learning. They gave me facts and definitions about recycling and the environment that seemed to be nothing more than a regurgitation of what I had taught, but I suspected that they were taking part in conservation activities only because I directed them to. (Arhar & Buck, 2000, p. 329-330)

Joanne: In what ways do you feel you are contributing to the problem?

Gayle: In my eagerness, I did not check out the assumptions my students had about the environment.

It was through a series of discussions around questions such as these that Gayle decided on her research question: What are the assumptions that my middle school students have about their relationship with the environment? While Gayle wanted to take immediate action to rectify this situation, she realized that before she could act, she needed to gather more information. The question "How can I improve my practice?" is the overarching question that framed her study. But her first subquestion related to understanding the perceptions of students.

How Will You Address Your Question?

Deciding on a plan of action is what most practitioners enjoy. But rather than making quick decisions about what to do, it may be better to first brainstorm many possibilities with a critical colleague. Once a list is drawn up, the actions can be evaluated and prioritized according to a variety of criteria, but foremost among them: How is this proposed action in line with my values and goals? Other criteria might include feasibility, imaginativeness, potential impact, hidden consequences, etc. Reflecting on these criteria and evaluating possible actions against them may take some time, but may also prevent wasted effort. Actions not selected form a back-up for the future.

Gayle decided to stop teaching anything about environmental education until she had done more reading and reflecting on what had happened. We talked during that year and then decided to brainstorm possible actions. Gayle decided to directly ask students about their assumptions concerning the environment. She planned to record their assumptions on the chalkboard, categorize them, and look for patterns.

During class, she tried to define *assumptions* for them and asked them in several different ways to tell her what their assumptions were about their relationship with the environment. But just as she was working hard to understand their perspective, they were working hard to give her the answers they thought she expected. After all, she *was* an environmentalist and they did not want to disappoint her. But beyond that, she wondered why it was so difficult for students to make explicit their assumptions about the environment and their relationship to it? Through reflection and collegial dialogue and much reading of the literature on environmental education, she came to understand that it is difficult, if not impossible, to state our assumptions because they are so embedded in our culture.

Another strategy was needed, so Gayle decided to form focus groups. She gained permission from parents and students to tape record the focus group interviews. Much to her surprise, almost all students agreed to be audio taped and provisions were made for those who did not. As a class, students developed questions: Should hunting be allowed? Should the population of people be limited? Should chemical fertilizers be allowed? In small focus groups scattered around the school, students began to explore the questions. Adults supervised but were not permitted to listen to the conversations. At the conclusion of each session, students wrote in their journals about what they learned and their attitudes about the topics they wrote about.

How Will You Document the Process?

Documentation is a natural part of teaching. As practitioners, we record grades, minutes of team meetings, and anecdotal records, keep journals and logs of activities, save student work to share with parents, interview students to find out what they are learning, and constantly observe student behavior, reactions, and responses. In this current environment of accountability, our ability to document student progress and our own efforts to support students is critical. While documentation is an everyday occurrence, in action research it takes on particular importance. We do this so that we can reflect on our experience and turn data into evidence to either support or challenge our emerging hunches.

Gayle used a variety of data collection tools: audio tapes, focus group interviews, and journal writing, to record observations and thoughts. Each was appropriate for her purpose and for the participants in her study. What is important to note is that once Gayle expressed her own frustration to her students and solicited their help in developing questions, students became part of the research process. At that point, data production became a joint venture and the research process became much more productive.

There are three basic ways in which data are produced: we record observations, interview others, and examine documents and artifacts (Wolcott, 1992). Many helpful and readable resources are available to middle level educators who want to know more about ways to produce data. *Action Research for Teachers: Traveling the Yellow Brick Road* (Holly, Arhar, & Kasten, 2004) is written with teachers in mind and has a chapter specifically focused on documentation. Other resources include: *You and Your Action Research Project* by Jean McNiff, Pamela Lomax, and Jack Whitehead (1996); *Curriculum Action Research: A Handbook of Methods and Resources for the Reflective Practitioner* by James McKernan (1996); and *Action Research in Education* by Ernie Stringer (2004). Jean McNiff's Web page contains a booklet titled *Action Research for Professional Development: Concise Advice for New Action Researchers*, which is a solid introduction to action research, but contains little information about data collection and analysis.

It is important to remember that in our zeal to address our questions, we may produce much more data than we can ever manage and organize. For every 1 hour of audiotapes, for example, it will take nearly 4 hours to transcribe. We need to temper our enthusiasm with reasonable limits so that our initial excitement does not turn into a nightmare of boxes and electronic files of information.

A final question to pose at this point of the design is related to ethics. How are participants to be protected from harm? Action researchers operating out of an ethic of care and concern for participants will want to make sure that any information gathered or actions taken do not harm participants in any way. A study would simply stop if such a possibility existed.

Written permission for participants (and parents if the student is considered a minor) is also needed. Gayle, for example, made sure that students and parents agreed to participate in the study and that they understood the purpose of the research. Securing such consent involves a promise of *anonymity* (pseudonyms are sometime used in writing up reports); *confidentiality* (information will not be shared with anyone other than those agreed upon); and the *right to withdraw*. Not only is verbal/written permission from participants a requirement of all universities and many school districts, but there are boards who review research proposals before researchers are permitted to begin a study. A good source of information about the ethics of action research is Jane Zeni's *A Guide to Ethical Issues and Action Research* (1998).

How Will You Interpret the Data?

Gayle listened to the tapes. She repeated the tapes many times. What she heard was initial laughter, joking around about nerdy environmentalists, and lots of comments about the tape recorder. But, students quickly began to listen to one another. They talked with seriousness about issues that she as an environmentalist cared a great deal about. She took notes. Then she read the journal entries and took more notes, paying attention to ideas/themes that recurred. Then she listened to the tapes once again, this time creating categories that helped her to make sense of student assumptions about their relationship with the environment. She also took notes about her own role in their assumptions. She listed quotes and journal entries under each category. Did all students have the same beliefs? To test her emerging categories and ideas, she looked for disconfirming evidence. Did some students hold different beliefs? Were there new categories that should be included? She then took some time off so that she could mull things over in her head, hoping they would jell into some statements about her students' beliefs that made sense in light of her experiences as teacher and research. She then wrote in her own journal – trying to synthesize what she had learned in her own words.

Interpretation is a process used to make sense of experience. Educational professionals constantly interpret people's actions, events, and data. Some interpretations are hasty and others take much more time and systematic effort. Action researchers take data apart through *analysis*, put them back together in new ways through *synthesis*, and develop *theories* to aid in taking action based on informed judgment.

How Will You Verify Your Interpretations?

A question that emerges during early stages of the design process is how to ensure that later interpretations will be truthful. It would be easy for Gayle, or any other action researcher, to set up barriers to hearing what the participants are really saying and doing. Triangulation is one way to provide multiple perspectives during the data collection process. By including all three sources of data (observation, interviewing, and documents/artifacts), we gain a more authentic picture of what is going on. We can ask ourselves: What do I see? What does student work tell me? What do students (and others) tell me? By viewing our situations and students from multiple perspectives, we can be more confident in any subsequent actions that are taken. Gayle takes such steps when she includes her own observations, student writing, and interviews in her data collection process.

But truth may be illusive. What researchers are now thinking is that truth may be partial and constructed through culture. Just as Gayle's students were not able to directly state their assumptions about their relationship with the environment, action researchers may not be able to *see* through the lenses of culture and habit that cloud perspectives. Although the quest for certainty and simplicity may be what prompts a research study, what typically emerges is complexity and depth of knowledge.

Action researchers aim for trustworthy accounts and interpretations; they want to be credible; they want to be respectful of others. Out of respect for the insights of others, they offer their interpretations only as possibilities, inviting others to also develop interpretations.

What Will You Do Next and How Will This Make Life Better?

Gayle learned several important things about student assumptions that changed the way she taught. First, students believed that the environment was separate from themselves. Gayle realized that she fostered this belief by arranging for students to study the environmental issues of far away places. Second, students believed that nature would not survive without human management. Without hunting, deer would breathe all of our oxygen and pine cones would never seed themselves and grow. Third, students believed that it was not *cool* to show interest in the environment. There was an underlying feeling that environmentalists were nerdy. Yet many students expressed conflicting emotions because they loved the environment and wanted to protect it.

How did Gayle use this knowledge that she and her students produced? She changed her teaching dramatically in order to help students become *fit inhabitants of the planet*. After doing more reading, reflection, and discussion with colleagues, she decided to make her environmental education classroom more authentic, holistic, integrated, and accessible for her students.

How Will You Make Your Work Public?

Gayle realized that she needed to share what she had learned so that others could share their perspectives. She made presentations at conferences (both local and national) and wrote about her experiences in journal articles. Other science teachers and action researchers developed new understandings of the assumptions of their own students and also offered new interpretations of Gayle's data. By sharing her knowledge, Gayle and others are creating a community of environmental educators, building their own knowledge about good practice. As Hiebert, Gallimore and Stilger (2002) point out in their article on creating a knowledge base for the teaching profession, "Over time, the observations and replications of teachers in the schools would become a common pathway though which promising ideas were tested and refined before they found their way into the nation's classrooms" (p. 12).

Public sharing takes many forms, formal and informal, written, oral, and performance, to audiences close by and distant. Dance, drama, poetry, video, first person narratives, case study accounts, newsletters, and formal research reports are just a few of the many ways that action researchers work to create a community of learners. The audiences are just as diverse: school boards, parent-teacher groups, team meetings, faculty meetings, social service agencies, and student councils, to name a few. Tailoring the presentation to the audience may ensure that the message is heard.

A FINAL NOTE

The format presented here is flexible and open to the interpretations of action-oriented educators seeking to transform middle grades education. The other chapters in this book include action research studies as well as theoretical and methodological insights that contribute to the knowledge base of good educational practice for the middle grades. While the federal government continues to discount the work of practitioners in favor of randomized controlled studies whose aim is to generalize to all settings, action researchers continue on their own path, developing a knowledge base about middle level practice that is accessible to both teachers and administrators. This volume is the beginning of that journey.

REFERENCES

Adelman, C. (1993). Kurt Lewin and the origins of action research. *Educational Action Research, 1*(1), 7-24.

Arendt, H. (1958). *The human condition.* Chicago: University of Chicago Press.

Arhar, J. M., Holly, M. L., & Kasten, W. C. (2001). *Action research for teachers: Traveling the yellow brick road.* Columbus, OH: Merrill Prentice Hall.

Arhar, J., & Buck, G. (2000). Learning to look through the eyes of our students: Action research as a tool of inquiry. *Educational Action Research, 8*(2), 327-339.

Atwell, N. (1987). *In the middle: Writing, reading, and learning with adolescents.* Upper Montclair, NJ: Boynton/Cook.

Carr, W., & Kemmis, S. (1986). *Becoming critical: Education, knowledge and action research.* London: Falmer.

Collier, J. (1945). United States Indian administration as a laboratory of ethnic relations. *Social Research, 12,* 265-303.

Corey, S. M. (1953). *Action research to improve school practices.* New York: Teachers College Press.

Dewey, J. (1929). *The sources of a science of education.* New York: Liverright.

Dewey, J. (1938). *Logic: The theory of inquiry.* New York: Henry Holt.

Elliott, J. (1976). Developing hypotheses about classrooms from teachers' practical constructs: An account of the work of the Ford Teaching Project. *Teacher Education Quarterly, 23*(3), 69-90.

Elliott, J. (2003, October). *The struggle to redefine the relationship between knowledge and action in the academy: Some reflections on action research.* Paper presented at the University of Barcelona, Spain.

Habermas, J. (1972). *Knowledge and human interests.* Boston: Beacon Press.

Hiebert, J., Gallimore, R., & Stigler, J. W. (2002). A knowledge base for the teaching profession: What would it look like and how can we get one? *Educational Researcher, 31*(5), 3-15.

Holly, M. L., Arhar, J. M., & Kasten, W. C. (2004). *Action research for teachers: Traveling the yellow brick road* (2nd ed.). Columbus, OH: Prentice Hall.

Jackson, A. W., & Davis, G. A. (2000). *Turning points 2000: Educating adolescents in the 21st century.* New York: Teachers College Press.

Lather, P. (1986). Research as praxis. *Harvard Educational Review, 56*(3), 257-277.

Lewin, K. (1946). Action research and minority problems. *Journal of Social Issues, 2*(4), 34-46.

McKernan, J. (1996). *Curriculum action research.* London: Kogan Page.

McNiff, J. (2002). *Action research for professional development: Concise advice for new action researchers* (3rd ed.). Retrieved January 16, 2004, from http://www.jeanmcniff.com

McNiff, J., Lomax, P., & Whitehead, J. (1996). *You and your action research project.* New York: Hyde.

Stenhouse, L. (1968). The humanities curriculum project. *Journal of Curriculum Studies, 23*(1), 26-33.

Stringer, E. (2004). *Action research in education.* Columbus, OH: Merrill Prentice Hall.

Whitehead, J. (1989). Creating living educational theory from questions of the kind, 'How do I improve my practice?' *Cambridge Journal of Education, 19,* 41-52.

Wolcott, H. F. (1992). Posturing in qualitative inquiry. In M. D. LeCompte, W. L. Millroy, & J. Priessle (Eds.), *Handbook of qualitative research in education* (pp. 3-52). San Diego, CA: Academic Press.

Zeichner, K., & Noffke, S. (2001). Practitioner research. In V. Richardson (Ed.), *Handbook of research on teaching* (4th ed., pp. 298-330). Washington, DC: American Educational Research Association.

Zeni, J. (1998). A guide to ethical issues and action research. *Educational Action Researcher, 6*(1), 9-19.

CHAPTER 2

EFFECTS OF ADOLESCENTS' PERCEIVED MOTIVATORS ON ACADEMIC ACHIEVEMENT AND SELF-EFFICACY

Laila Y. Sanguras

ABSTRACT

My research involves examining the effects of progressive motivators on middle school students. I have included a synopsis of the important research I compiled, as well as a detailed summary of my study. I tested the use of qualitative teacher praise, grades, and an incentive to see if I could improve my students' performance on vocabulary tests. The end of this chapter details my conclusions, limitations, and directions of further study dealing with motivation.

As I watched my seventh grade language arts students working on an assignment, I noticed varying levels of interest from desk to desk. Some students seemed completely engaged in the task; others needed prodding to continue working; and the remainder would not work at all unless I sat by them, monitoring their progress. I was puzzled because these were not troubled or disruptive kids. They were talented and imaginative students.

Making a Difference: Action Research in Middle Level Education, 17–39

Studying effective motivators for middle school students seemed a natural choice. I was interested in how and why some students were intrinsically motivated while others were not. I was curious about the long-term effects of external rewards on students' performance. I also wanted to know what each student's perceived motivator was and if their work improved when it was implemented. I was not convinced that I alone could change the behavior of my students, because I had tried and any success that I had was short-lived.

I wanted to understand further my students' motivation. I also wanted my students to feel pride when they completed an assignment well. I did not mind giving out rewards, but I needed to know if they were effective for middle school students. I did not want my efforts to be counterproductive and I wanted the positive results to last. Overall, I wanted to know that I was doing everything a good teacher should be doing to motivate students.

BACKGROUND

As I looked into the issue of motivation for academic achievement, it became evident that the issue perplexed many educators and researchers. The research literature began at the kindergarten level and extended through college, and was not limited by age group or profession. Much research exists to help understand the problems of motivating teachers and administrators within schools. Apparently, employers and teachers continue to struggle with motivation issues.

In a longitudinal study conducted by the National Center for Educational Statistics, researchers found that approximately half of the 25,000 surveyed eighth graders were bored in school half or more of the time (Hootstein, 1994). Although bored and unmotivated were not equated, they are closely related. When people are bored with a task, they tend to be unmotivated to complete it. This rate of boredom is cause for alarm, especially during a time when academic performance standards are high at the national and state level. Being a middle school teacher, I have observed that many students appear bored despite the intense efforts of their teachers to make the curriculum and instruction both interesting and meaningful. Understandably, I was troubled by the enormity of the boredom statistic.

According to Eller (1985), efficient motivators should be identified for each child, and then applied by school personnel. Due to the expanse of information available, many teachers become confused as to which are the most effective motivators. I gathered many sources to provide a clear snapshot of the available research. I explored the research on motivation, academic achievement linked to teacher praise, grades, and incentives as well as self-efficacy of students.

Maslow's Theory of Human Motivation

Maslow (1943) advanced a theory of motivation linked to the needs of humans. His theory became an integral part of this study because, as Maslow pointed out, people cannot move on to a higher level of achievement until their basic needs have been met. He called this a "hierarchy of pre-potency" and insisted that "every drive is related to the state of satisfaction or dissatisfaction of other drives" (p. 372).

The first of the Maslow's five levels of human needs are physiological needs, which include a person's basic needs for survival: food, water, air, and shelter. The second level addresses safety needs, which include security, freedom from fear, and order. The third level houses the need for love, affection, and belonging. The fourth level holds esteem needs for self-respect, achievement, and reputation. The last level of the hierarchy, self-actualization, is the need to be and do what a person was *born to do* and is rarely attained. Many teachers know students who come to school without attaining the first three levels of Maslow's *Hierarchy of Needs*. Because I examined specific motivational techniques that only I could control, I focused my study on the fourth level, the need for esteem.

Academic Achievement Linked to Teacher Praise

As with many aspects of education, research concerning teacher praise varied. Alber and Heward (1997) reported that teacher acclaim gave way to vast improvements in behavior across elementary, secondary, and special education classrooms. Miller and Hom (1997) found that the role of praise shifted from elementary to secondary school. They asserted that children, younger than fourth grade, who saw other children praised by teachers, believed them to be more intelligent. However, by eighth grade, Miller and Hom found that students saw the individual receiving praise as less capable than the others did. Evidently, students linked praise to failure and blame to success in school. In fact, Miller and Hom saw a connection between *praise* and low-achieving students, and *blame* and high-achieving students. In other words, students felt that if a teacher praised them, they were not very smart. In contrast, if students were blamed or received negative feedback from a teacher, they must be smart because the teacher had higher expectations of them. This dynamic demands that teachers examine their practices in the classroom. For example, I admit that I have higher expectations for my high-ability students and have blamed them for what I have seen as a lack of effort. I simply expected more of these students. To illustrate further, Stipek (1996) found the following:

> Children can interpret praise and criticism as indicators of teacher expectations. If a child is praised for succeeding on an easy task, the teacher probably has low expectations for that child. However, if a child receives criticism for failing it may be because the teacher had expectations of success for that child. (as cited in Gehlbach & Roeser, 2002, pp. 42-43)

On the surface, it may seem natural to praise a low-achieving student. However, teachers must think about the quality of praise offered and the effects of this praise on all students, regardless of ability level. Johnson (1998) pointed out that "praising at-risk students simply to encourage them is destructive and ineffective. Students recognize unearned teacher praise as indicative of their low achievement or typically inappropriate behavior" (p. 169). Hancock (2000) expanded upon this notion, when he suggested the following conditions for administering praise:

- Praise must be contingent upon the behavior being reinforced;
- Praise must specify clearly the behavior being reinforced;
- Praise must be offered soon after the occurrence of the behavior being reinforced;
- Praise must be believable to the recipient (p. 384).

Schwartz (1996) described teachers' roles in administering praise another way. She said that by distributing praise, teachers send three messages, the first one being good, and the other two being bad.

> The good message, which we want to send, is that the children's actions and products are valued by the adult. The two messages that we do not want to send them are that (1) we are always passing judgment on children's work and ideas and (2) we are the ones to decide if things are good or bad. (p. 396)

While in a study of 1,046 adolescents, Roeser and Eccles (1998) found that "the more adolescents perceived that their teachers thought they were good students, the more their valuing of school increased over time" (p. 142). Evidently, teachers must delicately balance the quality and quantity of praise given to their students.

Academic Achievement Linked to Grades

For some students, a grade carries a lot of weight. Grades are widely used because they portray a student's achievement very quickly and succinctly, but perhaps not always accurately. Often teachers grapple with the concept of attaching a grade to a student's work. Cizek (1996) asserted that grades do not communicate the information they intend to about a student's progress. He created this tongue-in-cheek analogy to describe more fully his point of view, "As communication devices, [grades] are more like two tin cans and a length of string than a cellular phone" (p. 222). Cizek (1996) explained that teachers consider attendance and participation when figuring final grades, although students and parents believe the grade only reflects the assignments for the class. This is where, he suggested, the communication falls short in using grades.

Researchers suggested that grades might be causing more harm than good for low achieving students (Kaplan, Peck, & Kaplan, 1997). For students at the top of their classes, grades did not have a negative effect. However, for struggling students, failure in school was a reason for dropping out. Poor grades can have a detrimental effect on a student's self-esteem (Kaplan, Peck, & Kaplan, 1997) and could lead to a drop in motivation.

Majesky (1993) was more outspoken about his disdain for formal grading. He found that grades place too much value on the judgment by teachers, rather than placing the value on the intrinsic benefits of doing one's best. Majesky also said that grades are "the source of that caste system we call tracking and the particularly hideous practice of assigning class rank" (p. 88). He urged teachers to place emphasis on the process of learning, rather than on grades at the end of a school year. Similarly, Anderman and Midgley (1997) recommended a task-focused middle school environment that recognizes improvement in learning. They called for a shift away from normative grading and pubic display of grades. Instead, teachers should use grades to acknowledge progress and involve students in the grading process.

Scant research was found in whole-hearted support of grades as successful motivators of adolescent learners. This is interesting because many schools rely primarily on grades for assessing student performance. Kaplan, Peck, and Kaplan (1997) supplied a surplus of information suggesting that poor grades do nothing other than make students feel badly about themselves. Now, this lack of support for grades being motivators for students poses a problem for educators. As teachers, we try to dispense grades fairly, based on performance. In order to increase the quality of this performance, we must motivate our students. We must also be sure that parents and students understand what each grade reflects.

Academic Achievement Linked to Incentives

In addition to considering the use of praise and grades in the class-room, teachers need to examine the use of incentives as motivational tools. Many of our students appear to be intrinsically motivated; they are compelled internally to achieve. Ryan and Deci (2000) defined intrinsic motivation as "the doing of an activity for its inherent satisfactions rather than for some separable consequence" (p. 148). They suggested, "Extrinsic motivation is a construct that pertains whenever an activity is done in order to attain some separable outcome" (p. 151).

Teachers also have students that are motivated extrinsically. For example, some students will try harder on an assignment because they want a good grade, a candy bar, or a pat on the back. Eisenberger and Armeli (1997) "found that reward for divergent thinking increased intrinsic creative interest" (p. 660). This implies that there is a place for rewards, as long as they emphasize the independence and creativity teachers hope their students' exhibit. McNinch (1997) found that external rewards were most useful when dealing with students at risk for failure. He stated that rewards were more successful in raising self-efficacy than if there were no rewards. When dealing with middle school students, it would be foolish for teachers to ignore the desire for these students to feel good about themselves. If McNinch's conclusions are accurate and teachers hope to increase motivation, then they cannot afford to *not* give rewards.

Eisenberger and Armeli (1997) described Eisenberger's *Learned Industriousness Theory* which "assumes that individuals learn which dimensions of performance are rewarded and generalize high or low effort more to these performance dimensions that to other dimensions in subsequent tasks" (p. 654). In other words, if a student receives a reward for a particular task, but not for another task, that student will concentrate more effort on the rewarded task. As a result, the person providing the rewards was the one pulling the strings on interest level, rather than a student controlling his/her own interest level. This is critical information when considering the issue of motivation.

Skinner (n.d.) suggested many times that positive reinforcement could achieve a desired effect without the messiness of punishment.

> For example, students who are punished when they do not study may study, but they may also stay away from school (truancy), vandalize school property, attack teachers, or stubbornly do nothing. Redesigning school systems so that what students do is more often positively reinforced can make a great difference. (A Brief Survey of Operant Behavior section, ¶ 14)

Evidently, teachers need to reflect on techniques used to motivate students to determine if the long-term effects are worth achieving the short-term goals.

Further, teachers should consider carefully Johnson's (1999) review of Alfie Kohn's (1988) book, *Punished by Rewards: The Trouble with Gold Stars, Incentive Plans, A's, Praise, and Other Bribes* when deliberating on the use of rewards in the classroom. Johnson aptly described Kohn's argument that regardless of age, people correlate a reward with an undesirable task. In other words, a task must be very distasteful if a reward is necessary.

Self-Efficacy in School

Self-efficacy is an issue that teachers must examine when dealing with students of all ages, especially middle school students. The core of the middle school experience is about increasing self-esteem and achieving an identity. Their successes and failures shape them more within these 3 years than at any other time in their lives. The success of different motivators will vary depending upon self-efficacy, and self-efficacy will vary depending on experiences.

When thinking about self-efficacy, teachers need to consider the last of the three prongs of Ford's *Motivational Systems Theory*. Gehlbach and Roeser (2002) summarized Ford's theory succinctly, "for motivation to occur one must: set goals for the future, generate sufficient emotion to produce action, and think that one has the ability to achieve the stated goals" (p. 40).

Zimmerman (2000) summarized Albert Bandura's ideas about and studies of self-efficacy. Bandura had "define[d] perceived self-efficacy as personal judgments of one's capabilities to organize and execute courses of action to attain designated goals" (p.156). Further, Bandura found that "self-efficacious students participate more readily, work harder, persist longer, and have fewer adverse emotional reactions when they encounter difficulties than those who doubt their capabilities" (p. 156). Bandura's findings demonstrate the importance of high self-esteem and give even more credibility to Maslow's (1943) *Hierarchy of Needs*.

Researchers found that even the shift from elementary to middle school has an impact on self-efficacy. Berndt, Hawkins, and Jiao (1999) noted that during the promotion from elementary to middle school, both boys and girls suffered a drop in their self-esteem. This was due to the number of changes involved in transferring schools, the absence of having solely one teacher, the trauma of being the youngest in a larger school, and other factors. As soon as adolescents walk through middle school doors, they were in a period of transition and faced with dealing with self-efficacy issues. Lopez (1999) found that the children who had positive thoughts about their success in school were generally higher performers than those who associated their performance with failure. This is extremely powerful. He ascertained that children's perceptions of their abilities are directly related to their capacity to reach their goals. Brophy (1998) created a label for children who lack this necessary self-efficacy. He called them *failure syndrome students* and defined them as "students who approach assignments with very low expectations of success and who tend to give up at early signs of difficulty" (p. 1). Brophy reported that upon experiencing failure after failure, some students would doubt themselves in relationship to success. He also suggested the need for efficacy training for these students, in order to remedy the problem, and increase motivation.

In an effort to increase students' self-efficacy by way of improving teacher quality, the National Middle School Association (NMSA) repeatedly called for high expectations for all students by all teachers. NMSA (n.d.) asserted that this "promotes positive attitudes and behaviors and serves as motivation for students to achieve" (Position Statement on Academic Achievement, ¶ 2). The association also encouraged educators to create opportunities for all students to succeed, thus increasing their self-esteem.

Gehlbach and Roeser (2002) cautioned teachers to find the balance between helping students improve their self-efficacy and maintaining high standards for their students. They summarized Eccles, Lord, Roeser, Barber and Jozefowicz's study that examined a science teacher who structured his instruction and assignments so that all students found success, no matter how menial the task (as cited in Gehlbach & Roeser, 2002). They also described another teacher who, by setting too high of standards, set her students up for repeated failure and eventual complete lack of effort. Again, balance is necessary to help our students reach goals and feel successful.

Woven throughout the literature in the areas of praise, grades, rewards, and self-efficacy, and their effects on academic achievement was a ribbon of similarity. Who do we want to control a child's ability to complete a task well and feel good about it? Researchers from Maslow (1943) to Gehlbach and Roeser (2002) emphasize the need to give children the power to control their own self-efficacy, thus increasing their level of motivation.

METHODOLOGY

Wy'east Middle School

Wy'east Middle School is located in a rural county and pulls from three different elementary schools. The school hosts an average of 408 students. The enrollment numbers waver throughout the year because of families moving around for work. The student population is 54% Hispanic with 52% of the students receiving a free or reduced lunch.

At the time of this study, my classes consisted of approximately 25 seventh grade language arts students. The population was split in my classroom along gender and racial (Caucasian/Hispanic) lines. The school ran on a block (A/B) schedule that allowed us to meet for 65 minutes two or three times per week.

Instructional Methods

I studied three different motivators: (1) teacher praise, (2) letter grades, and (3) incentives and their effects on young adolescents' academic achievement and self-efficacy. I began the study without any external motivators, so that I could establish a baseline. In stage one, I added teacher praise to the equation. Next in stage two, I used praise and letter grades. Finally in stage three, I ended with praise, grades, and incentives.

Before I began implementing any motivators, I conducted a survey in which I orally asked students general questions about motivation. I wanted to know the connection, if any, between their favorite perceived motivator and their performance during the stage when this motivator was implemented.

A major data source was the results of students' vocabulary tests, which I derived from *500 SAT Words and How to Remember Them Forever* (Gulotta, 2000). These are tests that assess a student's understanding of the meaning and spelling of each word. The book provides lists of words that are divided by grade level and reportedly seen on the SAT, a test administered by the College Board. Each word has a humorous story to help students remember the meaning. In addition to the students writing each word and definition, they also illustrate the humorous story. Students learned two words each day and took a test when they had learned ten words. Though I incorporated practice tests as instruction went along, I did not factor those data into this study. I referred to the formal vocabulary tests as the SAT tests, since the word lists came from the book, *500 SAT Words and How to Remember Them Forever*. For these SAT tests, I recited each word to the class and the students wrote the words and the definitions on their papers. For this study, I used the results from eight of the tests.

Stage One
As I began the new term, I did not assign my students any grades. They turned in their practice SAT tests, and I passed them back to the students without a grade or a point value on them. I wrote both positive and con-

structive comments on the students' tests to help them better understand my expectations. I put a positive comment on every paper and when necessary, how I thought the student could perform better. While the praise was evident, I tried to make it natural. I was also specific in my praise. My comments included notations such as, "I really like that you...," "This is a great example of ...," and "I have really noticed that you...." These specific comments were in addition to general ones such as, "Excellent work" or "Great job." Then, the students took the test that counted for their grades, followed by a survey asking how students felt when they received their tests back with the comments on them. This process of adding teacher praise to students' work lasted for approximately 3 weeks.

Stage Two

During this next stage, I assigned letter grades to the students' work. Because I did not want to cause any harm to my students' ability to perform well on these tests, I also continued with my praise though I did not emphasize it as heavily as in the first stage. I wrote praise, constructive comments, and letter grades on the practice tests. I gave a survey to determine how the students' feelings about their test changed from before they had a letter grade, if at all. I measured if the quality of work on the real test increased or decreased. This stage of assigning letter grades as well as praise took approximately three weeks.

Stage Three

The last component of my study was the incentive program. The incentives occurred in addition to the praise and grades, so as not to inhibit any increases in achievement. I determined the class average on their SAT tests during the first semester and set a realistic goal for them to achieve as a class. If the students reached or exceeded this goal, they would be rewarded with a pizza party. The goal that I set for them was to earn a class average of 16 points out of 20, which equated to a B.

Data Collection

I used surveys to determine self-efficacy throughout the study. These oral surveys were in the form of Likert scaled items and short answers. The items in the surveys questioned the students' attitudes towards practice and real tests, as well as general questions about their motivation.

My primary source of data was the results of the teacher-made SAT tests. I noticed changes in academic performance when I looked at the results of the tests over time. These tests were my measurement of academic success and were spread throughout the study. I also gathered data

(SAT tests) on a control group of similar students, and a baseline for both the control and experimental groups. These data provided a measuring stick for my analyses.

Data Analyses

First, I compared the SAT test scores of my control group and my experimental group from the first semester to establish a baseline. I used this baseline to determine how a specific variable caused any changes in the scores. I also needed to see how closely the control and experimental groups scored before I used any interventions with the experimental group.

I continued to compare the SAT test scores of both groups during the experiment. This provided a clear reference for me as I was trying to see any patterns in changes. It also served as an anchor upon which I could base my conclusions. I went through each variable: teacher praise, letter grades, incentives, and self-efficacy and to identify any connections between my actions and the achievement of my students.

RESULTS OF THE STUDY

I used the results of the first four SAT tests to establish a baseline before I introduced any variables (see Figure 2.1). The control group averaged a mean of 16 out of 20 points on these SAT tests from the first semester.

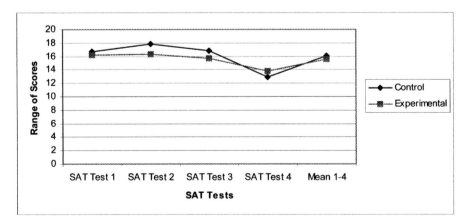

Figure 2.1.   Mean scores for control and experimental groups on the baseline SAT Tests 1-4

The experimental group averaged 15 out of 20 points. The control group appeared to be slightly higher academically than the experimental group when it came to these specific tests. The means of the averages of each test in the baseline showed that the control group (16.03) was slightly higher academically in the area of vocabulary than the experimental group (15.52).

Both groups performed consistently until the final test, when there was a decline in both groups' test scores. The reasons for this decline are unknown; perhaps the test was more difficult.

Stage One—Teacher Praise

I gave SAT Test 5 to my students after I had verbally praised each student as they studied for the tests. They had also taken practice tests. When the students received these tests back from me, the tests had only constructive comments on them, no scores nor grades. Then, they took the formal test.

The control group averaged 18.3, with a standard deviation of 2.15; most students scored fairly close to the average (see Figure 2.2). Two students earned the lowest score of 14, while eight classmates earned the highest possible score of 20.

Scores on the SAT Test 5 showed that the control group outperformed the experimental group when praise was used as a motivational technique. The experimental group averaged 16.55 with a standard deviation of 4.25. The range of scores for this group varied more than for the con-

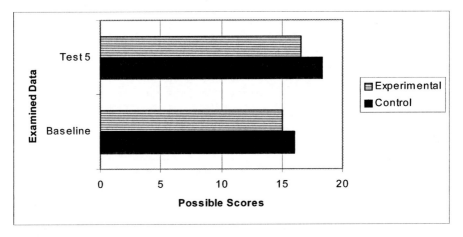

Figure 2.2.   Influence of teacher praise on groups' performance on SAT Test 5.

trol group. One boy earned the lowest score of 2, and four students earned the highest score of 20. Not only was the average significantly lower than the control group, but the students' scores were spread more widely apart from the average. Both groups scored higher than they did on the baseline; the control group scored over 2 points higher and the experimental group scored over 1.5 points higher. I was glad that there was an increase in scores; however, these cannot be attributed to my additional praise since both groups experienced a gain. Perhaps this test was not very difficult or maybe the students studied more for it.

Stage Two—Teacher Praise and Grades

During this stage, I continued to praise my students, but not as much; grades were added to the equation. On SAT Test 6, the control group averaged 15.65 with a standard deviation of 4.03 (see Figure 2.3). The lowest score earned was seven and four students earned the highest possible score.

Results from the SAT Test 6 revealed that the control group scored higher than the experimental group during the stage when grades were used to motivate. The experimental group averaged 12 with a standard deviation of 5.88. Two students earned zero points on this test and only one student earned the highest score of 19. The control group scored better than the experimental group, and, although lower, scored in close proximity to the baseline average. The experimental group not only declined in score compared to the baseline (3 point deficit), but they also

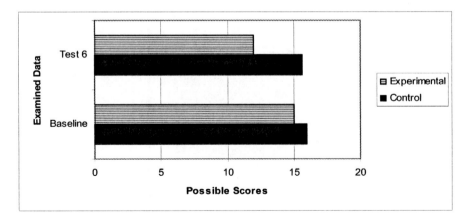

Figure 2.3.   Influence of teacher praise and grades on groups' performance on SAT Test 6.

scored lower compared to the teacher praise stage by itself. In this case, grades combined with teacher praise did not seem to work as a high motivational tool.

Stage Three—Teacher Praise, Grades, and Incentives

In this stage, the teacher praise was less evident than in stage one; the use of grades was maintained. The added variable was an incentive: a pizza party. I administered and examined the results of SAT Tests 7 and 8 during this stage.

On the SAT Test 7, the control group averaged 16.55 with a standard deviation of 1.99 (see Figure 2.4). The lowest score earned was 14, by four students. Three students earned the highest score of 20. Although this class did not know about the pizza party incentive, they met the requirement (16 points).

The control and experimental groups met the goal score (16) on the SAT Test 7, however neither group met this same goal for SAT Test 8. On the SAT Test 8, the control group averaged 14.35 with a standard deviation of 4.3. The lowest score was 7 earned by one student, while four students earned a perfect score of 20. It is also important to note that four students scored under 10 points. This group would not have earned the pizza party if that had been their incentive.

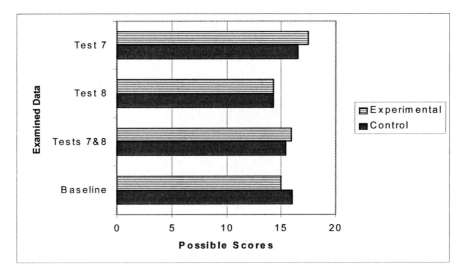

Figure 2.4.   Influence of teacher praise, grades, and incentives on groups' performances on SAT Test 7 and SAT Test 8.

On the SAT Test 7, the experimental group averaged 17.55 with a standard deviation of 3.28. The lowest score was 5, earned by one student and three students earned a perfect score. However, 90% of the students earned a score of 16 or better and the average exceeded my goal by 1.55 points. They earned the pizza party!

On SAT Test 8, the experimental group averaged 14.35 with a standard deviation of 5.23. Two students earned the lowest score, 7, and four students earned a perfect score. Forty-five percent of this group scored 16 points or better. The class did not earn a pizza party, so they were disappointed.

Compared to the baseline, the control group scored a bit higher on the first test and over 1.5 points lower on the second test. The experimental group, however, scored over 2.5 points higher than their baseline on the first test and over .5 points lower on their second test. Utilizing all three variables, in the case of SAT Test 7, was successful as evidenced by 13 higher scores and attainment of the class goal. When SAT Tests 7 and 8 were averaged, the experimental group outscored the baseline, while the control group did not. Notably, this was the only instance in which the experimental group outperformed the control group.

Conclusions Based on Baseline and SAT Tests 5-8

The control and experimental groups showed an interesting pattern for all eight SAT tests (see Figure 2.5). The groups scored the same whole score for the baseline test (16 points) and SAT Test 8 (14 points).

Results showed that the control group repeatedly scored higher than the experimental group except on SAT Test 7. In the baseline, the control and experimental groups scored the highest scores (17 and 16 respectively) on SAT Test 2. Also in the baseline, both groups scored their lowest scores (12 and 13) on SAT Test 4.

During the experimental period, the control group scored the highest (18 points) on SAT Test 5, while the experimental group scored the highest (17 points) on SAT Test 7. Interestingly, all variables were present when SAT Test 7 was given. Both groups scored the lowest on SAT Test 6 although the scores were widely varied (control mean score of 15 and experimental mean score of 12). The overall highest score for the control group was 18 points on SAT Test 5 and for the experimental group was 17 points on SAT Test 7. The overall lowest score for the control group was 12 points in SAT Test 4 and for the experimental group was 12 points in SAT Test 6. The control group began as stronger performers on the SAT tests than the experimental group. However, by the end, when I intro-

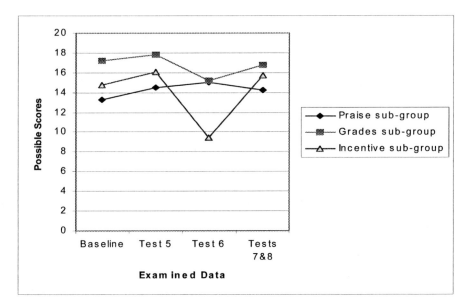

Figure 2.5.   Mean scores for control and experimental groups on baseline and SAT Tests 5-8.

duced all variables, the experimental group scored above the control group.

Praise Subgroup Findings

The students who chose praise as their preferred motivator in my first survey, i.e. the praise subgroup, averaged 14.5 points on the SAT Test 5; this was their second highest score over the course of the experiment and almost a point over their baseline score (see Figure 2.6).

This group did not have much variation in score, but did peak on SAT Test 6, which combined praise with grades. The remainder of the class averaged 16.4 on the same test during stage one. Although each subgroup improved their scores at least once from their baseline, none of the groups peaked when their preferred motivator was introduced.

Grades Subgroup Findings

The grades subgroup actually scored their lowest score (15.2) on the test that emphasized grades and teacher praise (SAT Test 6); they also

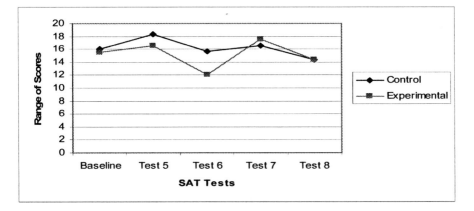

Figure 2.6.   Mean scores for praise, grades, and incentive subgroups on SAT
Tests.

scored lower than their established baseline (see Figure 2.6). They peaked
with a score of 17.8 on SAT Test 5, which only emphasized teacher praise.
The rest of the class averaged 10.2 on SAT Test 6, so this subgroup did
score higher than their classmates did when the motivational strategy
they preferred was used.

Incentive Subgroup Findings

The incentive subgroup scored their second highest score (15.7) on
SAT Tests 7 and 8, when an incentive was offered (see Figure 2.6). This
score was almost one point higher than their baseline. The other students
in the class averaged 16.2 points on SAT Tests 7 and 8, which does not
indicate that the incentive subgroup was more motivated than the others
in the class for these tests. They peaked at 16.1 points on SAT Test 5,
when praise was the only variable.

Self-Efficacy Findings

Throughout my study, I surveyed my students about their motivation
and feelings towards tests. I found the information I collected to be interesting and useful. I have only included the results that specifically pertain
to self-efficacy.

I had my class to rate on a scale of 1 (*terrible*) to 10 (*great*) how they felt
about the comments and their performance on the test I implemented

during stage one, when I introduced praise as a motivator. The average response for this question was eight. One student wrote down a number lower than six and four students wrote down 10. This shows that most students felt pretty good about the comments they received and/or their performance on the test. The student who gave the question a 1 on this scale earned 2 out of 20 points on the test, which gave my comments more of a constructive, rather than a praising, tone.

I asked the students to rate 1 (*strongly disagree*) to 10 (*strongly agree*) if they felt good about themselves when they earned a good grade. They answered with an average of 9.2. Two students reported scores of less than 6, but 14 students, 70%, answered that they strongly agreed (10) that they felt good about themselves when they received a good grade. Of course, *good* can be subjective, since for many students, good ranges from an A to a C.

I also asked the students to rate 1 (*strongly disagree*) to 10 (*strongly agree*) the opposite: if they felt bad about themselves when they earned a bad grade. My students answered the question with an average of 8.05, a little smaller than the previous question. This made me think that bad grades do not lend themselves to negative feelings as strongly as good grades do to positive feelings. Four students answered less than 6 and nine students (45%) gave a perfect score of 10. Again, *bad* is a subjective term.

After the students had their tests back with moderate praise and letter grades on them, I again asked them to rate on a scale of 1 (*terrible*) to 10 (*great*) how they felt about their performance. The class averaged a 6.9 on this item. This is not as positive of a reaction as I expected. Six students ranked themselves on the negative side of feelings about their test, while the rest of the class felt as though they were on the other half of the spectrum. These six students earned 0, 4, 6, 8, 11, and 14 out of 20. This is interesting, especially the boy who earned 14. Though 14 is higher score than other achieved, he did not feel great or even good about it. Three students gave themselves a 10, which indicates that they felt great about their performance. These students earned 15, 18, and 19 out of 20. It is interesting to see that these three girls did not need a perfect grade to feel good about themselves. Of course, the praise from me could have influenced this survey question as well.

When surveyed, 17 students (85%) reported feeling more motivated because of the pizza incentive, though two of them said they were only a *little more* motivated. The remaining three students reported feeling the same level of motivation regardless of whether there was pizza involved or not. Not one student said that the incentive caused them to feel less motivated to study for the tests.

CONCLUSIONS

During this study, I saw a small improvement in the test scores when I implemented teacher praise. As with any experience with middle school students, I felt the need to celebrate this small success. I could not determine if praise was the factor that led to this success; it could have been merely coincidental.

Students' test scores declined when I introduced the grades with a marginal amount of teacher praise. Compared to the baseline, the students performed less well during the experiment on SAT Test 6. Again, I was unable to pinpoint the variable as the cause for this failure.

When I added the incentive, a pizza party, to the teacher praise and grades, I noted a large improvement immediately on SAT Test 7. The students earned a pizza party and seemed very proud of themselves. On SAT Test 8, students showed an improvement from the baseline score, but it was small and they did not reach the established goal. The baseline score was not strong and the scores during the experiment were not much better.

Though I was unable to determine the relative success of each motivating variable independently, the surveys did supply me with students' opinions about the perceived values of the motivators. I found that the students did not score better during the stage in which their preferred motivator was employed. There was a discrepancy between students' performance and the motivator they appreciated the most. I gathered interesting data about my students' sense of efficacy towards a given variable, however the relationship between those scores and their motivation remains unclear.

Limitations

The scores from SAT Test 4 (the last baseline test) and SAT Test 8 (the last experimental test) were much lower than the other scores. I gave these tests towards the end of each semester when students were completing large writing projects. It is possible that students spent their time working on the projects instead of studying for the tests. Another possibility is that students may not have taken these tests as seriously since they had three other SAT test scores. Perhaps they thought these test scores would not affect their grade too much. In addition, SAT Test 8 fell during the week before school ended, which could have altered students' attitudes towards studying.

Word difficulty is another limitation. Though all of the words on the SAT tests came from the same source, the level of difficulty of each word may have influenced my students' success. Some words were more difficult; some words were easier. Some students may have had prior knowledge of some of the words, so already knew the meaning and/or spelling. This would have made of the tests easier for some of the students than others.

Student absence from school was a limiting factor. During the last phase of my study, I taught my language arts students on a Monday and gave them the test on the next Wednesday. However, on Tuesday, many of the students went on a band field trip. I noticed in the past that students forget what is happening at school when they go off campus. This absence from school could be a possible factor for their weaker performance on the final test.

Student choice of incentive and motivators were other limitations. During stage three, I did not allow my students to choose the incentive, which could have influenced their motivation level. Although it worked for SAT Test 7, a pizza party did not motivate them to study for SAT Test 8. This leads me to believe that perhaps the students needed a choice in their extrinsic motivator. I also did not give my students a voice in what they believed motivated them. I decided that I would test the effects of praise, grades, and pizza. Then, students chose which of those motivators helped them the most, when it is possible that none of the options were motivating. In addition, I did not give students a choice when coming up with a goal to reach in order to earn the incentive. If we had created the goal together, I believe it would have been more effective. The importance of offering choices became more evident as I continued to review the research literature. Gehlbach and Roeser (2002) suggested that intrinsic motivation will increase when students have some choices in their assignments.

Reflections and Implications

Through surveys and conversations with students, I learned that almost every student welcomes true praise and that it can be powerful. Sometimes that power comes in the form of a great performance on a test, but very often, it comes in the form of seeing a child smile. My study made me think about the kind of praise I give to my students. I need to remember to praise specific actions instead of offering generic praise.

I struggle with how to use grades. Administrators, the community, students, and parents rely heavily on grades to judge students' performance. I must ensure that each grade reflects exactly what I want it to reflect. It is imperative that I base grades on what my students know. In the past, it seems that I assigned grades based on how responsible students were in completing assignments. In light of the research on the possible harmful effects of grades, I am becoming more thoughtful about my grading practices.

I remain unsure about the use of incentives. I suppose that, in moderation, they have their place. I think that it is nice to celebrate our learning as a class, rather than to attach celebrations to accomplishing a specific task. I did see a high level of motivation in many of my students to study for the test, but I do not think that an incentive can change behavior long term, as the results from SAT Test 8 show. My students were less excited about the offer of pizza the second time and they did not reach the target goal. I am not certain if incentives have to increase in value to be successful. Perhaps for incentives to be effective, students need input into their selection, as I mentioned in the limitations section.

Although I did not learn as much as I had hoped about self-efficacy, this action research study reinforced what I already know: that self-efficacy has a large impact on a student's motivation. As I continue to improve as an educator, I need to remind myself of this fact. If my students feel capable of learning the material that I am teaching, their chances of success increase dramatically.

Further Study

First, I would like to find a way to collect concrete data linking self-efficacy to motivation. This is very important and definitely warrants a closer look. Next, I would conduct this study over an extended period, at least 2 years. Additional time would allow me to examine the motivation variables independently and gather more data. Ideally, I would include more students and test results to reduce possible skewing of an average because of a high or a low score. Finally, I believe it would have been more useful to me if I had isolated each variable. As I moved through the study, I added another variable without eliminating a variable. Consequently, it is difficult to draw strong conclusions about the motivation variables on student performance.

Through communication with my students and studying the research of those before me, I came to a realization. Students, particularly young adolescents, do not conform to what is convenient for us: educators and researchers. What motivates one student one day may not work for another or even for the same student on a different day. This challenge makes each student unique and keeps me coming back for more. Despite all of the qualifiers to my study that I mentioned earlier, I realized several truths. We need to encourage all of our students to exceed their perceived limitations, help them work through their failures, and celebrate their successes in a way that makes them feel confident and capable. This is our job.

REFERENCES

Alber, S., & Heward, W. (1997). Recruit it or lose it! Training students to recruit positive teacher attention. *Intervention in School and Clinic, 32,* 275-282.

Anderman, L. H., & Midgley, C. (1997). Motivation and middle school students. In J. L. Irvin (Ed.), *What current research says to the middle level practitioner* (pp. 41-48). Columbus, OH: National Middle School Association.

Berndt, T., Hawkins, J., & Jiao, Z. (1999). Influences of friends and friendships on adjustment to junior high school. *Merril-Palmer Quarterly, 45*(1), 13-41.

Brophy, J. (1998). Failure syndrome students. *ERIC Digest.* (ERIC Document Reproduction Service No. ED 419 625). Champaign, IL: ERIC Clearinghouse on Elementary and Early Childhood Education.

Cizek, G. (1996). Grades: The final frontier in assessment reform. In K. Cauley, F. Linder, & J. McMillan (Eds.), *Educational Psychology* (pp. 221-224). Guilford, CT: McGraw-Hill/Dushkin.

Eisenberger, R., & Armeli, S. (1997). Can salient reward increase creative performance without reducing intrinsic creative interest? *Journal of Personality and Social Psychology, 72*(3), 652-663.

Eller, B. (1985). An examination of the effect of tangible and social reinforcers on intelligence test performance of middle school students. *Social Behavior and Personality, 13*(2), 147-157.

Gehlbach, H., & Roeser, R. W. (2002). The middle way to motivating middle school students: Avoiding false dichotomies. *Middle School Journal, 33*(3), 39-46.

Gulotta, C. (2000). *500 SAT words and how to remember them forever.* USA: Mostly Bright Ideas. [Available: www.mostlybrightideas.com]

Hancock, D. (2000). Impact of verbal praise on college students' time spent on homework. *The Journal of Educational Research, 93*(6), 384-389.

Hootstein, E. (1994). Motivating students to learn. *Clearing House, 4*(67), 213-217.

Johnson, D. (1999). Creating fat kids who don't like to read. *Book Report, 18*(2), 96.

Johnson, G. (1998). Principles of instruction for at-risk learners. *Preventing School Failure, 42*(4), 167-174.

Kaplan, D., Peck, B., & Kaplan, H. (1997). Decomposing the academic failure-dropout relationship: A longitudinal study. *The Journal of Educational Research, 90,* 331-343.

Lopez, D. (1999). Social cognitive influences on self-regulated learning: The impact of action-control beliefs and academic goals on achievement-related outcomes. *Learning and Individual Differences, 3*(11), 301-320.

Majesky, D. (1993). Grading should go. *Educational Leadership, 50*(7), 88, 90.

Maslow, A. H. (1943). A theory of human motivation. *Psychological Review, 50,* 370-396.

McNinch, G. (1997). Earning by learning: changing attitudes and habits in reading. *Reading Horizons, 37*, 186-194.

Miller, A., & Hom, H. (1997). Conceptions of ability and the interpretation of praise, blame, and material rewards. *The Journal of Experimental Education, 65*, 163-177.

National Middle School Association. (n.d.). *National Middle School Association's Position statement on academic achievement.* Retrieved June 26, 2001, from http://www.nmsa.org/news/pospapacachieve.html

Roeser, R. W., & Eccles, J. S. (1998). Adolescents' perceptions of middle school: Relation to longitudinal changes in academic and psychological adjustment. *Journal of Research on Adolescence, 8*(1), 123-158.

Ryan, R., & Deci, E. (2000). Intrinsic and extrinsic motivations: Classic definitions and new directions. In K. Cauley, F. Linder, & J. McMillan (Eds.), *Educational psychology* (pp. 148-155). Guilford, CT: McGraw-Hill/Dushkin.

Schwartz, S. L. (1996). Hidden messages in teacher talk: Praise and empowerment. *Teaching Children Mathematics, 2*(7), 396-401.

Skinner, B. F. (n.d.). *A brief survey of operant behavior.* Retrieved June 21, 2002, from http://www.bfskinner.org/operant.asp

Zimmerman, B. (2000). Self-efficacy: An essential motive to learn. In K. Cauley, F. Linder & J. McMillan (Eds.), *Educational Psychology* (pp. 156-159). Guilford, CT: McGraw Hill/Dushkin.

CHAPTER 3

THE USE OF MANIPULATIVES IN MATHEMATICS CLASS

Theresa A. Shrum

ABSTRACT

This action-based research project explores whether the use of math manipulatives improves student performance in a middle school mathematics class. Research about the advantages and disadvantages of manipulative use is summarized. Ideas are included from several sources about successfully using manipulatives. Five lessons focusing on different mathematics content strands were presented to a class of 24 seventh graders highlighting manipulative use. Results from pre and posttests showed student learning gains in four out of five concept areas. During the study, the classroom setup changed to cooperative learning groups and peer tutoring became a norm.

INTRODUCTION

On a hot August afternoon, I entered a classroom where I would start a job teaching seventh and eighth grade mathematics within a few short weeks. I found boxes and boxes of unopened or little used math manipulative materials. I pulled out some of the familiar materials to organize,

Making a Difference: Action Research in Middle Level Education, 41–61

like protractors and rulers and pushed the others aside until time allowed me to go through them more thoroughly.

As I lived through the first months of setting up a new classroom, I wondered how to make use of the manipulative materials. I started to organize them on shelves in containers and thought of ways to incorporate their use into mathematics lessons. I experienced failed attempts as students said they did not need hands-on materials to learn difficult division problems. I found materials scattered and not properly stored after a study on probability. Nevertheless, I also experienced some initial victories. I started to wonder: How do I effectively incorporate the use of manipulatives into my middle school mathematics teaching? How do I organize the materials and the classroom management of these materials? Why do many mathematics teachers at this level stick to teaching abstractly and not incorporate hands-on activities using manipulatives? Are manipulatives best used in the lower grades? How do I prepare and give a lesson using manipulatives? Could the use of manipulatives spark interest in the mathematics classes I now found myself teaching?

These kinds of questions led me to undertake an action research project with the following questions. How does the use of math manipulatives improve student performance in middle school mathematics class? More specifically, how does the use of math manipulatives improve student performance in the areas of computation and estimation, measurement, algebraic relationships, geometry, and probability and statistics? How does the use of math manipulatives improve student attitudes towards learning mathematics at the middle school level? To begin addressing these questions, I explored the research literature dealing with use of math manipulatives.

REVIEW OF THE LITERATURE

Teachers engage in a cycle of inquiry. They research and incorporate what they feel is most important into their curriculum. Then they select the instructional methods they feel best. Finally, they evaluate the students and themselves on this process. Incorporating math manipulatives is one part of putting the puzzle together.

> Effective teachers recognize that the decisions they make shape students' mathematical dispositions and can create rich settings for learning. Selecting and using suitable curricular materials, using appropriate instructional-tools and techniques, and engaging in reflective practice and continuous self-improvement are actions good teachers take every day. (National Council of Teachers of Mathematics, 2000, p. 18)

Teachers' daily planning decisions influence directly the mathematical achievement of students (Mercer & Miller, 1992). Therefore, teachers keep in mind that they want students to value mathematics and to become confident in their mathematical abilities. They want students to become good problem solvers and to learn to reason and communicate mathematically (Joyner, 1990).

This literature review describes how educational researchers define math manipulatives. I also examine the advantages and disadvantages of using math manipulatives. Finally, I look at suggestions for successful classroom management and a lesson design made specifically to incorporate manipulative use.

Definition

Math manipulatives are objects that appeal to several senses and which a student is able to touch, handle, and move (Driscoll, 1981). Marzola (1987) agrees with this definition adding they are concrete models that incorporate mathematical concepts. Examples of manipulatives include: Cuisinaire rods, multilinks, unifix materials and stamps, base ten blocks, math balance, place value activity cards, dominoes, stamps, coin matching cards and stamps, coins and bills, money flash cards, clock dominoes, puzzles and stamps, geared clock face, trundle wheel, metric and customary measurement kit, fraction circles, dominoes, tiles, decimal squares, geoboards, beans and bean strips, sticks, straws, abacuses, and so forth (Marzola, 1987).

Advantages and Disadvantages of Using Math Manipulatives

Boling (1991) cites several ways that manipulatives can help middle school students not lose interest in mathematics. In middle school the content becomes more difficult. Some students still need concrete learning experiences. Peer influence increases. Students are experiencing rapid physical growth. "The average student is still in the concrete to semi concrete learning stage in fifth grade and only just beginning to be able to understand abstract concepts in seventh grade" (p. 18). Suydam (1984) points out student attitudes towards mathematics tend to remain positive until sixth grade and become increasingly less positive as students progress through school.

Is the use of mathematical manipulatives too childish for the middle school student? Quinn (1997) states middle school students do enjoy activities with manipulatives when learning new material rather than to use manipulatives to remediate or review prior knowledge.

Stein and Bovalino (2001) believe manipulatives are a tool, which help students to think and reason in ways that are more meaningful. Manipulatives may increase a child's ability to develop the structure of a concept, increase his/her attention span, and motivation to learn. They provide more immediate and concrete feedback than working with symbols. Remediation is reduced when students are allowed to build and reflect on their own personal knowledge (Ross & Kurtz, 1993). Children who use manipulatives may better understand mathematical ideas and applications to real-life situations (Marzola, 1987). Deep mathematical learning situations are seldom generated on blackboards. With manipulatives the child can create something not there before and builds it into his personality (Dienes, 1960).

Manipulatives are often used while students are in cooperative learning groups. This deepens understanding as students handle the concrete materials, discussing and describing the processes and results (Ball, 1992). Cooperative work aligns with Vygotsky's cognitive theory. His theory proposes learners need to verbalize in order to direct attention, solve problems, and form concepts (Woolfolk, 1993). Vygotsky (1978) asserts, "The most significant moment in the course of intellectual development, which gives birth to the purely human forms of practical and abstract intelligence, occurs when speech and practical activity, two previously completely independent lines of development, converge" (p. 24).

Why do teachers resist the use of manipulatives? Tooke, Hyatt, Leigh, Snyder, and Borda (1992) identify several reasons for teacher resistance. Teacher's guides in textbooks are the most widely used resource for selecting activities and instruction and many guides provide lessons with limited student interaction or manipulative use. Teachers resist their use because they feel manipulative instruction for students above fourth grade is inappropriate and students above fifth grade *need* abstract teaching. Furthermore, teachers experience pressure from administrators to cover the curriculum and manipulative use is too time consuming. Additionally, some teachers say that manipulatives confuse their students (Tooke et al., 1992). Preservice teachers, in particular, cited a lack of confidence in their own abilities to use manipulative materials correctly (Trueblood, 1986).

Teacher reluctance to manipulatives is quite varied. Some teachers believe students will become too dependent on the materials and not master basic computational algorithms (Trueblood, 1986). Other teachers have found lessons involving concrete materials difficult to manage (Ross & Kurtz, 1993). Another fear is that students will just play with the manipulatives (Heuser, 2000). Teachers feel that manipulatives are too time consuming to make, organize, and implement with their students. Additionally, it is expensive to buy many commercially produced manipulatives (Hollingsworth, 1990).

Indeed using a variety of different kinds of manipulatives can help children think about ideas in different ways (Burns, 1996). However, Driscoll (1981) cites this variance in thinking as a potential weakness rather than a strength. Children can be distracted by irrelevant details such as colors or numbers written on manipulatives. Teachers need to use caution as they teach children to generalize from one representation to another.

Successful Use of Manipulatives

Researchers and educators note the benefits of incorporating a concrete activity, then pictorial representation, and moving on to abstract or symbolic mathematical representation. Then, those students not at the symbolic level can eventually understand the topic (Boling, 1991; Quinn, 1997; Stein & Bovalino, 2001).

Mercer and Miller (1992) and Ross and Kurtz (1993) suggest the following process. Teachers model the concept using the manipulative with an overhead projector if possible. The teacher guides the students to practice and provides feedback. Students practice independently. Several researchers encourage cooperative learning and group work as students practice on their own (Burns, 1996; Weaver as cited in Ohanian). In this process, students communicate reasoning with others in their group or partnership and discuss related components in their reasoning (Battista, 1999). A final step is to have students reflect on what they have learned and state these reflections in writing (Ross & Kurtz, 1993).

An important part of incorporating manipulatives into math lessons is knowing when to intervene. "Direct teacher intervention is sometimes critical to the students' progress" (Battista, 1999, p. 447). Within reason, it is important to let the student struggle. This is an essential component for establishing the validity of their mental model and enumeration.

To facilitate manipulative use teachers should *think aloud* about what they are representing (Joyner, 1990). However, teachers should not work through the problems step-by-step nor immediately correct any deviation from the prescribed procedure. Teachers need to lead students toward discovery, not jump in and supply the way to do it (Stein & Bovalino, 2001).

The majority of teachers who successfully use manipulatives have training devoted to learning to incorporate manipulatives (Stein & Bovalino, 2001). Tooke et al. (1992) state, "the largest part of those teachers who did indicate they used manipulatives in their classroom said they did so because their colleagues had informed them of the effectiveness of the materials as well as how to use them" (p. 6).

Key to successful use of manipulatives is making sure teachers have a clear understanding of why the materials are important to the lesson (Joyner, 1990). Students should not be left too much to their own devices. This may happen if little of a mathematical introduction is given and students do not know the overall objective or goal. Teachers experience more success if they design their own lessons and try things out first (Stein & Bovalino, 2001).

When selecting which manipulatives to use the materials should suit the concept and the developmental stage of the learners. There should be a clear connection between the meaning and the symbol (Marzola, 1987). Manipulatives should be varied to help students generalize math concepts (Mercer & Miller, 1992).

One of the biggest challenges to is how to organize the manipulatives. Package the materials to avoid chaos and so that their distribution becomes a smooth process. Students need to help organize the materials, and then, should be taught to store and put manipulatives away. Students need guidelines for what is acceptable and not acceptable (Joyner, 1990). Classroom procedures regarding their use should be in place (Stein & Bovalino, 2001).

Finally, teachers need to be aware that when first using manipulatives students will want to actively participate (Ross & Kurtz, 1993). Let students become active agents as soon as possible (Marzola, 1987). Students will have a stronger desire to investigate in their own manner than to follow the teacher's directions (Joyner, 1990).

Summary of Literature

In conclusion, this literature review defined math manipulatives, discussed the advantages and disadvantages of their use, and listed suggestions for their effective use. Overall the literature favored the use of manipulatives in teaching mathematics. However, as Driscoll (1981) states in the conclusion of his study on math manipulatives:

> The research into manipulatives and mathematics instruction shows that the quality of learning is not inevitable and that children cannot learn mathematics well with manipulatives alone. For an experience with mathematics that is firmly planted and easy to build on, children need the guidance of aware, informed, and caring teachers. (p. 27)

METHODS

Information on Student Population

The action-based research took place in a rural community with a population of approximately 20,000. It is the hub for smaller agricultural towns. The research was conducted with seventh graders at a middle school. The teaching staff at this middle school included three mathematics teachers for seventh and eighth grades.

The average student enrollment for this school ranged between 450 and 500. The total number of students eligible for free/reduced lunches was 49.6%. The total enrollment for the seventh grade class was 149. Seventh grade individual classes average 28 students. The total seventh grade class was 58% female and 42% male. The ethnic population distribution was 78% White, 13% Hispanic, 4% Asian, 3% Native American, and 1% Pacific Islanders.

Twenty-four seventh graders served as the population for this study. Since two students moved during the year, I analyzed data sets for 22 students. This school district has a high mobility rate and frequent absenteeism. So, any student missing for either the pre or posttest was excluded from the analysis.

Instructional Methods

I designed a lesson for each of the major mathematics strands: computation and estimation (C&E), measurement (Meas), algebra (Alg), geometry (Geom), probability (Prob) and statistics. Below are the ways that I incorporated manipulative use into the lessons for each of strand:

- The C&E lesson used Cuisenaire rods to find the least common multiple (LCM). The LCM is used to help students find the common denominator when adding or subtracting fractions.
- For Meas a concept attainment lesson was presented on recognizing when to use one-dimensional (1D), two-dimensional (2D) and three-dimensional (3D) measures. Manipulatives were separated by students into 1D, 2D, and 3D categories and then assigned a proper measurement label. For example, a line would be measured in inches, a square piece of cloth in square inches and a sugar cube in cubic inches. On the follow up worksheet students were asked to do conversions such as: $1 \text{ft}^2 = \underline{} \text{in}^2$.
- The Alg lesson was a problem solving activity using wooden tiles. Students tried to find the *nth* term. For example, a sequence with

one tile in the first term, two tiles in the second term, and three tiles in the third term had *n* tiles in the nth term.

- The Geom lesson involved measuring various round objects and discovering pi or 3.14.... Students divided the circumference and diameter of the round objects.
- The Prob lesson made use of student created dice. Students marked the dice with uneven probabilities and created probability problems.

To support the inclusion of manipulatives in my teaching, I developed and used a lesson plan template (see Appendix A).

Data Collection

I collected three sources of data: teacher made pre and posttests, a student survey, and a teacher journal. For the student attitude survey, I used a 5-point Likert scale to provide quantitative information about student's beliefs (see Appendix B). The five levels of response were strongly agree, agree, undecided, disagree, and strongly disagree. I administered this teacher-made survey before lessons in the fall and after lessons in the spring. I also recorded informal journal observations throughout the school year about the selected class. My observations were noted before or after the testing or manipulative lesson. I included my own observations and opinions along with statements I heard from my students.

Data Analyses

I entered the pre and posttest scores into an Excel spreadsheet, which permitted me to compare the mean scores for the pre and posttests as well as construct tables and figures to illustrate these means. I also computed a learning gain score, the difference between the mean pre and posttest scores. Then, I constructed a table and figure to show the learning gain for each math strand.

Due to the nature of the attitude survey, I chose not to average the results. Instead, I combined the strongly agree and agree responses for a percent agreement level and combined the strongly disagree and disagree responses for a percent disagreement level. I tallied the undecided responses as well. I used this information when reporting students' levels of agreement or disagreement and whether these levels changed over the course of the year.

To analyze the teacher recorded informal journal observations, I highlighted comments dealing with manipulative use, attitudes towards mathematics and any other ideas associated with the action research. I coded words or phrases as positive, negative or neutral. I used this information to make generalizations about the study from the fall to the spring.

RESULTS

I obtained the following results from analyzing 22 students' pre and posttest scores before and after the C&E, Meas, Alg, Geom, and Prob lessons (see Table 3.1). The students' mean scores for C&E were 39% on the pretest and 51% on the posttest. Students' mean scores for Meas rose from 23% on the pretest to 96% on the posttest. Mean scores on the Alg pretest and posttest were 65%. Students' mean score for Geom were 17% on the pretest and 62% on the posttest. The students' mean score on the Prob pretest was 40% and on the posttest was 69%.

Results of the manipulative pre and posttests showed an increase from the fall to the spring, except for the Alg scores, which remained the same.

I calculated learning gains from pre to posttest for each of the tests (see Table 3.2). The learning gains increased for the concepts of C&E (12%), Meas (73%), Geom (45%) and Prob (29%). No gain was evidenced for the Alg concept. In general, these results seem to indicate the use of math manipulatives helped students learn in all strands except Alg.

Attitude Survey

The results of the student attitude survey provide some insights into my students' perceptions of manipulatives in the math class. First, Table 3.3 summarizes the survey results. Then, I discuss the students' responses to each survey question.

Table 3.1.   Math Manipulative Test Results

Strands	Pre	Post
Computation & Estimation	39%	51%
Measurement	23%	96%
Algebra	65%	65%
Geometry	17%	62%
Probability	40%	69%

Table 3.2.   Learning Gain from Manipulative Pre to Post Test

	Strands				
	C & E	Meas	Alg	Geom	Prob
Learning Gain	12%	73%	0%	45%	29%

In Question 1 (Q#1), the students indicated whether math manipulatives helped them to better understand math concepts being taught. Both the pre and post surveys showed a strong percentage of agreement, from 75% to 81%. The percent of disagreement remained the same at 6% for the pre survey and 6% for the post survey. The undecided was at 19% for the pre and 13% for the post survey. Therefore, students appeared to think using math manipulatives helped them to understand better the math concepts taught in both the fall and the spring.

For Question 2 (Q#2), students were to respond about whether they liked doing math. A 62% majority said they liked doing math in the pre survey and 44% said they liked doing math in the post survey. The pre survey percent of disagreement was 25%, while the post survey was 31%. The big change from pre to post survey came from one-fourth more of the students expressing an undecided opinion on the post survey. Therefore, students appeared to like doing math at the beginning of the year more than at the end of the year.

Question 3 (Q#3) involved deciding whether using math manipulatives was confusing and if students would prefer a teacher explaining how to complete the task without the use of a manipulative. Sixty-two percent of the students disagreed in the pre survey as compared to 38% in the post survey. For the percent of agreement, 19% of the students in the pre survey agreed, while in the post survey it increased to 31%. This would seem to indicate more students would rather not use manipulatives or changed their opinion to undecided, because the undecided opinions went up from 19% to 38%.

For Question 4 (Q#4), students indicated their agreement or disagreement with the statement: "I don't think I get enough real work done when using math manipulatives." Sixty-two percent disagreed in the pre survey, while 38% disagreed in the post survey. The level of agreement remained at 13% for both the pre and post survey. However, 24% shifted from agreeing to being undecided. It appeared more students did not feel the use of math manipulatives was a factor in whether they were really accomplishing work in math class.

Question 5 (Q#5) dealt with whether the student thought math manipulatives helped them like math class better. Fifty percent of the students at the beginning of the year agreed, while 6% disagree, and 44% were undecided. Opinions shifted a little in the post survey with 44% showing a level of agreement, 13% showing disagreement and 38% undecided. It seemed that less students in the spring thought that math manipulatives helped them like math class better.

Students also responded to this open-ended question: "What do you like or dislike about math manipulatives?" In response, students made

Table 3.3. Math Survey Results

Question Synopsis	Pre Survey Agreement	Post Survey Agreement	Pre Survey Disagreement	Post Survey Disagreement	Pre Survey Undecided	Post Survey Undecided
Q#1 Math manipulatives helped student to better understand math concepts.	75%	81%	6%	6%	19%	13%
Q#2 Student indicates whether they like math.	62%	44%	25%	31%	13%	38%
Q#3 Math manipulatives are confusing to use. Student would prefer teacher explanation.	19%	31%	62%	38%	19%	38%
Q#4 Student indicates they do not think the use of manipulatives helps them achieve objective.	13%	13%	62%	38%	25%	50%
Q#5 Student likes math class better because s/he may use manipulatives.	50%	44%	6%	13%	44%	38%

considerably more positive comments than negative or neutral comments. Examples of positive wording included: "I like," "helps me," "easier for me to understand," "they're fun," "hands-on," "cool," and "can physically see a problem." The word "like" appeared in two-thirds of the pre survey responses.

Negative student responses included: "confuses," "dislike," "get in the way," "take longer," and "teacher makes you use them." These types of responses came from less than 15% of the survey respondents for the pre and post surveys.

About the same percentage of students were neutral about whether they liked or disliked using manipulatives. Typical responses included: "don't care," "don't know if I'll like it," "not sure," and "okay."

Teacher Journal

I recorded observations in my teacher journal throughout the school year. Though the comments were qualitative rather than quantitative data, several repetitions in ideas occurred. Descriptions and examples of my entries follow:

- Students expressed pleasure, enjoyment or having fun while using manipulatives.
- Students used words such as "fun," "happy," "cool," and "liked it."
- Several incidents occurred where students wanted to check understanding with peers.
- The most frequently recorded observation involved the teacher having to answer many individual questions. For example, students needed follow-up attention because they did not understand what they were supposed to be doing.
- Several times during the year, the teacher noted some students discovering very quickly the intended math concept when using the manipulative. Sometimes these students were then bored while waiting for other students to understand.
- Four discipline incidents were recorded.

In summary, my journal entries indicated that students enjoy using math manipulatives. Overall, my recorded observations were more positive than revealed by the students' survey responses (see Table 3.3).

CONCLUSIONS

In formulating my conclusions, I review my original research questions, consider my actions, and speculate on what the data and analyses showed. I also discuss how the results will influence my future practice.

How Does the Use of Math Manipulatives Improve Student Performance in the Area of Computation and Estimation?

I presented a lesson using Cuisenaire rods to improve student performance in the area of C&E. I allowed students playtime to help them become familiar with the manipulatives. The next day, I presented the concept portion of the lesson and students were supposed to see the connection between matching up different rod colors to find the least common multiple (LCM). Many students did not seem very comfortable with the manipulative, even on the second day of the lesson. Very few seemed to understand the connection by the end of the lesson. For example, three purple rods or two green rods equaled twelve white rods (12 is a common denominator for fractions like 1/4 and 1/6).

Results of the pre and posttests showed only a 12% learning gain (see Table 3.2). In my opinion, the reason for this may be the pre and posttests covered too many fraction objectives besides LCM. The manipulative, Cuisenaire rods, was unfamiliar to students, so the results for the use of this particular manipulative may be skewed. In the future, before I try to use Cuisenaire rods again, I will involve the students in more practice beforehand. Afterwards, they may be able to transfer a concrete idea to an abstract computational concept.

In my teacher journal notes, I stated that I could barely get around to the many groups needing help because they did not understand. The class had at least four students on a Learning Assistance Program, but did not have an instructional aide helping me. I learned how difficult it is to work with some manipulatives when students do not understand the use of the Cuisenaire rods. As indicated by the attitude survey (see Table 3.3), more students decided that using math manipulatives was confusing or became undecided as to whether they thought they were confusing or not. After this particular lesson, some students were confused how to use the manipulative to understand the C&E concepts.

In conclusion, the Cuisenaire rod manipulatives could have increased student performance in the area of computation and estimations, though they did not notably help many of the students in this class. I would recommend to other teachers to practice using the Cuisenaire rods with an individual student first to increase confidence before using in the classroom for the first time (Trueblood, 1986).

How Does the Use of Math Manipulatives Improve Student Performance in the Area of Measurement?

I presented a concept attainment measurement lesson to help students recognize the use of 1D, 2D, or 3D measures. Most of the class members seemed to be able to make the necessary conversions after categorizing the concrete examples into 1D, 2D and 3D groups. However, I taught the lesson a second time to several individuals in the class the next day who did not understand the mechanics of converting (deciding whether to multiply or divide by the correct smaller or larger unit and accompanying number). I recognized the wide gap in developmental levels between class members and one-on-one help was the only way some of the students would probably ever understand the concept.

The pre and posttests closely matched the follow up assignment for this measurement objective. The manipulatives helped students transfer knowledge about the look and feel of 1D, 2D, and 3D objects (concrete understanding) to the abstract task of converting the measurement labels. I decided students in future classes would benefit from these manipulatives being used and should experience learning gains. Unlike my pre and posttest for the Cuisenaire rod lesson there was alignment between what was taught and what was tested in the Meas testing.

In conclusion, the use of math manipulatives did help to improve student performance in the area of Meas. I believe reteaching some students in the class after they failed to understand the initial lesson might have made the learning gains for this concept greater than for the other concepts I taught.

The manipulatives used were things familiar to students like paper, sand, pieces of fabric, gravel, etc. Manipulative use is often more successful if teachers design their own lessons (Stein & Bovalino, 2001). In this case, I did not use a commercially purchased product, but designed the lesson myself and used everyday items familiar to students. I believe this contributed to the success of teaching this measurement concept.

How Does the Use of Math Manipulatives Improve Student Performance in the Area of Algebraic Relationships?

I presented a visual math lesson after the pretest with the final objective being a student showing evidence of finding the missing number sequence terms. Another objective was being able to find the nth term, an algebraic rule that would help the student find the number of items in later sequence terms. No change occurred in the average test scores from the pre to posttest. Looking closely at how individuals scored on the pre and posttests, I found inconsistency. Evidently, the students did not learn the algebraic concept that I was trying to teach. I noted in the teacher journal notes that a few students caught on readily to the concept of finding the nth term rule. The second day of the lesson many more class members began to understand the concept but class members of lower developmental level still had little understanding of what the concept was at all.

In the future, I would be more careful to explain slowly during the guided practice portion of a visual math lesson. Students can be confused if a teacher tries to make them jump too soon from one type of representation to another (Battista, 1999). I caution other teachers to proceed slowly and to check student understanding frequently as a visual math lesson progresses, perhaps breaking up the content into more minilessons to help the student's concept formation.

If students with different developmental levels are present in the same class, I recommend the more mathematically gifted students be allowed to go on and try to find the algebraic representation for more difficult sequences, while the teacher reteaches the concept to other students. Peer tutoring is also recommended.

How Does the Use of Math Manipulatives Improve Student Performance in the Area of Geometry?

The pretest given to students contained 10 questions about essential vocabulary terms, subskills, and how to find the circumference of a circle. The activity used several round manipulative objects with the goal being a student understanding pi or 3.14… comes from dividing the circumference by the diameter of a circular portion of an object. There was a 45% increase in learning gain from average pre to posttest scores. Many students had 0% on the pretest. Only one student still had 0% on the posttest.

Analysis of my teacher journal notes revealed some initial confusion about how to use the measuring tape and the concepts of circumference and diameter. I taught these subskills in previous lessons and students helped each other cooperatively in their work groups to figure these out. Indeed, Ball (1992) recommends cooperative learning groups when students use manipulatives.

Strong learning gains occurred because the majority of students improved from pre to posttest. I taught the test concepts as subskills and reinforced using the manipulative activity. My teacher journal notes indicated that students retained concepts and were able to transfer them to the new task involving manipulatives. I was pleased that students consistently went from low scores indicating a lack of understanding to higher scores. The majority of the students did indeed make learning gains. I anticipate similar results with another class of students.

In conclusion, the use of math manipulatives did improve student performance in the area of Geom. I highly recommend the measuring of round objects activity to other teachers so students have a concrete sense of diameter, circumference and pi. I also recommend this activity because it did not use expensive, commercially prepared manipulative objects, but round objects familiar to students such as cans, oatmeal containers, round toys, and so forth.

How Does the Use of Math Manipulatives Improve Student Performance in the Area of Probability and Statistics?

The lesson taught to students used a manipulative to help students understand a probability concept. Uneven probability is a difficult idea for students to comprehend if only presented abstractly. Therefore, I asked students in the lesson to create their own paper dice and to decorate them with uneven probabilities.

The teacher-made test asked students questions about the probability of events occurring, the difference between experimental and theoretical probabilities, and uneven probabilities. Although the test contained many different concepts, students improved overall from pre to posttest. The average learning gain from pre to posttest was 29% (see Table 3.2). In addition, no student score decreased from pre to posttest. Because the results were consistent, I believe other classes would gain from doing this activity and transfer the learning from creating their own dice to abstract problems on paper. Additionally, my teacher journal entries further support these assertions. One of the comments I recorded stated, "As I examined the dice the class members had made, I only found a few with dice faces having even probabilities."

In conclusion, I feel strongly that the use of math manipulatives improved student performance in the area probability. In this case, most of what the students were learning was new to them. Middle school students will not find the use of manipulatives childish if the manipulative relates to new material and not just for remediation purposes as was often seen as their primary purpose in the past (Quinn, 1997). I recommend other middle school teachers try this hands-on approach to teaching probability because it seems to promote deeper understanding of the concept.

How Does the Use of Math Manipulatives Improve Student Attitudes Towards Learning Mathematics at the Middle School Level?

Before answering let us look more closely at the survey questions most closely relating to students liking mathematics. Six percent more students in the attitude post survey compared to the pre survey agreed math manipulatives helped them to understand better the concepts. The final percent of agreement was 81%, which seems to support my initial assertion. However, other results make this assertion not as clear. Student attitudes towards liking math actually decreased 18% in the post survey (see Table 3.3). Looking at the teacher journal notes, the number of positive wordings used by students overall was in a three to one ratio for the pre survey but decreased to a two to one ratio for the post survey. Overall attitudes were more positive than negative towards using manipulatives to help with understanding in the spring; however, there was a decrease in liking math class and liking math class when manipulatives were used.

I do not think I can say conclusively the use of manipulatives helped improve student attitudes towards learning mathematics because some of the data showed a decline in positive attitudes. Nevertheless, the students seemed to appreciate how the manipulatives helped them to understand the math concepts. Perhaps their attitude toward liking math decreased because some of my lessons did not prepare the students to use the manipulatives adequately before I began teaching the concept. The students needed me to guide them more slowly from concrete to pictorial and abstract representations. Students also did not perform well on testing when the manipulatives were not the familiar objects.

How Does the Use of Math Manipulatives Improve Student Performance in Middle School Mathematics Classes?

I would assert that in many cases the use of math manipulatives does indeed improve student performances in middle school mathematics classes. My students showed learning gains for four out of five of the concept area tests. A majority of students were in favor of the idea that math manipulatives helped them understand math concepts better.

What problems did I encounter in my study and would I want other teachers to be aware of? Some of the lessons failed because students were not able to make a successful connection between the concept to be learned and the concrete materials. Many students in these classes seemed not to understand the overall objective. Another problem was trying to measure too many objectives in my teacher made tests. When doing action research, the teacher needs to develop activities and tests with consistent objectives so valid data may be collected.

To facilitate the teaching of the lessons incorporating manipulative use, I set up my classroom in cooperative learning groups. I had never organized a classroom physically for such an extended period of time (most of the school year) in this manner. It really helped when using manipulatives because the groups were established, so materials were easily distributed and retrieved.

Peer tutoring became a norm whether the lesson used manipulatives or not. As part of the action research process, I changed my teaching practice and became known as one of the teachers who regularly use cooperative learning in our building.

The lesson plan I designed included a section where I asked students to reflect in writing. The idea of the design itself proved valuable and helped me in writing lesson plans. Unfortunately, I abandoned the written reflection piece because it became too burdensome to review regularly for each manipulative lesson. However, I do incorporate reflection responses in other areas such as warm up questions and practice problems for state math assessments.

Another positive outcome was organizing successfully my many math manipulatives and in essence training students to retrieve them, use them, and put them away. Many studies suggested establishing procedures to help with the distribution of these extra materials proceed much more smoothly (Joyner, 1990; Stein & Bovalino, 2001). Once I had on hand a supply of small boxes, large boxes, sandwich bags, lunch sacks, etc., preparing for the day's lesson really did not take an inordinate amount of extra time.

Finally, I do not recommend the use of all the commercial math manipulatives available. Teachers can sometimes be more successful in using more readily available items that students are more familiar with. Sometimes these commercial items, as was my experience with Cuisenaire rods, present many problems to successful use.

The use of math manipulatives in mathematics classes can spark interest in mathematics and help students achieve deeper understanding of abstract concepts. However, the quality of the learning depends on the skill of the teacher in adequately preparing for their use.

Final Reflection

In conclusion, I was doubtful that an action research study would yield meaningful results. For example, I did not think the use of teacher made tests would be as reliable as perhaps using state testing results. I also doubted that the study's results would not be as meaningful as when comparing control and experimental groups. However, after going through the entire action research process: problem identification, literature review, intensive study of one class, data collection and analysis, and looking at data results from three sources, I feel this method was a powerful learning experience for me. Not only do feel I answered my questions, but it had an overwhelmingly positive impact on my teaching.

APPENDIX A

Lesson Plan Model for Using Math Manipulatives

Materials:

PreLesson or Introductory Lesson (students initially explore the manipulative):

Objective:

How does the use of the manipulative tie into this objective?

Introduction (usually includes modeling, use of overhead projector encouraged):

Lesson Plan (demonstate, guided practice, feedback):

Independent Practice:

Will cooperative grouping be used? If so, then discuss group size, how materials will be distributed and collected, etc.

Will students be asked to respond in a math journal? If so, journal question:

Debriefing or reflection session:

Suggested Follow-up:

APPENDIX B

Math Survey

Please respond to the following items by drawing a circle around the response that most closely shows your opinion.

Key:
Strongly Agree (SA) Agree (A) Undecided (U) Disagree (D) Strongly Disagree (SD)

1. I believe the use of math manipulatives helps me to better understand the math concepts being taught.

    SA   A   U   D   SD

2. I like doing math.

    SA   A   U   D   SD

3. Math manipulatives are confusing for me to use and I would rather just have my teacher explain how to do the work.

    SA   A   U   D   SD

4. I don't think I get enough real work done when using math manipulatives.

    SA   A   U   D   SD

5. Math manipulatives help me like math class better.

    SA   A   U   D   SD

Write a response on the blanks provided (at least two sentences).

6. What do you like or dislike about math manipulatives? Why?

    _____

    _____

    _____

REFERENCES

Ball, D. L. (1992). Magical hopes: Manipulatives and the reform of math education. *American Educator, 16*(2), 14-16.

Battista, M. T. (1999). Fifth graders' enumeration of cubes in 3D arrays: Conceptual progress in an inquiry-based classroom. *Journal for Research in Mathematics Education, 30*(4), 417-448.

Boling, A. N. (1991). They don't like math? Well, let's do something! *Arithmetic Teacher, 38*(7), 17-19.

Burns, M. (1996). How to make the most of math manipulatives. *Instructor, 105*(7), 45-51.

Dienes, Z. P. (1960). *Building up mathematics.* London: Hutchinson.

Driscoll, M. J. (1981). *Research within reach: Elementary school mathematics.* Reston, VA: National Council of Teachers of Mathematics.

Heuser, D. (2000). Mathematics workshop: Mathematics class becomes learner centered. *Teaching Children Mathematics, 6*(5), 288-295.

Hollingsworth, C. (1990). Maximizing implementation of manipulatives. *Arithmetic Teacher, 37*(9), 27.

Joyner, J. M. (1990). Using manipulatives successfully. *Arithmetic Teacher, 38*(2), 6-7.

Marzola, E. S. (1987). Using manipulatives in math instruction. *Reading, Writing and Learning Disabilities, 3*, 9-20.

Mercer, C., & Miller S. P. (1992). Teaching students with learning problems in math to acquire, understand and apply basic math facts. *Remedial and Special Education, 13*(3), 19-35, 61.

National Council Teachers Mathematics. (2000). *Principles and standards for school mathematics.* Reston, VA: Author.

Ohanian, S. (1992). Energizing your math program. *Instructor, 101*(8), 48.

Quinn, R. (1997). Developing conceptual understanding of relations and functions with attribute blocks. *Mathematics Teaching in the Middle School, 3*(3), 186-190.

Ross, R., & Kurtz, R. (1993). Making manipulatives work: A strategy for success. *Arithmetic Teacher, 40*, 254-257.

Stein, M. K., & Bovalino, J. W. (2001). Manipulatives: One piece of the puzzle. [Electronic version]. *Journal of Research in Mathematics Education, 6*(6), 356-359.

Suydam, M. N. (1984). Attitudes toward mathematics. *Arithmetic Teacher, 32*(3), 12.

Tooke, J. D., Hyatt, B., Leigh, M., Synder, B., & Borda, T. (1992). Why aren't manipulatives used in every middle school mathematics classroom? *Middle School Journal, 24*(2), 61-62.

Trueblood, C. R. (1986). Hands on: Help for teachers. *Arithmetic Teacher, 32*(6), 48-51.

Vygotsky, L. S. (1978). *Mind in society: The development of higher psychological processes.* Cambridge, MA: Harvard University Press.

Woolfolk, A. E. (1993). *Educational psychology* (5th ed.). Boston: Allyn & Bacon.

CHAPTER 4

TEACHER COLLABORATION

The Missing Link in Inclusive Education

Diane Stanton

ABSTRACT

A special education teacher and an eighth grade social studies teacher
endeavor to provide instruction that is more meaningful to six special needs
students with learning and/or emotional difficulties and 22 general education students in a civics class. During the semester of collaboration and
inclusive teaching, meaningful changes included: (1) the development of
positive behaviors in the special education students, (2) a growing respect
for individual differences among the general education students, and (3)
enhanced feelings of self worth for both groups of students.

INTRODUCTION

Louisa County, located in central Virginia within the Charlottesville—
Richmond—Fredericksburg triangle, is a rural residential and agricultural community. This 514 square mile county has only one middle
school, Louisa County Middle School (LCMS), though the region is

Making a Difference: Action Research in Middle Level Education, 63–82
Copyright © 2005 by Information Age Publishing
All rights of reproduction in any form reserved.

undergoing rapid change and growth. In fall 2001, it served 1,020 students. The student population was not very diverse and included 71% Caucasian students, 27% African American students, and 2% from other backgrounds and cultures. Approximately 33% of the students were eligible for free lunch and 12% of the students received special educational services.

The team concept is very important at LCMS. Teaming enables a group of two to four classroom teachers to work with and monitor a smaller number of students. It is an integral part of the school culture and is the basis for the organizational framework of the school. Students attend assemblies as teams, sit in team groupings, and participate in competitions, such as the number of cans for a food drive or number of books for a reading campaign, based on team configuration. Students do cross team lines for exploratory classes, though they do not cross grade designations. In addition, special education teachers provide service to identified students from all grades and teams, and at times, teach more than one subject at a time. The unifying element of these classrooms is students with a special education label.

During the first year of my masters program in education at George Mason University, I focused on an action research project. The project compelled me to look at my situation as a special education teacher from a different angle. Why is it that the students designated as needing special assistance are placed in an environment where they could not possibly receive a full period of instruction in an academic subject, since the teacher provides simultaneous instruction of two subjects? I used this question to guide my action research on inclusion education.

Inclusion and inclusive practice interested me. Previously, I attended conferences specific to inclusion. Then, at my principal's request, I organized a team of eighth grade teachers willing to participate in inclusion. This team and I visited model inclusion programs. However, we were disappointed when the administration divided the team and made no move toward more inclusive scheduling of students. We questioned why we were not moving forward to comply with federal mandates for serving special education students in the least restrictive environments (LRE).

As a result of the administrative action to dissolve the team, I approached one general education colleague, Mr. M., with my concerns about serving special education students in a less restrictive setting. I proposed that we work together, since we taught eighth grade civics during the same block. Mr. M agreed to have my class join his. Our vision was to work together collaboratively. We raised the following questions. Could we through our own moral agency, successfully effect a change and effectively implement a form of more meaningful instruction through inclusion at our school? Would we be able to collaborate and scaffold pedagogy inclusive of all our students' needs?

BACKGROUND

The philosophy of inclusion acknowledges the importance of the real world for student learning (VanDyke, Stalling, & Colley, 1995). It emerges from the belief that we all work in inclusive communities with people of different races, religions, aspirations, and disabilities. Segregation in a school setting does not prepare an individual for the inclusive community of today's world (University of North Iowa, College of Education, n.d.). Inclusive education therefore builds on the premise that classrooms need to be designed to provide all students opportunities to receive effective educational services with appropriate supplemental or supportive services. Inclusive classrooms vary greatly, and look and run very differently from one another.

In many cases, inclusive classrooms were a school's response to the legal mandate of The Individuals with Disabilities Education Act (IDEA) that students with disabilities be educated in the LRE. Congress declared that every child has the right to be educated in the education setting most appropriate for that child. While the law did not contain the word inclusion, it defined the most appropriate setting as least restrictive:

> To the maximum extent appropriate, children with disabilities ... are educated with children who are not disabled, and that special classes, separate schooling, or other removal of children with disabilities from the general environment occurs only when the nature or severity of the disability is such that education in general classes with the use of supplementary aids and services cannot be attained satisfactorily. [IDEA Sec. 612 (5) (B)] (as cited in ERIC Clearinghouse on Disabilities and Gifted Education, 1993)

Currently, advocates of IDEA view the least restrictive environment as the general classroom, and they support an inclusive model unifying the special education and general education systems. Much of recent literature adheres to this view of inclusive education that essentially requires general educational reform in which supports and instructional approaches benefit all students.

Many inclusion proponents claim that segregated programs do not meet the original goals of special education. Walker and Ovington (1998) reference the National Study on Inclusive Education which reports that with separate special education "drop out rates are high, in excess of 20%, and persons with disabilities have the highest drop out rates of any population" (National Center on Education Restructuring and Inclusion, 1994, p. 5). The National Study on Inclusive Education (as cited in Walker and Ovington, 1998) notes that services in the mainstream model were not being delivered and

> there were failures for students in both general and special education settings, lack of appropriate services ... monitoring ... and the placement if students in educational settings for other than their educational needs ... and the absence of supplementary aids and support services for those students in general educational settings. (¶ 14)

Still, others assert that segregated special education programs benefit the student regardless of disability. Such segregated programs are only legally valid when discussions address how to meet the individual student's needs and limitations. LRE is a civil right of special education students. This legal precedent requires that placement in the general classroom should be the first consideration when planning instruction (Stout, 2001).

Effective inclusive programs result largely through the initiatives of administration (Walther-Thomas, Korinek, & McLaughlin, 1999). Sapon-Shevin warns, "Inclusion without resources, without support, without teacher preparation time, without commitment, without a vision statement, without restructuring, without staff development, won't work" (as cited in University of North Iowa, College of Education, n.d.). Effective inclusive programs rest on the commitment of a general and a special education teacher to work collaboratively in providing appropriate educational services for all students in their classroom. Then, inclusive education is viewed as a process that evolves successfully as a collaborative working relationship between two teachers in a student-centered classroom characterized by good teaching. Such a classroom brings to mind Dewey's concept of a classroom environment, the objects, materials, resources and actions selected by the teacher(s) to establish a democratic environment (see Chapter 4 of Hansen, 2001).

At Louisa Middle School, the eighth grade teacher and I hoped to establish such a student-centered learning environment through our collaborative work. Together, we addressed these research questions: Could we through our own moral agency, successfully effect a change and effectively implement a form of more meaningful instruction through inclusion at our school? Would we be able to collaborate and scaffold pedagogy inclusive of all our students' needs? Specifically, we wanted to know if we would be able to implement an inclusive model that would positively influence the academic behaviors and attitudes of our students.

METHODS

Context for Inclusion

Following my conversation regarding inclusion with Mr. M., the eighth grade general education teacher, I discussed our endeavor with my principal and the director of special education. Both were supportive of our efforts and saw my students' exposure to the general curriculum as important to their preparation for the required Virginia Standards of Learning Tests (SOL). However, they expressed concern that I not be viewed as a mere assistant in the general education classroom. They seemed to view inclusive education as limited to a coteaching model. In response, I expressed my perspective that our teaching roles need not be prescribed, but needed to evolve as we developed a cooperative relationship in the classroom, which would allow us to meet the needs of all the students. At this point, the director of special education also advised me to look at the positive effects of inclusive practice on the general education students.

Ideally, any inclusive effort would have occurred at the beginning of the school year when teachers typically state their expectations, classroom procedures, and student responsibilities. Our efforts did not have an ideal start, since we began our inclusive work at the beginning of the second semester. When I joined Mr. M.'s class, my intention was to offer curriculum support and modification primarily for my students, but also for his students. His class included some mainstreamed special education students, students with 504 plans (which prescribe accommodations for students with minor disabilities in the general education setting), and other students identified as slow learners. This approach followed an established model of inclusive teaching cited in the literature (University of North Iowa, College of Education, n.d.). Mr. M., the general education teacher, would take the lead, and I, the special educator, would offer the support. We acknowledged that a coteaching model might evolve.

We based this initial arrangement upon our respect and trust for each other as coworkers. Over the past 5 years, special education students on my caseload received mainstream instruction in Mr. M's class. Because of this mainstreaming, I conducted numerous observations in his classroom. His curriculum characteristically addressed different modes of learning and provided opportunity for a variety of ways for the students to demonstrate mastery of material. At first, my role would be to increase the level of support available to all students in the classroom, and further substitute and modify the curriculum during our shared planning period.

In general, the special education students in my class constituted a small number who had not been mainstreamed into general education social studies classes. Their characteristics include low reading levels (second to fourth grade level), and most notably, poor student skills such as not arriving on time for class, not bringing supplies, and not completing any out of class homework assignments or projects. These special education students seemed to have become accustomed to living up to the low expectations they have for themselves, whether these are self defined or placed upon them by others. They interpreted their LD (learning disabilities) labels to mean Louisa Dummies.

The goals of including my special education students in the general class were to: (1) address attitudes and build positive student behaviors through peer models; (2) enhance feelings of self respect and competency through the development of teamwork and collaborative skills; (3) promote social values of equality and respect by demonstrating a variety of ways of addressing student skills; and (4) increase student achievement through improved positive student behaviors.

Interventions

As part of our efforts to create an inclusive classroom, Mr. M. and I made various accommodations to the curriculum and instructional materials including unit organizers, graphic organizers, Think Doodle, as well as cloze versions of class notes for students having difficulty taking notes. We also provided assistance in completing assignments and projects during Bobcat Block (homeroom period) assistance in completing assignments and projects. In addition, we made available instruction in the use of a tape player or computer for alternative means of representation and expression.

Data Collection and Analysis

To evaluate our goals, I collected and examined data from a variety of sources including point sheets, anecdotal records, informal interviews, and surveys. Point sheets provided documentation of students' behaviors. Specifically, my special education students could earn 10 points per class:

1 point for being *prompt* (in assigned seat when the bell rings);

2 points for being *prepared* (with supplies and homework);

2 points for being *polite*;

3 points for being *productive* (paying attention and completing assignments, participating in small group work); and

2 points for being *responsible* (for following directions, accepting redirection without argument).

I calculated the monthly averages at two time points, November and March, to determine changes in student behavior.

In addition, I kept anecdotal records on each student, as well as documentation of my dialogue with Mr. M., who noted any changes of behavior or achievement in his students. As we each began to get to know our collective students better, we viewed changes in all of the students' behavior and work. To analyze the anecdotal data, I reviewed my notes and looked for patterns as well as specific examples of change.

I conducted informal interviews and surveys with students to gauge the impressions and views of the students' attitudes in the class. For the informal interviews, I asked my special education students a series of open-ended questions and noted their responses. For the surveys, I constructed five open-ended questions and uploaded these to an online Web site (www.quia.com). Twenty-seven students took the survey in school's computer lab. Afterwards, I tabulated the student responses and then, coded their responses as positive, negative, or neutral.

ACTIONS AND RESULTS

Goal 1

The first goal of this action research project was to address attitudes and build positive student behaviors through peer models. A review of my students' initial and subsequent experiences illustrates movement toward this goal.

Initial Experience

From day one, attention to student attitudes and behavior was a primary concern. I had debated with myself over whether to tell my students in advance of our proposed inclusion with Mr. M.'s class, but decided not to forewarn them. They would have asked many questions, and for some it would have only provided an opportunity for high anxiety. Quite frankly, I was concerned that I might be setting up a disaster. Intellectually, I knew this was the right thing to do and I was very confident that both Mr. M. and I would do what we can do to provide a successful experience for all the students.

The first day of the term, I greeted my eighth graders at the door. James was the first to arrive. I addressed him: "Hi, James! We're going to be doing something a little bit different today, and join Mr. M.'s class."

James, looking at me warily, said "Okay" and did not make any move to sit down or leave the room. He stood by my side as Larry entered. I gave Larry the same greeting and received a similar reply. The same was true for Jason and Brian, however, Brian points out that he is not on that team. I replied, "That's okay, neither are James or Larry." The four boys went back into the hall.

It was getting time for the bell to ring, and as I started to walk with them to Mr. M.'s class next door, Marcie and Gary came flying down the hall. I told them that we would be joining Mr. M.'s class. This time, I heard an adamant refusal. Marcie asserted, "I don't want to go in with all those kids!" I explained, "But Marcie, they're on your team and in your math class. You know a lot of them." By this time, Marcie was red in the face with tears welling up in her eyes. She replied, "No. Ask Gary. He doesn't want to go either." As I look at Gary, he blurts, "NO! No way. I'll fail!" As I reached out a hand to pat Marcie on the back, she continued, "I don't want to be with all of them."

While I talked with Marcie and Gary, the other four boys looked for direction. I asked them, "Do you guys want to go on ahead? Mr. M. knows you're coming." They responded with variations of "okay" and moved down the hall to Mr. M.'s classroom.

I moved into the classroom to speak with Marcie and Gary. Leaning on a desk, I addressed Gary, "Gary you're a smart kid and you're doing well in here. Just keep doing what you're doing and you'll be fine. I wouldn't bring you anywhere where I thought you would fail." I sensed he was wavering. He glanced over at Marcie. I turn my attention to her and said in a somewhat firmer tone, "Let's go Marcie, you might have fun." Both students turned and preceded me down the hall.

As we entered the general education class, Mr. M. was making some seating assignments. When he was called to the door, I assumed the task of assigning seats. I spread my special education students throughout the classroom to intermingle with his general education students. Mr. M. said little by way of introduction; he stated simply that we have some new students. Then Mr. M. announced the agenda for the day.

I walked around to each of my students and distributed cloze note-taking sheets. As Mr. M. began his instruction, I continued to circulate around the room to ensure that each student was on task. Jason stopped me as I went by his desk. "I can't see." I replied, "Put your glasses on." Jason countered, "I don't have them." So, I suggested, "You can move up to the front, Jason, so you can see to take your notes." Jason responded: "Nah, that's alright." The girl beside him showed Jason her notes. A minute or so later as I circled back, Jason stopped me again. He asked, "Can I go to the bathroom?" I answered, "Lunch is in about 20 minutes. You can go then."

I circled toward the front of the room and noticed that Brian had not filled in any of the notes on his paper. I prompted him in a whisper, "glasses." He complied and began to take notes. I glanced around the room at my students. James had hidden the cloze note-taking sheet that I gave him. As I circled back around to Jason again, he asked, "Can I go to the nurse?" I replied, "No."

A reading assignment followed. I asked one student to work with Marcie on the reading and another to work with Larry. A girl volunteered to work with Jason, but James refused any assistance from a peer. Gary completed his assignment independently. Gary got up to sharpen a pencil, and Mr. M. questioned him about having gum in his mouth. "Gary, I hope that's not gum in your mouth. If it is I suggest you find a more appropriate place to put it." Gary put the gum in the trash, then glanced back at me and narrowed his eyes. The bell rang for lunch, which divided this class in half. It was a spilt block running 42 minutes with a 28 minute lunch break followed by the remaining 42 minutes of class. As Gary passed me on his way out the door, he mumbled, "I hate this class!"

The students returned promptly from lunch and continued with the reading assignment. James, Larry, and Brian were also in my English class the next period. When I asked how they liked the inclusive class, their responses varied. James asked, "If I do my work in that class can I be mainstreamed next year?" Larry replied, "It was OK." Brian offered, "I dunno...we can try it."

Upon reflection, I had many thoughts about this first day. Jason's attempt to solicit attention through avoidance behaviors was very similar to his behaviors in my special education class. I was concerned with James bluffing behavior. I recalled that earlier, James would not admit to having any kind of reading problem, and would fill in anything on an assignment just to get it done. Marcie concerned me with her discomfort in being around the general education students. My first thoughts were that we must be doing something wrong when simply entering a group of their peers caused the special education students so much concern over their differences.

Subsequent Experiences

As the days progressed, I continued to emphasize to my special education students the importance of coming to class prepared. I reminded them of how they earned their points and the value of theses points (one-third of their class grade). James, Larry, and Gary participated in the instruction by asking and answering questions. I noticed that Jason received assistance frequently from one of his young female friends, and he continued to make requests for the bathroom, nurse, and band-aid requests. Brian demonstrated a head down, withdrawn behavior that was

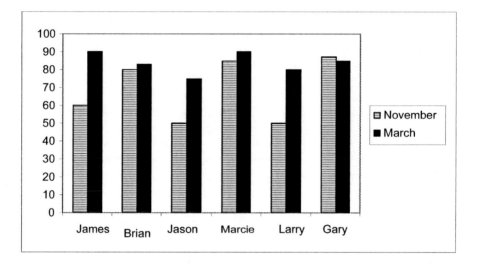

Figure 4.1.   Behavior points earned by special education students.

characteristic of his demeanor in my special education English class as well and his other special education and exploratory classes.

I gave passes to my students to come to my room during Bobcat Block to complete assignments. On more than one occasion, I set up notebooks with Larry and Jason. By class number seven, my students demonstrated more of the targeted student behaviors. With notebook, pen, book they were in their assigned seats when the bell rang. Evidence of changes in student behavior appeared.

Figure 4.1 depicts individual special education students' monthly averages for November (baseline) and March (third month of inclusion). For Jason, James, and Larry, the percentage of points earned increased, which reflects an improvement in desirable student behaviors. Gary and Marcie, who were reluctant to participate in a general class, were able to maintain their desirable behaviors in a large group setting. For Brian there was also a slight improvement.

Goals 2 and 3

The second and third goals of my action research focused on students' beliefs. The second goal was to enhance the special education students' feelings of self-respect and competency, while the third goal was to promote values of equality and respect among the general education students. The advancement of these social values included the development of teamwork and collaborative skills. Changes in students' attitudes and behaviors emerged slowly.

During the fourth class, Mr. M. distributed an assignment, a tic-tac-toe of the development of the U. S. Constitution. This tic-tac-toe assignment offered students some choice in selecting activities to complete. The students chose three activities in a row, such as making a time line, t-chart, poster, or traditional activities such as writing a newspaper article on a selected topic. Mr. M informed the students that they should start with the activity of constructing a time line about the U. S. Constitution and its formation. This would provide a solid starting point for the overall assignment.

To accommodate student differences, we modified the instruction with teacher-prepared lecture notes, computers, and small cooperative pairings. First, I provided full copies of teacher-prepared lecture notes for my students use, since we were aware that my students did not have lecture notes because the lesson occurred prior to their joining Mr. M.'s class. We observed that these copies of notes became very desirable items to many of the general education students. Second, we had access to the mobile computer lab, and the assistance of one of our computer support personnel to support the time line activity. With the availability of computers and lecture notes, the class was much more animated. Even with three adults circulating among the students, we kept very busy. Third, some of the students worked in pairs because there were not enough computers for each student. In some cases, my special education students took the lead.

This class is a breakthrough class. I interacted more and so did my students. I began to provide individual instruction for every student in the class and my students began to demonstrate their strengths and skills in technology. My special education students knew how to use the program and were able to assist Mr. M's general education students. My students were no longer simply on the receiving end of instruction; they were actively engaged in the curriculum. Computer technology was an area where my students could shine. For the first time, I was absolutely, positively sure that we were going to be successful with our attempt to provide a meaningful experience in inclusive education.

Marcie, however, was absent during the class when we constructed the timeline. I sent the information about the assignment to her resource teacher. During the following weeks, Marcie came to my class during her resource class, and she requested a pass to my room during Bobcat Block. Two of Mr. M.'s girls also came to my room to get help with their time line. These general education students, in turn, encouraged Jason to see me during Bobcat Block for additional help. Ultimately, Marcie as well as the other five of my students all completed this assignment. My student,

James, initiated a request for assistance of his resource teacher and turned in a very impressive project. His assignment was one of 10 or so in the entire class submitted on time, and he was very pleased with his accomplishment.

Mr. M. incorporated into his pedagogy two activities, which tapped students' individual strengths. One was his use of small groups to complete assignments and which fostered an ever changing grouping of students of mixed abilities. The other technique was his use of what he called a Think Doodle, which afforded our more visual students to demonstrate their competence. The task did not involve written language per se, but rather a graphic presentation of events. Mr. M. used it for civil rights legislation as well as a representation of how a territory becomes a state. In each instance, the students drew items as visual reminders for the events.

In another instructional variation, Mr. M. provided students with a graphic organizer about how bill becomes a law. During this activity, the students made visual representations of events. Mr. M., an excellent artist, offered suggestions and drew examples on the board for the students to view. He also acknowledged students' efforts. Mr. M. scanned the class and commented on some innovation on the part of the students, called attention to them, and congratulated them on their idea. As I circled the room and commented on drawings, I passed Larry, whose work was very neat and precisely drawn. I pointed out what an excellent job he was doing. Katie, who sat next to him, commented, "Look at mine, you can't even read it!" Larry, beaming from my positive comment, reached over, added a few lines to Katie's drawing to improve it, and said, "There you go!" Katie, smiled, "Hey, thanks!" She turned to show it to a classmate on the other side of her. Another of Larry's classmate passed her Think Doodle to him, so he drew a line or two on hers, too. Larry, who frequently received help from these young ladies, was smiling proudly. I commented to Larry, again, "Way to go!"

In early March, prior to the large groups' survey in the computer lab, I asked my students to respond to some informal interview questions, "Do you like joining Mr. M's class for social studies? Why or why not?" Five out of the six students replied with comments such as "we learn more, we get to do more different kinds of things with more different people, and there are more girls." Only one student, Marcie, responded negatively. She maintained that there were "too many people in there."

Marcie's response did not come as a complete surprise. I recalled that in January, Mr. M. and I were concerned with Marcie's apparent unhappiness. My observation was that Marcie, the only girl in my eighth grade group, was extremely quiet and withdrawn in her classes. In the following weeks, Mr. M. noticed a major difference in her behavior as she became friendly with her new classmate, Amy. She appeared to be engaging in very enjoyable conversations as she smiled and worked cooperatively with this student. Though she expressed concerns about the number of students, Marcie appeared to be making progress in the general education classroom.

Mr. M. noted changes in his students as well. He commented that many of his students had stepped into leadership roles. When they worked with the special education students, their own work improved because of their attempts to lead by example. He felt that his students kept up with supplies better and brought extras to share. Further, he noted that his more advanced students were better able to appreciate the struggles many special education students face in class. They became more aware that those special needs students were not, as one of his students observed, "weird, dangerous, bad, or dumb."

In late March, Mr. M. and I scheduled the computer lab for one-half of a class period or 45 minutes and informed students that we would be doing something special the next class meeting. The students were very excited. "This is the best class," commented a student from somewhere in the class. Another asserted, "You like this class best!" Mr. M. responded that he could never say that he preferred one class over another since that would not be fair.

My students, I noticed did not saying anything, but when we returned to my classroom for their next class, both James and Larry asked me about the special activity. I would not tell them, so they continued to ask. Next, they tried the same ploy they heard in Mr. M.'s class, "You like our class best!" I replied that they were my favorite civics class. They laughed at first, until James, pointed out that they were my only civics class.

Though we did not reveal the nature of the special activity to them, the students would complete a survey that I prepared using an online Web site to assess student attitudes regarding inclusion, special education, and learning styles. The survey included five open-ended questions (see Table 4.1). I hoped to get some feedback from the class about their knowledge of what Mr. M and I were doing, and how they felt about having special education students in the general education class. Because I knew the students worked at varying rates, I selected some social studies games as part of their assignment.

After the students completed the survey, I reviewed and coded their responses in three categories: positive, neutral, and negative. Student responses are summarized in Table 4.1.

Question 1 invited students to describe special education. Positive responses to this question included "a class for students who need help with certain things." I coded responses that used the term slower in a nonpejorative as neutral. These included responses such as "kids who learn things slower." I coded responses that used more charged or

Table 4.1.   Student Responses to Questionnaire

Questions	Positive	Neutral	Negative
1. What is special education?	6	16	5
2. What is inclusive education?	5	22	—
3. If you were told that what Mr. M. and Mrs. X were doing is inclusive education would you know that it is?	17	7	3
4. Can you suggest anything that we could do differently in this class?	17	7	3
5. Different people learn differently. How do you learn best?	20	6	1

demeaning comments such as "for kids who lack intelligence" or "kids who are retarded" as negative.

The second question asked students to define inclusive education. There were no negative response for question 2, and only a few positive responses. Students responded neutrally to this item. Their neutral response were variations of "I don't know," or "sorry, but I don't know." I viewed and coded as positive responses expressions such as "a class where everyone is included in the activity" and "where everyone works together."

Question 3 probed students' understanding of inclusive education as practiced in our class. For question 3, I counted a simple "yes" or variant of it such as "gives people the help they need" as positive, and I viewed a "no" as a neutral response. In contrast, I coded responses regarding too many kids and large class size as negative.

The fourth question inquired about what we could do differently in our inclusive class. I viewed responses to question 4 as positive when students offered constructive comments such as "more projects" and "more activities like this one." I counted a response as neutral when a simple "no' was given. I viewed as a response such as "a smaller class would be better" and "less kids."

The final item asserted that people learn differently, and asked students how they learned best. When coding question 5, I tallied responses as positive when they targeted specific ways students learn. These responses included "notes and class discussions," because "it [information] gets to me faster," group projects "lets you think out loud" and "more hands on activities because when I hear something and then do the activity, I learn the information fast." I viewed responses such as "I don't know" or "no" as neutral. I counted one response as negative since it included a litany of the word 'not': "not notes, not the text book, not projects, but everything else." As I pondered this response, I surmised that perhaps the student liked discussion.

Although the results of the survey were generally positive, most of the negative comments had to do with the size of the class. One negative comment was that the "new" students should return to their other class, because the classroom was too crowded. In January, I brought six eighth grade students to Mr. M.'s class of 22 students. By late February, two more special education students were added to my class. The reason that one of these students was added to my class was precisely because we provided an inclusive setting. At the time of this research, general education classes in our school ranged from 18 to 22. Our inclusive classroom total was 30 students, which made for a very crowded room.

In addition to the survey responses, students sent me e-mail messages about the activity. Their messages gave me feedback on the activity in the computer lab and requested that we come to the lab more frequently.

Goal 4

Our fourth and final goal was to increase student achievement through improved positive student behaviors. Given the short time frame, I was not sure that I would see much improvement in increased student achievement. At the beginning, I debated whether to require Bobcat Block or an additional resource period. I decided against this pull-out approach of adding another resources period, since this meant taking away their exploratory class. For the most part these exploratory classes were classes such as agricultural science, technology, and band that the students enjoyed. In addition, Bobcat Block was a time when many of the exploratory classes practiced or met for clubs. I did not want to penalize them in any way for their involvement in an inclusive class. Nevertheless, I told students they were welcome to come to me for help with homework, project, or studying for tests. I provided the students with passes, and indicated when I thought that they needed to come back. Furthermore, Marcie and James had resource periods where they could get help. James met with success as evidenced by the on-time completion of his tic-tac-toe assignment and earning an A grade. Frequently, Marcie came to me during her resource period for extra assistance.

On test days, my special education students returned to my classroom, and I helped them with the reading of the test. Test performance scores do not, in general, demonstrate that the students are mastering the curriculum. However, administrative expectations, as stated in my conversations at the beginning of this endeavor with the principal and director of special education, were that the students' achievement levels would improve as measured by Flanagan assessments and the SOL tests. Such expectations seemed unrealistic to me. When students have been in a restrictive self-contained special education setting and given a watered down curriculum, one semester of access to the general education curriculum is not at all likely to produce higher scores on standardized achievement tests.

The increased level of the engagement on the part of my students as evidenced by their points was a more realistic assessment of their academic progress. I assigned productive points to assess on-task behavior and task completion. In November, students earned points at a 47% rate, while in March they increased to 87%. Prompt and prepared rates were 45% in November and climbed to 85% in March. Students who came prepared and on time, participated in class discussions and activities, completed homework and in class assignments, and finished content area projects were making academic progress. Predictably, the Flanagan and SOL tests did not measure this type of academic growth.

My eighth graders' attitudes and behaviors improved during this endeavor. They wanted to participate in the general education curriculum. For example, one day, Mr. M. was absent, and the work he had assigned required independent reading. I pulled out my students to work with them on it. They all wanted very much to return to *their* class...even Marcie and Gary. I sent a few students back, among them Marcie and Gary because they had earned 100% on the last in-class assignment. The rest agreed that we needed to review the required material. Student attitudes, behaviors, and sense of self worth had improved and their percentage of points earned (Figure 4.1) reflected this change. Although some students had difficulty, they worked continually toward mastering the student behaviors (prepared, prompt, productive) that facilitate academic success.

DISCUSSION

Inclusive education is based on collaboration and is a process that evolves. Inclusion cannot be prescribed. As the semester progressed, I became increasingly more involved in classroom activities to support the curriculum, but Mr. M. assumed major responsibility for teaching. Initially, my role was one of a coach for my special education students and for some of Mr. M.'s general education students.

Our collaborative inclusion approach emerged. Bauwens and Hourcade (1995) referred to this approach as a supportive teaching model—not quite what the school administration prescribed. In Bauwens and Hourcade's model, both disabled and nondisabled students are in the same classroom, the general education teacher is responsible for the content of the material, and the special education teacher focuses on the adaptations. If Mr. M. had not been so skilled at weaving various techniques and strategies into his pedagogy, I would no doubt, have needed to come forward with more effective strategies. For example, I provided visual copies of his notes for use on the overhead. I also adapted writing assignments and developed word banks for open-ended questions. Further, I generated vocabulary quizzes and puzzles for the entire class. Importantly, Mr. M. was skilled in generating graphic organizers and unit organizers, which were an integral part of his teaching.

We both grappled with the issue of grading. For my students, I averaged the scores from completed work, tests, and projects. Students with diverse needs have not always been graded strictly against curriculum standards, rather they were judged against the goals set in their individualized education program. What their grades reflected has been a growing concern among educators. How can a student who is working below grade level earn a B or even a C in a class? At a staff meeting, we discussed how even general education students earning Bs on his/her report card may not pass the SOL. Parents and other students also did not understand the relationship of grades and the standardized test score. I began to question whether we needed to indicate that students could be working below grade level. Moreover, I wondered how grades affected the special education student's view of reality. Are students marginalized by the lack of adequate feedback? For example, a student earned a B in class, but did not demonstrate independent work habits and mastery of course level material, and only earned a 40% on the SOL. While Mr. M. gave some value to effort, he did not weigh it as systematic a way as I did with the point structure. Evaluation of student work remained an issue. It was not simply a special education versus general education issue; it was a school wide policy concern.

As I grappled with issues related to inclusion, I came upon a new, at least to me, paradigm—The Universal Design for Learning (UDL). It draws on brain research and new media technologies to respond to individual learning differences and extends the principals of universal design used by architects in product design. Architects that employ universal design create structures to address the widest spectrum of possible users. Designing for the divergent needs of a special population increases usability for everyone. A classic example is the curb cut. Although originally designed to help those in wheel chairs to negotiate curbs, curb cuts ease travel for those pushing baby carriages, riding skateboards, pulling suitcases or simply walking.

The UDL shifts old assumptions about curriculum, teaching, and learning. Orkwis (1999) reminds educators that students with disabilities fall along a continuum of learner differences rather than constituting a separate category. He contends that teacher adjustment for learner differences is necessary for all students. Curriculum materials should be varied and diverse including digital rather than simply text materials. Instead of offering students a remedial approach to learn a specific curriculum, curriculum must be flexible in order to accommodate learner differences. It must be flexible in the essential areas of representation, expression, and engagement.

So often teachers make accommodations for representation, ensuring multiple modalities in how we present a lesson, but often overlook a student's ability to engage actively in the manipulation and interpretation of the material presented. Voltz, Brazil, and Ford (2001) remind us that inclusion does not refer to physical space. Inclusion implies a sense of belonging and acceptance; it is active meaningful participation. As the school year was ending, I began to address the level of *active* participation of my students, particularly those who do not read on grade level. It was commonplace to read tests and materials to the students identified with learning disabled at my school. I had used audiotapes of texts and such, but time became an issue in locating and or recording all the text that we tend to present visually to our students. To support my special education students, the school secured a separate computer for my classroom that did not run on the school network. In addition to this computer, we used a scanner and CAST e-Reader software (text-to-speech program) that reads virtually any scanned text or information from the Web. My students learned how to scan text and access the converted text. Not only were able to access independently the curriculum at their level of engagement, but also became increasingly motivated to do so. My inquiry led me to understand that accommodations should reflect the goal of the teacher and the student (Meyer & O'Neil, 1999). Perhaps the effective use of accommodations and of assistive technology will also be the subject of future teacher research.

Mr. M. and I agreed that our collaboration and inclusion of my special education students in his general education class was the right action. We were effective; we were able to collaborate and scaffold pedagogy that was inclusive of all our students' needs. Although I did not attain the administration's goal of coteaching, I became increasingly more comfortable in asserting the role of the special education teacher as one who facilitates meaningful accommodations for the students. As Mr. M. and I came to view our students on a continuum, they were no longer his or my students, no longer part of a separate category. They were our students. They were students whose needs must be addressed. I discovered that somewhere along the way, educators have lost sight of IDEA's mandate that supplementary aids (not aides) and services (not necessarily human) are how to meet student needs in a least restrictive environment.

As my school struggles to prescribe ways to instruct effectively a diverse group of learners, it seems that more credence needs to be given to allowing collaborative relationships to develop and grow. Collaboration is the essential link to effective inclusion.

AUTHOR'S NOTE

Diane Stanton has taught special education for the 20 years and has been at LCMS for the past 8 years. This action research study was completed as part of the first year requirement for the M.A. degree in education through George Mason University.

REFERENCES

Bauwens, J., & Hourcade, J. J. (1995). *Cooperative teaching: Rebuilding the schoolhouse for all students.* Austin, TX: Pro-Ed.

CAST Universal Design for Learning [Computer software]. (1999). *CAST eReader.* Wakefield, MA: Center for Applied Special Technology.

ERIC Clearinghouse on Disabilities and Gifted Education. (1993). Including students with disabilities in the general education currriculum. *ERIC Digest #E521.* (ERIC Document Reproduction Service No. ED 358 677). Reston, VA: Author.

Hansen, D. T. (2001). *Exploring the moral heart of teaching: Toward a teacher's creed.* New York: Teachers College Press.

Meyer. A., & O'Neil, L. M. (1999). Beyond access: Universal design for learning. *Educational Leadership, 58*(3), 39-43.

National Center on Education Restructuring and Inclusion. (1994). *National study of inclusive education.* New York: Author.

Orkwis, R. (1999). Curriculum access and universal design for learning. *ERIC/ OSEP Digest #E586.* Reston, VA: ERIC/OSEP Special Project, Council for Exceptional Children.

Stout, K. S. (2001). *Special education inclusion.* Retrieved August 1, 2004, from the Wisconsin Education Association Council Website: http://www.weac.org/ resource/june96/speced.htm

University of North Iowa, College of Eudcation. (n.d.). *What does an inclusive classroom look like?* Retrieved August 1, 2004, from http://www.uni.edu/coe/ inclusion/strategies/inclusive_classroom.html

VanDyke, R., Stallings, M. A., & Colley, M. (1995). How to build an inclusive school community: A success story. *Phi Delta Kappa, 76*(6), 474-76.

Voltz, D. L., Brazil, N., & Ford, A. (2001). What matters most in inclusive education: A practical guide for moving forward. *Intervention in School and Clinic, 37*(1), 23-30.

Walker, K. E., & Ovington, J. A. (1998). *Inclusion and its effects on students*. Retrieved August 1, 2004, from http://www.cehs.wright.edu/~prenick/JournalArchives/Winter-1999/inclusion.html

Walther-Thomas, C., Korinek, L., & McLaughlin, V. L. (1999). Collaboration to support student success. *Focus on Exceptional Children, 32*(3), 1-18.

CHAPTER 5

EXPERIENCING ACTION RESEARCH

A Preservice Collaborative Team Studies a Middle School in Crisis

Sandra L. Stacki

ABSTRACT

The New York State Education Department provided finances and consultation to personnel of a failing school to develop and implement an action plan based on the middle school concept to enhance the overall academic environment. A faculty member and six master's students used a qualitative approach to understand and describe the perceptions of school community members, primarily teachers, concerning the success, strengths, and weaknesses of the action plan, and what improvements and barriers exist in the relationships among the community stakeholders. The master's students learned about daily life in a minority middle school and valuable action research lessons to use in their own classrooms and schools.

Making a Difference: Action Research in Middle Level Education, 83–106

BACKGROUND

In 1990, the New York State Education Department (NYSED) recognized the one junior-senior high school of the Regentsville School District (RSD)[1] for measures of low performance, particularly in scores on standardized English language arts (ELA) and math assessments. The NYSED placed this school on the School Under Registration Review (SURR) list.[2] In 1995, a special state panel issued a harshly critical review of this district and state oversight began. The following year, the legislature granted the unprecedented request of New York Governor George Pataki to enact legislation authorizing a partial state take over of all the schools in the district and removing the school board. After new school board members were elected, the RSD continued to be operated by its new school board with the advice of the NYSED. Yet improvements in academic performance were slow in coming despite the efforts of both the NYSED advisors and the school board, who often disagreed.

Many cite the high poverty rates and virtually no commercial tax base as continual problems in school improvement for this small, primarily minority district. RSD is on Long Island, which has the most racially isolated, and segregated suburbs in the country as measured by school and housing patterns (Powell, 2002). In 1999, more than 80% of this district's eighth graders failed to meet state standards on ELA and math exams (Wyatt, 2000b). This district was called "one of the worst-performing public school systems on Long Island" (Saslow, 2000) and had employed four superintendents in 5 years since the state intervened (Wyatt, 2000a).

In response, in 2000, education Commissioner Richard Mills stated publicly,

> This is the last opportunity for [this district] to provide an appropriate education for the children and to demonstrate that by meeting reasonable performance targets. If they do not, I will recommend that they lose the opportunity to operate a [grades] 7-12 program. ([Regentsville's] Last Chance, 2000)

Mills later amplified his position by proposing that lack of improvements would require the closing of the junior-senior high school, and either transforming it into a charter school or transferring the current student body to schools in surrounding districts. However, Mills did not articulate until November 2000 what specific benchmarks of improvement would need to be met to avoid decertification. Represented in Table 5.1 are the average target scores for 8th and 12th grade Regents assessments in 2001.

Table 5.1.   Target Scores for [Regentsville] 2001 State Assessments

	Target Score	*Last year's score*	*Increase*
8th grade English language arts	78 out of 200	65 out of 200	13 points
8th grade math	45 out of 100	31 out of 100	14 points
12th grade English	55% seniors passing	41% seniors passing	14%
12th grade math	55% seniors passing	50% seniors passing	5%

Source: Adapted from Pratt (2000, November 10).

A NEW MIDDLE SCHOOL ACTION PLAN

Beginning in spring 2000, the NYSED provided more finances, advice, and consultation to help the junior high personnel in the junior-senior high school to develop a middle school action plan based on the New York state Middle-Level School Improvement Initiative for the 2000-2001 school year and the New York state Essential Elements of Middle-Level Education (EEMLE),[3] an implementation guide for state middle level policy (www.emsc.nysed.gov) that echoes the National Middle School Association guidelines. The new middle school action plan was developed to assist school personnel to implement the concepts, structures, and practices of a middle school, enhance the overall academic environment in the middle school, and thereby improve the eighth grade ELA and math test scores. Among other components, the middle school action plan included teacher professional development, which began with a required 3-day training session before the beginning of the fall 2000 school year. In addition, middle level personnel could attend an optional 6 weeks of professional development sessions. Throughout the year, teachers planned to administer monthly *intermediate assessments* to monitor test score improvements. Furthermore, the superintendent planned to sponsor a number of public meetings throughout fall 2000 to present to the community the further structural and communication changes that the middle school would be undertaking.

Concurrently in spring 2000, the middle school also participated in a NYSED study. With the help of the Statewide Network of Middle-Level Education Liaisons, an advisory group, the NYSED began preliminary research in 10 middle schools: five with high scores and five with low scores on the state eighth grade assessments in ELA and mathematics. A two-member team from the middle level education liaisons group observed and conducted informal interviews for a day at one middle school, and then, quantified their results on a checklist with units that conformed to the EEMLE. Different teams throughout the state completed these visits to the 10 middle schools. Regentsville was among the five lowest performing schools.

This chapter highlights the research purposes, process, and findings of a qualitative, action research study that I, as a member of the middle level liaisons and a faculty member from Hofstra University's School of Education and Allied Human Services, engaged in with six graduate students.[4] As a collaborative team, we explore the liaison's preliminary research at the junior high and the implementation of a middle school action plan. First, I discuss my purposes for involving these graduate students in a preservice research assignment requiring field experience in local schools, our team's goals in this collaborative project, our research process, highlights of our findings, and reflections on preservice teachers engaging in research. During this process, these graduate students learned about not only action plan implementation difficulties, troubling school conditions, and day-to-day life of various personnel at this SURR, but also valuable research skills and lessons to take with them to their own teaching positions. By learning about research during our class and our team meetings, as they also actively researched among teachers at Regents Middle School (RMS), they began to discern that certain problems in their own classrooms or in their schools can be proactively explored and hopefully improved before failure occurs. By gaining an understanding of action research and its purposes, these graduate students will be able to take ownership, become engaged as part of a change process, and conduct their own study or lead and contribute to a collaborative study.

WHY RESEARCH IN SCHOOLS?

Every semester, I teach a course called *Perspectives in Educational Practice*. This is an introductory course in the master of science program; however, a few master of arts students take the course as an elective. A major component of the master's students' work includes completing a research project. In a class with typically 25 students from all subject areas—some to receive 7-12 and others K-12 certification—three to six might be the master of arts, inservice students who are already teaching full time in their own classrooms. After initial readings about doing action research, we discuss how these inservice students can complete action research in their own classrooms. They can "initiate and control the research in conjunction with the other day-to-day activities of leading a school or classroom" (McKay, 1992).

Action research is a way to provide more indigenous perspective to the research as teachers explore their own classrooms and schools. One advocate describes it as a "fancy way of saying let's study what's happening in our school and decide how to make it a better place" (Calhoun, 1994, p. 20). Most action research implies a process in which planning, researching, taking action, and assessing the action are involved. Ideally, all stakeholders would be involved in "identifying, defining, and struggling to solve the 'problem'" (Schensul & Schensul, 1992, p. 196). Thus, practitioners decide to study scientifically their problems and make decisions or take action to affect changes in their classrooms or school (Arhar, Holly, & Kasten, 2001). Yet, action research also includes self-reflective inquiry, an individual reflection on practice, or a collaborative process to support teachers in their professional development and school-based improvement (Allen & Calhoun, 1998).

Most preservice teachers are uncertified and have little or no experience with a teacher's perspective of daily life in the classroom and school.[5] How can I help these graduate students to learn about action research and experience school-related research even though they are not yet teaching in their own classrooms? Each of these preservice students explore a classroom or school problem or issue similar to those the inservice students selected, though this exploration is through the perspectives of other teachers (and sometimes other school personnel) in one or more local school districts. Thus, since they cannot complete an action research project in the purest sense as teachers in their own classrooms, they will still complete active, field research in schools.

Although this course is one of the few not requiring a field component, I set up visits to three different middle and high schools each semester and encourage students to attend at least one with me. I arrange more trips to middle schools than high schools because I believe the 7-12 certification program usually emphasizes high school. I choose schools primarily through my contacts among the middle level education liaisons, who have been involved in the evolving process of middle level education in New York (Stern & Stacki, 2004). Therefore, my students and I visit those schools that I know are implementing the New York state Board of Regents policy (2003) and the seven New York state Essential Elements of Middle-Level Education (Board of Regents, 2000). If students are not doing field observations in other classes, these group trips can provide them with ideas and perhaps a point of access for a study in the schools. I also encourage them to read the newspaper and review essays in *Kaleidoscope: Readings in Education* (Ryan & Cooper, 2004) among other texts to gain additional topic ideas.

Throughout the semester, we discuss their research in a step-by-step process. I let the students know that this is how we will proceed, which helps to allay their initial fears of doing field research—something I discover that only a few have done before, perhaps as part of a senior project in their undergraduate studies. I help students to understand that this is qualitative, exploratory research with a general goal of better understanding the perspectives of the respondents and the environment at the schools. They do not need to hypothesize an outcome; they begin to understand that ideas emerge during their data gathering, particularly in conversations with teachers, which they may not anticipate. We also discuss that these are small studies, like pilot studies, and that making generalizations beyond the immediate setting can be problematic and require careful analysis. The general steps we take as a group are next to visit the library and receive instruction in the most up-to-date methods for researching topics and accessing books, journal, and newspaper articles, and information from reliable internet sites. The following week, students submit a research proposal, which indicates their chosen topic, a rationale for this study, and how they hope to gather their own data using a combination of observations, interviews or surveys, and documents.

Often at this point, the students do not have complete access to an observation site and are contemplating issues such as whether or not to interview several teachers in one school or work in two schools so that they may compare findings. I encourage them to take advantage of access to teachers gained through observations in other classes or through other contacts in the schools. The students submit 10 interview or survey questions that they formulate based on articles read on the topic. I review their proposals and questions providing comments, questions, or further reading ideas to assist them. We take time for a brief discussion or a few questions in most class sessions. Next, students read two or three short examples of published action research for discussion. To help them organize, I provide an outline of research paper sections. In particular, we discuss looking for patterns or themes as they integrate their findings from their various data sources. Two weeks before the papers are due; they discuss their ongoing work in small groups to try out ideas, ask questions, and determine if they have common concerns or questions to bring to the larger group. In the final 2 weeks of class, the students present to each other their topics, process of data gathering, major findings, conclusions, and implications. They distribute a one-page overview of these areas to aid classmates during the presentation.

A Team Project Emerges

In the fall 2000 semester, I provided my students with an opportunity to participate in a group research project at the newly emerging RMS.

The research that the two-member teams of the middle level education liaisons had completed in spring 2000 in the 10 middle/junior high schools was a beginning. Yet the one-day observation and anecdotal information that two people gained was insufficient to provide any meaningful information in a school such as RMS that was one of the lowest performing schools.[6] As a member of the liaisons group, I had discussed with the supervisor of the NYSED's Middle-Level Education Program and the New York state Middle School Association vice president and consultant for the state in program and staff development for RMS, an idea for a more inclusive, semester-long qualitative study. Both of these middle level experts worked as consultants with RMS to improve the school since RMS was placed on the state's list for possible closure unless state assessment scores improved.

These middle level experts introduced our research idea to administrators and teachers in the middle school. I introduced the research in my three master's level courses and discussed the opportunity for students to join me in this research project; six agreed—three women and three men. Even though some had doubts about observing at this school, the group was motivated by the goal of conducting research to produce a report which was of immediate interest and need for the NYSED. In addition, I was heartened that two African American male students had volunteered for the project; the remainder of our group was European American. Because the school has a majority of minority students and staff, having at least two African Americans among our group I think eased concerns among some of the respondents. Although diversity is defined in many ways beyond color, in a politically charged environment where the state has already stepped in and issues of power and privilege are questioned, a totally white research group could more likely be viewed as *them* coming to learn about *us*.

OUR GOALS AND RESEARCH PROCESS

As the study began, I reviewed the initial research conducted through the NYSED and middle level education liaisons in spring 2000. Our new team of seven, six graduates students and myself, discussed the state's interest in learning more about and understanding the action plan's progress at RMS primarily from the perspectives of those charged with its daily implementation. Then, we summarized our general goals as follows:

1. To understand and describe the perceptions and attitudes of members of the school community—teachers, administration, staff, and student body—concerning the success of the action plan; and

2. To describe the strengths and weaknesses of the action plan in terms of fostering intellectual, academic, personal, and social development of the middle school students.

However, as our research observations and interviews began and our in-class readings and discussions in such areas as policies, community context, social and cultural reproduction theory, funding, racial inequalities, and parental involvement continued, we decided to broaden our scope to gain information that allowed us to understand the situation at RMS more clearly from a variety or perspectives. We included these additional goals:

3. To describe what barriers exist and what improvements have evolved in the relationships among the community, parents, students, teachers, administrators and staff because of or despite the action plan.
4. To describe how the school and community cultures not addressed by the action plan affect the middle school and stakeholders.
5. To describe what larger problems affect the middle school, which cannot be addressed by the action plan.

A QUALITATIVE APPROACH

A qualitative/naturalistic methodology allows researchers to conduct research in the places where the respondents interact daily and emphasizes discovering the meaning and culture of the environment through the perspectives of its various stakeholders (Eisner & Peshkin, 1990; Wolcott, 1992). In our nonparticipant observation study, our fieldwork consisted of observing, interviewing, and examining documents at the middle school with administrators, teachers, students, and other staff. This approach opposes using methods such as mailed surveys or interviews over the phone that do not study the work site/school in the research process (Eisner & Peshkin, 1990).

One of the methods we used to gain a more comprehensive view were observations of various events and sites in the school, for instance team meetings, classroom teaching, hallways during and between classes, and the cafeteria. We completed 18 formal interviews using an interview protocol with teachers and administrators and informal interviews with other staff. We interviewed 15 teachers from various subject areas including special subjects such as Spanish and home and careers, the principal, a vice principal, a guidance counselor, and talked informally with a few security personnel. Most formal interviews were audiotaped and transcribed. My students interviewed African American, European American, and His-panic American female and male teachers in an attempt to provide varied perspectives. A majority of these teachers had 2 to 5 years of experience in teaching or administrating at RMS. Only four respondents had been in the district for more than 10 years, one being an assistant principal.

We also reviewed documents from the school including policy state-ments, handouts at team meetings, and flyers sent home to parents; docu-ments from the NYSED; and newspaper articles about the school and district. We discussed these artifacts at our team meetings and analyzed them as part of the data.

Our team began this process with deciding on a time for the team to meet outside of class. In addition to attending regular class meetings, stu-dents met 6 times for at least 2 hours as a group with me to understand the goals of the research; learn more about research and their roles and responsibilities; discuss documents, findings, questions, and interpreta-tions; and eventually turn in their assigned written parts of the project. We discussed goals for the project and additional handouts on qualitative research. For our second meeting, the students each developed a list of questions for the interview protocol to meet our goals based on their reading of the action plan, the New York State Middle-Level School Improvement Initiative for the 2000-2001 school year, the EEMLE, and newspaper reports. We talked about students' questions and then revised and finalized one interview protocol that each of us used during teacher interviews. For administrative interviews, we created several additional questions.

DATA COLLECTION AND INTERPRETATION

Over a period of 9 weeks, the six graduate researchers and I visited the school at least 5 days each to observe, interview, and gather document data. Three students and I visited 7 times. Usually groups of two to four would visit the school at the same time, but we observed different class-rooms and other locations and conduct interviews individually. One of the reasons for this, at least initially, was the fear that two of the women stu-dents expressed about going to the school. From hearsay and newspaper articles, all of the preservice students knew about the school and district's problems. They talked about an unsafe school and community where vio-lent events occurred, so security guards and metal detectors were needed. Yet their curiosity to gain first-hand knowledge and the challenge of our task engaged them more; they did not let their fear prevent them from participating. We accommodated their reluctance to go to the school alone by traveling in groups. Many of the students' initial observations included much about the discipline and violence they witnessed. However, as they became more comfortable in the environment and realized that positive moments occurred, they were able to focus on the wider scope of events and interactions. Because our individual schedules varied, occasionally one researcher would visit alone. I visited several times alone and attended, with the two state education consultants, one earlier planning meeting in early September of the team charged with leading the implementation of the action plan.

As the researchers observed and interviewed, descriptive notes were taken and each researcher transcribed the audiotaped interviews. Five teachers preferred not to be audiotaped; therefore, students took copious notes. The students and I brought copies of the transcripts of interviews completed thus far to the meetings to disseminate to each group member to read. To analyze content, we each highlighted words and phrases we believed were important and those that they saw repeated by many respondents. Then, we discussed possible meanings and interpretations of the data, and whether or not any patterns were developing. As we brought new data to each meeting, we used a constant comparison method (Huberman & Miles, 1998) to look at previous understandings and patterns in light of new interviews completed or insights gained from additional observations. This allowed us to be reflexive in our analysis as we used initial ideas and interpretations to help us inform further data collection and writing (Coffey & Atkinson, 1996).

As we neared the final weeks of the semester and the interviewing and observing ended, we completed our analysis of patterns found in interviews and observations. We used documents to support, illuminate, or offer conflicting evidence. Interpretation of meaning—"making sense of what has been learned" (Denzin, 1998, p. 313)—involves creating a text that communicates these understandings to the readers. It also requires the "reconstruction of social worlds and often emphasize[s] the unique rather than regularities of incidence or pattern" (Coffey & Atkinson, 1996, p. 7). Our research team decided to write the report by creating sections that demonstrated the most prominent patterns in the world of teachers in this school, yet we wanted also to share individual voices that offered unique perspectives. Although no rendering of qualitative research is totally without the writers' interpretations, in general, our writing represents descriptive realism as we primarily "allow the world being described to speak for itself" and share a multivoiced story (Denzin, 1998, p. 327).

Each group member wrote two or three sections. After further group discussion of these drafts, each member revised their sections, often to include more data. We also determined the need to include more individual quotes to share the teachers' or other staff members' voices and views.

Many of these initial drafts summarized too much and lacked enough individual perspectives to support the general points. Once students turned in their revised individual sections, I wrote an overview of our research approach and collated the parts providing transitions and making editing decisions. I sent the report to the student researchers for final feedback. Then, I sent the report to the two state education experts who had facilitated our access to the school. The NYSED could use the information to aid in the assistance to RMS and the school district.

RESULT HIGHLIGHTS

This chapter focuses primarily on the preservice students and their involvement in active field research. However, what the students and I discovered in relation to our original goals is also important to understanding their experience. Here I present highlights of findings that the team garnered about the strengths and weaknesses of the action plan, the relationships among stakeholders, and the larger community problems.

The RMS Action Plan

All 18 respondents interviewed praised universally the RMS action plan for attempting to bring a holistic approach to foster an environment that promoted individual intellectual development, academic achievement, and personal and social development of students. However, not everyone expressed the same level of familiarity with the action plan or the same sense of involvement with its implementation; some noted only learning of the plan when the school year started. The responses to the action plan are categorized under three subheadings: perceived strengths, perceived weaknesses, and perceived obstacles.

Perceived Strengths
The respondents perceived the greatest strengths of the RMS action plan to be in its provisions for: (1) teaming, (2) master scheduling, (3) staff development, and (4) increased in-school social events.

Teachers described teaming as the most important support system for them, helping to improve communication and curriculum coordination, to address students' needs including finding learning disabilities, to integrate disciplinary actions, and to share teaching skills. In regard to benefits for the students, a social studies teacher felt that the plan "socially keeps kids together." Since the students are scheduled on interdisciplinary teams, they have more classes with the same other students, which allows them to build relationships and develop study buddies. One English teacher felt that "teaming has given the students more support on both the academic and personal levels. When advisory begins, this will increase student support. Without teaming there would be no support and total chaos would occur." Most respondents also believed that teaming fostered collaboration and collegiality among teachers, but especially empowered them as responsible participants within the decision-making process of the school. As one teacher said, "At least now we have a voice. Before we had none." Yet, several teachers cautioned about the need for more support from administrators and a solid infrastructure.

Respondents perceived the master scheduling as an improvement. The schedule changed to include more classes per day for students. Another change in the structure of the school day allowed for common planning time for teams; however, many teachers indicated that lack of attendance at team meetings was a problem. Yet, some teachers noted that class scheduling sometimes worked to conflict with the time of team meetings, especially for special subject teachers. This conflict, common to many middle schools with teams, undermined the teams' effort and led to diluted team cohesiveness. It also fostered teacher isolation and worked against the action plan.

Most teachers responded that the professional development classes designed as part of the action plan were extremely helpful to individual respondents' enhancement of professional skills and knowledge. They perceived the content shared at team meetings such as teaching strategies, rubrics, and focus on eighth grade assessments as useful information. Teachers recommended more workshops in learning classroom management skills, dealing with social problems, and handling student discipline.

Each member of our research team observed at least one team meeting. Several members described in their observation notes the teachers' discussion of proactive events to motivate the students and recognize their good behavior and achievement. The teachers spoke of using social events such as a pizza party for students who had honored their obligations under the action plan and school policies. Events such as these provided a sense of community and common purpose for students. The teachers did not want to respond to situations only after the fact in a punitive manner.

Perceived Weaknesses

The weaknesses often generated more comment than did the strengths of the plan, and some of the weaknesses teachers' elaborated on went beyond the action plan and focused on the school in general. The respondents perceived the greatest weaknesses of the action plan to be its failure to address: (1) clear and relevant enforcement of discipline by the administration, (2) adequate time to implement the action plan to achieve NYSED assessment standards (thus creating anxiety), (3) basic skill levels of incoming elementary students, and (4) the need for positive, coherent communication and support from the NYSED and the administration that will encourage work towards the action plan rather than fears of the school closing.

The perceived failure of the administration to enforce school rules and discipline unruly students was voiced unanimously by the teachers as being the result of "no consequences." No issue elicited as an intense a reaction as that regarding safety and discipline. Most respondents related stories of attempting to deal with disciplinary problems in the classroom or hallway, ranging from chronic lateness to class to physical violence, or sending students to the administration, and later discovering that the students returned to normal school activities without disciplinary measures. The teachers expressed levels of frustration, despair, and fear; most of the preservice interviewers witnessed violent incidents firsthand. Only recently had the school developed in-school suspension.

In both classrooms and hallways, disorder is highly visible. Teachers felt that the administration should do more to enforce the rules (appointment of deans was repeatedly mentioned), and that the lack of control interfered with learning, consumed time on classroom management and at team meetings, and frustrates the other efforts being made under the action plan. Teachers believed that they were put into untenable positions of having to enforce rules without administrative support or having to deal with emotionally distressed students in need of other professional help. They expressed a desire to see parents take a more active role in the discipline of their children and most thought that the security guards were either disrespectful to the children, not well qualified or trained, or not numerous enough to make much difference in the school climate. However, the security chief noted that the sheer number of students presented a serious problem to the few security officers attempting to manage them and that the students attending the school knew that "next to nothing" would happen to them if they broke school rules.

Administrators viewed the discipline and safety issues differently than the teachers, admitting the problems, but disagreeing about remedies used. The principal noted, "We have policies and I certainly follow through with whatever we can, but we have people who just sort of pick at the children." The administrators witnessed teachers who have become so stressed themselves that they appear to be overreacting to even the slightest digression on the part of the students. Administrators acknowledged that the children come to school with a variety of differences and problems. They seem frustrated seeing children who suffer through harsh living conditions and subsequently act out when they are in school. As our interviewers continued their observations at the school, it was clear that most classes proved to be challenging in regard to discipline. The experiences ran the gamut: from the teacher who had to keep leaving the room because she was about to burst into tears to the skillful veterans who deftly handled each disruption. However, many precious minutes of class were wasted during the various attempts to quiet unruly students. In one disruptive class, one girl became visibly upset over the chaos and began crying. She turned to the observer, believing him to be from the state, and pleaded through tears, "Please, mister, don't close us down!"

Although most respondents did not believe that NYSED would close the middle school, divide the students, and send them to other districts—one of the remedies threatened if the assessment targets were not reached—many questioned whether or not the state had allowed sufficient time for those goals to be reached by June 2001 given the history of the district and the radical changes being attempted under the action plan. Optimism on the ultimate achievement of the state's assessment targets ranged from guarded to enthusiastic, and respondents expressed belief in the students' abilities to succeed given time and a more orderly environment.

The looming specter of needing to pass the state's various assessments affected many of the students and teachers. "I think that many people are uncomfortable," reported one teacher, echoing a sentiment heard time and time again. "I wouldn't say nervous, but apprehensive as to whether or not we can follow or fulfill the requirements that are being set down by the state.... I would say there is a general feeling of unrest."

The teachers believed that the students had never been adequately prepared academically to take these tests; the very concept of a state issued test is daunting in and of itself. Thus, the teachers' complaint was that the action plan failed to address the basic skills of students, especially elementary students new to their school, and provide adequate time to prepare students for the standardized examination format. Teachers placed blame on poor performance by the elementary schools and students receiving inadequate education through the seventh grade. Many teachers questioned how students could possibly come up from the elementary school having such remarkably low levels of reading and math skills and suggested that perhaps the state should examine these problems. Teachers felt that they had to work harder to teach their lessons if they also had to attempt to give remedial instruction in basic skills. Intervention programs, which might assist skill-deficient students, took place after school and were nonmandatory.

Overall, the teachers sensed that the students were not going to be ready to take these tests, especially the bilingual and special education students. One teacher responded, "I think that the Regents' plan that all students must pass the Regents is totally ridiculous." Another teacher acknowledged a lot of pressure exists in the classroom, and that the teachers are working before and after school to try and help the students. A third teacher cited that no materials were available prior to this year for students to practice, and, therefore, assessing students based only on this year is unfair. The changes that could possibly affect a positive outcome were just too recent. A fourth teacher, although acknowledging that the students are scared of the tests, believed that by using the practice tests each quarter, the students will benefit and improve their performance (adding the caveat, "The ones that [sic] are in class.") Another teacher felt that the practice tests serve to keep the students focused and give them a sense of what they need to work on. A comment from an administrator was the most open minded of all: "I think the students, for the most part, are seriously handling it.... There's some balking...but many of them are very cooperative and they know that this is something that we just have to do." This interviewee also noted, "The teachers are certainly working hard."

Responses concerning the perceived lack of communication and support from the NYSED and the administration varied in their focus. Most respondents reported having little or no contact with state education representatives and felt disenfranchised by the very agency that had threatened to close the school. A number of respondents expressed the feeling that the action plan was dropped on them in September, and that it would have made more sense to get everyone involved with it sooner. A major problem appeared to be lack of information regarding what the state was actually doing in the school. Several teachers reacted to questions concerning the plans of the state with "I know the school was taken by the state but, to be honest with you, I don't understand the concept," and "I'm not sure what's going on, the nuts and bolts, as far as the administration and the state and what they're trying to do." Although our research team knew state representatives were helping to facilitate the RMS action plan and did spend some time at the school, some teachers expressed that they did not see a state presence on the school premises.

Several teachers and nonteaching staff had positive reports regarding the efforts of the administration to communicate. For example, during staff meetings, teachers received encouraging suggestions and ideas for classroom implementation; a few discussed positive guidance. Yet the administration, according to other teachers, did not seem available or well known to the teachers. Rather the administration was a faceless entity not directly or consistently involved in the day-to-day running of the school. Clearly, the high principal and superintendent turn over rate complicated a positive continued communication with teachers. For some respondents, inadequate communication from the administration such as not being informed in a timely manner of meetings was a problem. In the case of the 6-week summer training program (professional development), a few teachers said they had never been aware of it, and one reported having submitted an application to attend but was never contacted.

One teacher described administrators and the state as making promises they could not keep. Supposedly, they both offered books and money to the school if the teachers put together a list of what they required. Though supplies were ordered in September of 2000, they still had not been received by November 2000. Another teacher acknowledged that colleagues had begun to order supplies out of catalogs and were buying them in stores with their own money. One English teacher noted that although "they are trying," the administrators are "in a quandary." Another teacher claimed, almost identically, "They [administration] don't know what to do with RMS." The findings indicate that the teachers need more awareness of how the state and administrators are implementing the plan.

Teachers would also like to see more guidance and support offered by members of the administration and the state. One teacher had this suggestion for selecting members of the administration: "We need distributive leadership, individuals with strong academic backgrounds and a love of learning." Most teachers seem to want to make a difference, but they can only do so with the help and guidance of those implementing the rules from higher up.

This lack of communication contributed to teachers and students anxieties about the school closing. Uncertainty, outrage, loss of hope, apathy, and fear, public announcements by Commissioner Mills, newspaper articles about the school closing, and the unknown future had dramatically affected the school stakeholders and resulted in numerous mixed feelings. Some teachers expressed optimism about the action plan and seemed observably to strive toward its goals in the classroom and at team meetings; some students responded to the positive regard and creative classroom lessons. Yet most respondents believed that uncertainty was causing many staff and students to lose hope. Some administrators and teachers left the school last year as threats of closing loomed. The large turnover rate hurt the school and made performing well on state tests even more difficult.

Teachers thought the students accepted Mills' threat to close the school as being as good as done; they believed that the students had already quit, some stating that students had actually vocalized the sentiment, "The school's going to close, so what does it matter what we do?" The "children are mentally departing from the situation; they are stressed out and getting short tempered." The emotional instability the students experienced due to the negative publicity and the uncertainty of their school's future added to a perceived lack of motivation to do well. Other respondents reported that some students expressed a sense of outrage that *their* school could be closed even if they try hard. Many students had not clearly expressed any feeling, but teachers reported that lateness to class and disruptive behavior had increased. The principal agreed that students believed that studying was pointless; they lost respect for their principal and their teachers who appeared powerless to them. He thought that this feeling of hopelessness was a major contributor to increased levels of violence.

Perceived Obstacles

All respondents commented on factors, which are tangential to or outside the scope of the RMS action plan, summarized as: (1) financial concerns, (2) social-emotional needs of students, (3) interpersonal concerns, and (4) parental involvement.

The school district was in its second year of austerity when voters again failed to approve an increased school budget. Many teachers cited lack of resources and the deteriorating physical plant as examples of how the lack of money affected the school. Respondents reported having no texts for some classes, few computer resources, and having to purchase nontext materials out-of-pocket for classes because the school has no system or means to provide them. Many people also pointed to specific examples of how the building needs repairs or replacements, such as missing floor tiles, roof leaks, and thermostats that did not work. The lack of working thermostats resulted in the overheating of classrooms that must be vented by opening the windows, wasting the energy used in generating the heat.

With regard to difficult students, most respondents recognized that a significant number of students had social-emotional needs that were not being met outside the school. Some respondents reported that many children were in foster care, attended the school transiently, were inadequately supervised after school, or did not live in a home environment that provides for adequate adult guidance and nurturing. Although many stated that they tried to be as encouraging and caring of students as possible, the scale of the population of students in need outstripped the school's ability to provide testing and professional intervention.

Interpersonal concerns touched upon conflicts between and among the community, parents, administrators, faculty, and students. At some team meetings, divisiveness and unwillingness of some team members to participate were observed. Some comments seemed to reflect turf protecting or that others were not pitching in and doing their job. Many other comments, however, reflected teachers' confusion, frustration, and fear about the action plan and the possible outcome of the 2000-2001 school year.

Most respondents recognized the opportunity at hand and stated that everyone needed to continue to work together towards achieving the action plan. As one person put it, "Everyone needs to own up to their own problems and fix them. They need to stop blaming each other and look at what needs to be done and how to get there."

Responses were mixed on whether or not parental involvement with the school had improved; however, effort on the school's part to involve parents and community was obvious. The school held open house nights (meet the teacher) including one in August and another in September, and parent-teacher conferences. Many teachers noted increased attendance at open house and parent teacher student association meetings with more questions being asked. A few parents had even attended team meetings. The local religious community appeared supportive, as well. Local church leaders are trying to get a community response. One teacher stated that, because parents are responsible for looking after their children when they are suspended out of school, they are "starting to get the message and be supportive." One administrator felt that "most of the students who have support from home, where home is demanding something, are coming in here everyday and doing what they're supposed to do because they get some consequences, repercussions from home." Another administrator said,

> I look at the students here as not necessarily bad kids, a lot of them are sick kids, and they need help and they need love. And that's what it's gonna take. We need to ensure that the students have full support from parents, teachers, and administrators, so their minds will be prepared for success.

Many teachers echoed that more parental involvement could only bring about more positive change. When their parents care, the children may be inclined to do well. One male teacher said of parents: "Just by talking to them and explaining what the problems are, the behavior improves dramatically. Just because the parent walked in and talked to me."

One concern of several teachers was the lack of access some parents had to their child's educational experience, which could account for why these parents did not actively participate. Some parents were nonnative speakers and may not be able to understand what was being discussed at meetings. One language teacher noted, "There is a big number of immigrants; I'm talking about the Spanish children. They [parents] cannot do homework with their children."

One teacher discussed her concern about contacting certain parents about their child's behavior. "A lot of these parents are violent. It's scary to call your [student's] houses because they [students] are going to get a beating. I am afraid to call some people's parents." Another reason teachers noted for lack of parental involvement was the discouragement and stress of some parents regarding the uncertainty of the school's future. If the school risks the chance of closing, the parents may think that they have little influence or control over the situation. A teacher explained: "And the parents are gonna figure, 'Well why should I bother; the school's closing down anyway?'"

Suggestions for trying to involve parents included making it mandatory "that parents attend various kinds of workshops." Teachers advocated showing parents that teachers really care, that "parents need to be approached by teachers as someone who cares about their child." Overall, teachers were willing to do nearly anything to gain the support of more parents in bringing about positive results in the school as a whole.

CONCLUSION

The team of six graduate students who participated in this active field study learned valuable lessons on many topics. Based on all the data, experiences, and discussion that the preservice students and I shared in this research project, one student drafted the following conclusion. After our team reviewed the conclusion, I made minor editing changes.

Team Conclusion

> After a while a school and the individuals in the school start to take on a culture. They begin to share what makes you, who you are, which is why this situation becomes scarier. Education is the key for success. They cannot close down the school, since they would be destroying their culture (a teacher).

RMS needs an administration that looks at the long-term goals as well as the short-term goals. With a high teacher and administrative turnover, this school needs consistency—a difficult task to achieve. RMS must implement a system of discipline in which the administration is firm and sympathetic at the same time. Most teachers felt that the children need a strong stable atmosphere that focuses on the basics. It appeared as though many of the students were entering the middle school without a strong foundation of skills from the elementary schools. One Spanish teacher stated, "The state, I know, has very high standards, and sometimes our kids, unfortunately, have not been trained to pass these tests. I have noticed that they don't have any test skills." It is a difficult task to prepare students for tests that assess skills that students have not yet acquired.

For the most part, teaming has been positive and supportive at the same time; however, it still has its kinks. Most teachers felt that it has helped in identifying children with special needs versus children with disciplinary problems. Teaming has also become a support group for the teachers. One staff member believed that the development of teaming has led to teachers "speaking more with one voice." Still teaming is not perfect, with three teams and an adjunct team, the special education students are spread throughout.

Structural and financial problems also need to be addressed at RMS. The schools' physical appearance needs care. One social studies teacher asked, "What message does this send to the kids?" This can cause the students to feel that administration and teachers do not care for them. To improve the infrastructure of the school, it is imperative that the school has the finances available. More often than not, the school has not had the budget for the upkeep, while teachers have enough problems getting the resources they need in the classrooms for the students. The administration and the state promised to get teachers the resources they needed. In response to one question about the adequacy of resources, one English teacher replied, "We need much more." As a result, several teachers even purchase their own resources to fulfill their lesson plans.

RMS needs a stronger disciplinary process. One teacher suggested that the school needs two deans: one male and one female selected from the staff. These deans need to know the community and students and have a strong disciplinary classroom. They need to teach for two or three periods, be with the students the rest of the time, and receive a paid stipend. Instead, RMS has become a culture in which blame is spread, where administrators do not want to handle the problems, causing inconsistency and the child to go back and forth between parents, administration, and teachers. Most often, the parents blame the teachers for any problems that occur, while the administration also blames the teachers.

It is imperative that parents, teachers, and administration become further educated. Education is a key to success, so that mistakes are not repeated and growth may occur. Teachers should attend staff development and share their experiences with the other teachers. Parents should also attend the free workshops and daily team meetings whenever they can, so they are aware of what is going on in their children's lives.

Through teaming, meetings, staff development, community support, and communication, teachers, parents, and students are pulling more together to improve the school. The action plan provided a framework and direction, and the teachers are trying to be more positive and encouraging with the student population. Still many strides must be taken and work completed—with the cooperation of all.

A DISTRICT UPDATE

In March 2001, the Board of Regents recommended a state takeover of the district school system. This action relieved the school board of its duties, removed the power of residents to vote for annual school budgets, and gave management power to Commissioner Mills who appointed a new board and could appoint a new superintendent and/or a private management company.

Scores improved for eighth graders on the ELA and mathematics state exams for 2001, yet the district still lags behind most Long Island districts (Lambert, 2002a). Although the RSD school board vigorously and legally opposed their own removal, this occurred when the state finally took over the district in early May 2002. By that time, six superintendents had held the position in the last 7 years. The take over included state-appointed trustees—three of whom must be from the district; residents retaining the right to vote on the school budget; and the infusion of millions of dollars into the district including $100 million to construct three new schools to open in fall 2004 (Lambert, 2002b). New York's funding formulas have been challenged in court to provide a fairer distribution of state aid, and residents of Nassau County on Long Island filed suit and forced correction of the over assessment of residential property, which could help this district provide more of its own financial support for schools. However, the state could continue to administer the district for up to a decade. Notably, RSD was the first and only district taken over by the state due to educational failure. In 2004, the district was seeking to hire its seventh superintendent in 10 years (Saslow, 2004), and the promised new schools were not yet opening.

REFLECTIONS ON THIS ACTION RESEARCH

The collaborative research project at RMS was an opportunity to involve preservice students in a research study that provided us as researchers and, perhaps more importantly, NYSED a broader perspective on RMS and the implementation of the action plan from the perspectives of many stakeholders at the school. Through 43 observations among the researchers and interviews formal and informal, important themes emerged that helped identify what was working with the action plan and what was not. We successfully completed our goals and the students learned additional valuable lessons, some may generalize to similar middle schools in crisis.

Out in the field, students eyes were opened wide with regard to the numerous and complex events and interactions that teachers are a part of every day in a poor, minority school with deeply rooted financial, social, and political problems. They overcame fears about going to the school and realized that these teachers and students share the same desires, concerns, needs, and joys as those at other schools, whether on the SURR list or not. They understood that students want to feel ownership and security while in their schools. New York teacher certification requires that part of student observation hours be in high needs and diversely populated schools. The students' research in this school added to these important experiences. These extended observations and interviews at RMS allowed these graduate students to get an under the surface understanding of the professional life of teaching, of teacher as not just an instructional leader in the classroom, but also a political participant in the culture and direction of a school. Unfortunately, although we provided the state with valuable information, our research team was not part of making the decisions or taking action to affect changes in the classrooms or school as is the expected outcome of action research projects (Arhar, Holly, & Kasten, 2001).

One newspaper editorial discussing the district's situation commented:

> Schools of education should incorporate into their mission the explicit recognition of the effect of race on educational practices and decisions. The nation's future teachers and administrators must know more about our country's racial history and implications of race on instructional and administrative decisions. Better informed teachers and administrators will not only assist students in improving their interpersonal relationships, but will assist all students (and their parents and communities) in better understanding and anticipating the dynamics of race. (Bernstein, 2003)

The goals of our teacher education programs and many of our classes do explicitly recognize racial issues in schools through a critical pedagogy approach. Yet, as this study demonstrates with its complexity and interdependence of issues, the problems and the solutions are both external and internal to the school and go beyond the dynamics of race. External standardized tests, funding issues, and politics—internal obstacles of poor conditions, a history of low expectations, and high teacher and administrative turnover are among the key reasons for the lack of success. In this larger sociopolitical realm, and connected to many discussion areas in our course together, these students learned that larger structural and institutional issues must also be understood and examined.

On the process level, several of the student researchers told me that they enjoyed the collaborative work as they learned to listen to each other's observation stories and ideas, discuss, interpret, and compromise with each other over the findings. Overall, this field-based action research provided many teachable moments for those students involved and will benefit them in their future teaching positions and in action research endeavors to improve their classrooms and schools.

NOTES

1. The school and community name are pseudonyms.
2. In a letter to the New York state Board of Regents (January., 2004), James Kadamus, a deputy state education commissioner, indicated that over the last 3 years, more schools with middle level grades have been designated SURR schools than have other types of schools, such as elementary or high schools. More middle level schools on the SURR list close rather than improve. Over 80% of schools with middle grades in New York City are designated as schools in need of improvement, a stage prior to being placed on the SURR list. In 2000, 105 failing schools existed in New York, 97 of them in New York City (Wyatt, 2000).
3. The Essential Elements of Middle Level Education was revised and updated by the state in late 2000. The new title reflects the state's strengthened emphasis on the 28 New York state learning standards: *The Essential Elements of Standards-Focused Middle-Level Schools and Programs* (www.emsc. nysed.gov).
4. I would like to acknowledge and thank the six students who collaborated with me on this research: Laury Herzlin, Theresa Orosz, Lauren Verlizzo, Scott Batson, Ken Leman, and Cardinal Valery.
5. Students are encouraged to substitute teach or work g as inclusion aides in the classroom, sometimes one on one with a particular student.
6. The goal of this study of 10 schools was to determine if a significant correlation existed between schools scoring highly on the state assessments and schools implementing the highest degree of units from the EEMLE. The results did indicate a correlation, but statistical analysis to determine significance has yet to be completed.

REFERENCES

Allen, L., & Calhoun, E. (1998). Schoolwide action research: Findings from six years of study. *Phi Delta Kappan, 79*(9), 706-710.

Arhar, J. M., Holly, M. L., & Kasten, W. C. (2001). *Action research for teachers: Traveling the yellow brick road.* Columbus, OH: Merrill Prentice Hall.

Bernstein, M. F. (2003, February 2). The tone of inequality in education. *The New York Times*, p. LI13.

Board of Regents of the State of New York. (2000). *Essential elements of standards-focused middle-level schools and programs.* Albany, NY: Author.

Board of Regents of the State of New York. (2003). *Supporting young adolescents: Regents policy statement on middle-level education.* Albany, NY: Author.

Calhoun, E. (1994). *How to use action research in the self-renewing school.* Alexandria, VA: Association for Supervision and Curriculum Development.

Coffey, A., & Atkinson, P. (1996). *Making sense of qualitative data: Complementary research strategies*. Thousand Oaks, CA: Sage.

Denzin, N. K. (1998). The art and politics of interpretation. In N. K. Denzin & Y. S. Lincoln (Eds.), *Collecting and interpreting qualitative materials* (pp. 313-344). Thousand Oaks, CA: Sage.

Eisner, E., & Peshkin, A. (Eds). (1990). *Introduction. Qualitative inquiry in education: The continuing debate*. New York: Teachers College Press.

Huberman, M. A., & Miles, M. B. (1998). Data management and analysis methods. In N. K. Denzin & Y. S. Lincoln (Eds.), *Collecting and interpreting qualitative materials* (pp. 179-210). Thousand Oaks, CA: Sage.

Kadamus, J. (2004). *Conceptual framework for middle-level reform strategy*. Retrieved January 17, 2004, from http://www.regents.nysed.gov/January2004/0104emscvesidd4.htm

Lambert, B. (2002a, January 9). [Regentsville] educators point to improving test scores. *New York Times*, p. B6.

Lambert, B. (2002b, April 17). State moving to take over [Regentsville] school district. *New York Times*, p. B6.

McKay, J. A. (1992). Professional development through action research. *Journal of Staff Development, 13*(1), 18-21.

Powell, M. (2002, April 22). Separate and unequal in [Regentsville], Long Island. *The Washington Post*, p. A3.

Pratt, C. (2000, November 10). State gives [Regentsville] standards to reach: If scores are not met, high school could close. *Newsday*, p. A44.

[Regentsville's] last chance to shape up. (2000, September 10). *Newsday*, p. B3.

Ryan, K., & Cooper, J. M. (2004). (Eds.) *Kaleidoscope: Readings in education* (10th ed.). Boston: Houghton Mifflin.

Saslow, L. (2000, April 30). Charter school plan approved for [Regentsville]. *New York Times*, p. LI7.

Saslow, L. (2004, March 14). [Regentsville] challenge: Hiring school chief. *New York Times*, p. LI2.

Schensul, J. J., & Schensul, S. L. (1992). Collaborative research: Methods of inquiry for social change. In M. D. LeCompte, W. L. Millroy, & J. Preissle (Eds.), *The handbook of qualitative research in education* (pp. 161-200). New York: Academic Press.

Stern, J., & Stacki, S. L. (2004). Creating common middle-level knowledge: A New York story. In S. C. Thompson (Ed.), *Reforming middle level education: Considerations for policymakers* (pp. 189-203). Greenwich, CT: Information Age.

Wolcott, H. F. (1992). Posturing in qualitative research. In M. D. LeCompte, W. L. Millroy, & J. Preissle (Eds.), *The handbook of qualitative research in education* (pp. 3-52). New York: Academic Press.

Wyatt, E. (2000a, July 13). Little improved despite an overhaul, L.I. school district is at a crossroads. *New York Times*, p. B1.

Wyatt, E. (2000b, September). Interim [Regentsville] schools leader quits after two months, citing board interference. *New York Times*, p. B4.

CHAPTER 6

ON THE JOB TRAINING

Action Research in a Middle Level Alternative Certification Program

Melinda Wilder, Dorie Combs, and Cynthia Resor

ABSTRACT

An integral part of the middle level alternative certification program at Eastern Kentucky University is the action research project. The action research project is designed to fulfill the research component of this master's program while promoting career-long reflective teaching. The project is introduced, developed, revised, and completed throughout the four semester program. To determine if this action research project met our goals, data were gathered through analysis of the summative program assessment questionnaire and comments. We ascertained that both goals were met for the student, though some adjustments were needed to the scheduling and support provided to students as they plan and carry out their research. Recommendations for future programs are provided.

Making a Difference: Action Research in Middle Level Education, 107–124

INTRODUCTION

According to the National Center for Education Statistics, 2.2 million teachers will be needed over the next 10 years (Hussar, 1999). The education community in the United States is struggling with ways to meet this shortage while addressing the mandate of the No Child Left Behind Act for a highly qualified teacher in every classroom. Meeting these challenges is especially difficult for middle schools. Approximately 53% of classes in high poverty middle schools are taught by a teacher who lacks a major or equivalent in their teaching field. This problem is not limited to math, science, and special education either. Even in seventh and eighth grade social studies and English classes, there is a shortage of credentialed teachers (Ingersol, 1999). One avenue for filling the need for qualified middle grades teachers is through the development of fast-track, alternative certification programs.

One critical aspect of developing these programs is figuring out how to ensure that they meet rigorous, master's level academic standards while providing practical experience for the students. Traditionally, research has been considered a necessary academic component of any postbaccalaureate program. The National Council for Accreditation of Teacher Education's (NCATE) standards for teacher education programs expect that candidates in education related graduate programs will, "develop the ability to apply research and research methods" (The National Council for Accreditation of Teacher Education, NCATE, 2002, p. 20). How can a fast-track alternative certification program realistically include research? Action research may be the best way to answer this challenge. This paper presents the results of an action research project about action research in a master of arts in teaching program.

In 2001, Eastern Kentucky University (EKU) began a master of arts in teacher (MAT) degree program for individuals with bachelor's degrees in a certifiable teaching field (e.g., biology, English, history, and math). Completion of this program yields initial secondary level certification (grades 8-12). However, it was immediately clear that there was a critical need for middle level teachers in our region. In addition, a number of individuals were coming to us wanting to teach, but who did not hold a traditional teaching degree or even a degree in a teaching field. These individuals with degrees in nursing, journalism, forensic science, pharmacy, social work, and other areas seem to be a natural fit for middle level instruction. Effective middle level teachers use instructional approaches such as teaming, integrated learning, and interdisciplinary investigations, as well as making real-world connections within their content specialty (National Middle School Association, 2003). These nontraditional teacher candidates know how to use interdisciplinary planning and team-work on a day-to-day basis. They do not just know the science, math or language arts, or social studies content, they know how to apply that content in practical ways. The question, then, was how to prepare these individuals to meet the unique needs of young adolescents and meet the dual emphasis requirements of the NCATE / National Middle School Association standards for initial certification (National Middle School Association, 2001). In Kentucky, teachers in grades 5-8 must hold a specific middle level certificate in *two* areas of emphasis and pass the PRAXIS exam in each of those content areas.

The EKU department of curriculum and instruction begin the middle level MAT program with 14 candidates in 2002. By layering the MAT in middle level education over the previously established MAT in secondary teaching, we only needed to develop one additional course, a methods course that focuses on the unique needs of young adolescents, middle school curriculum, as well as content specific and general instructional strategies. The middle level MAT candidates must take additional content courses in order to demonstrate successful completion of at least 27 credit hours in each of two emphasis areas, including previous undergraduate and graduate coursework. A total of 12 credit hours must be completed as part of the MAT program, including at least 3 hours in each area. For example, an individual with a pharmacy degree, who has completed over 30 hours of biology and chemistry, might take an additional 3 graduate hours in earth science and 9 additional hours in math in order to complete a total of at least 27 hours in both science and math. Each student's planned program will be unique and based on prior coursework.

EKU is fortunate to have a series of graduate level content courses designed specifically for middle grades teachers, e.g., inquiry physics for the middle grades, approaches to poetry, economics for teachers, and math concepts for teachers in grades 5-9. Eight candidates of the first cohort of the MAT completed the program, and five more are scheduled to graduate in May 2004. Of the original 14, 13 of these now hold full-time teaching positions. (One individual dropped out of the program during the first year.) A second cohort of 12 graduate students will complete student teaching in spring of 2004, while a third group begins the program at the same time.

An integral part of EKU's alternative certification, MAT program is the action research project. This project is designed to fulfill the research component of this graduate level program while promoting career-long reflective teaching. The action research project is introduced, developed, revised, and completed in four courses throughout the four-semester program. Students conduct the project during the student teaching semester. They complete the final research paper and give a multimedia presentation to their peers and professors during the capstone seminar following student teaching.

Because it is based on the individual teacher candidate's needs and interests and serves as a critical reflection on that individual's classroom practices, using action research in an alternative certification program promotes understanding of research and reflective practice. Action research allows teachers to play a more active role in their professional development, helps them make wise and informed decisions to improve their teaching, and facilitates limiting the gap between educational theory and classroom practice (Johnson, 2002).

PURPOSE

The purpose of our action research project was to determine if the middle grades MAT candidates' action research projects met our program goals of (1) involving students in educational research, and (2) promoting career-long, reflective teaching. Specifically, this project answered the following question: Is action research an effective practical research model that promotes reflection in a middle grades alternative certification master's degree program?

This is an important question since not only is it necessary to find a practical yet rigorous way to incorporate research into the master's level alternative certification programs, but it is also essential to prepare these teachers to meet their professional responsibilities. One traditional expectation of teacher preparation programs is to prepare teachers to link educational theory to classroom practices. This expectation has been difficult to achieve in traditional programs and is a greater challenge in alternative certification programs due to their fast-track nature. Another expectation comes from the redefinition of teachers' professional responsibilities by the local school districts to include the role of researcher (Fullan & Hargreaves, 1992). This change is based on the premise that school change is most effective when it advocated by the teachers themselves. If school districts expect teachers to be able to participate in school change, action research is a logical methodology. *This We Believe: Successful Schools for Young Adolescents* (National Middle School Association, 2003) encourages middle school teachers and leaders to use of action research in the development of a middle school's vision.

When a shared vision and mission statement become operational, middle level educators pursue appropriate practices in developing a challenging academic program; they develop the criteria to guide decisions and a process to made needed changes. Reviewing new ideas as they apply to this vision and its subsequent mission is a task that must be revisited regularly as circumstances change and new research and practices emerge. (p. 12)

For the purpose of this study, action research is defined as "the process of studying a real school or classroom situation to understand and improve the quality of actions or instruction" (Johnson, 2002, p.13). The goal of action research is twofold: to improve practice and to improve understanding of the educational context in which teaching takes place. Action research is seen as a paradigm for doing research rather than a specific set of qualitative or quantitative research techniques.

REVIEW OF THE LITERATURE

A review of the literature regarding action research components of alternative certification programs indicates a deficiency of published research on this topic. When doing a search of four different databases and an Internet search with two different search engines, no published studies of the use of action research in alternative certification were found. The Educational Resources Information Center database includes many unpublished action research projects developed as graduate theses and dissertations. Many sources cited that action research was a part of their alternative certification program but no accounts studied the effectiveness of this component. Therefore, the following review focuses on the effectiveness of using action research to promote understanding of and appreciation for education research as well as its efficacy in promoting reflective teaching in graduate teacher education programs.

Several studies showed that participation in action research does indeed increase teachers' appreciation for and understanding of educational research. In a study by Bennett (1994) designed to determine teachers' attitudes toward educational research and perceptions of themselves as researchers, she found that action research effectively improved attitudes toward educational research and was successful in promoting reflective teaching practices. This study used an open-ended questionnaire and follow-up interviews to assess the attitudes of three groups of teachers participating in a traditional MAT program: one group was beginning the program, the second had completed one of the required research classes, and the third had completed the two required research courses and required action research project. The findings of this study indicated that (1) teachers' attitudes toward research do change favorably after participating in an action research project, and (2) the action research project was the key to allowing teachers to connect practical knowledge with educational theory that resulted in systematic reflective thinking about teaching practices.

In another study done at four institutions, researchers concluded that action research did indeed help both graduates and undergraduate students learn the process of educational research (Sparapani, Abel, Easton, Edwards, & Herbster, 1996). This study summarized four colleges' uses of action research in both graduate and undergraduate programs. They concluded that although action research can take a variety of forms depending on the institution, three outcomes were obvious. The research projects helped students (1) identify their interest areas, (2) closely examine that interest area through data gathering and analysis, and (3) formulate conclusions and recommendations based on that data. Again, these abilities fostered graduates' and undergraduates' abilities to connect educational theory with classroom practice.

When looking at how teachers perceive their own capabilities to do educational research, DeCorse (1997) found that the teacher trait of novice versus experienced made a significant difference in teachers' perceptions. This project studied 13 masters' level students: eight were in-service teachers and five were preservice teachers who had completed student teaching. Based on data collected through interviews and journal writings, the researcher concluded that master's students who are teachers were more likely to plan and develop research projects that were *meaningful and feasible* (DeCorse, 1997, p. 14) whereas novice teachers were unsure of the significance of their ideas. DeCorse proposed that there may be a *magic window* (p. 14), of moderate experience, in the range of 6 to 10 years, for involving inservice teachers in action research. When looking at the spectrum of experience from novice to very experienced, it appeared that moderate experience generates a variety of questions for which these teachers are willing to investigate solutions.

A study of the stakeholders in graduate teacher education programs also indicated that action research is an appropriate methodology to involve teachers in educational research. When studying the traditional teacher education curricula with questionnaires, Ravid (1997) found that graduate students, faculty, schoolteachers, and school administrators believed three research skills to be most important. They were "the ability to use library resources, the ability to conduct action research in a classroom setting, and the ability to critically analyze professional literature" (p. 12). In her conclusion, Ravid cautions that action research by students in a graduate level initial teacher education program may be problematic when these students do not have their own classrooms other than their student teaching placement.

Planning and conducting action research projects can also help teacher candidates develop reflective teaching practices. In an action research project by graduate students on their use of action research, it was determined that reflective practice was one of the issues that was important to this type of research (Feldman et al., 1996). This study involved seven doctoral students and one professor in examining their roles in teacher education programs and was conducted during their participation in an action research course. They concluded that peer collaboration was an essential component of action research required to change perceptions of classroom teachers and that this collaboration promoted individual growth and development.

Dolbec and Savoie-Zajc (1995) found similar results. The researchers determined that despite several institutional constraints, the primary benefits of graduate students participating in action research included promoting both reflective thinking and changes in practices. Their conclusion was based on four research projects completed by the graduate students. They found several factors that affect the effectiveness of using action research. First, the action research process was incompatible for traditional, systematic, linear research done in academic graduate programs since it requires different collegiality and participation elements. That is, action research has to accommodate to the realities of the school setting. For example, schedules had to be changed because of inclement weather, unannounced school assemblies, or teacher absences. A high transient population within the classroom can destroy the sample size. Second, there seemed to be a mismatch between the requirements of the project proposal and the actual project implementation, which often required significant changes. This mismatch created tensions among the graduate student, the classroom teacher, and the student's advisor. Third, the implementation schedule often required the candidates to perform their research after completing other academic requirements. To be effective, the project needs to be synchronized with the candidate's student teaching schedule and completed within the scope of a course or series of courses. However, Dolbec, and Savoie-Zajc (1995) concluded that even under challenging circumstances, action research was an effective way to learn about the process of educational change while providing an opportunity to reflect on one's own strengths and areas for growth.

Daniels (2002) encouraged middle school teachers to collaborate within interdisciplinary teams to reflect on their instructional practices. She pointed out that action research lends more structure to the reflective process through thorough planning, comprehensive review of data as well as thoughtful and insightful writing. Though Daniels (2002) does not advocate one type of action research, she does believe the collaboration within interdisciplinary teams are essential for school improvement.

Although there is a scarcity of published inquiry on the effectiveness of action research in alternative certification programs, research of traditional graduate teacher education programs indicates that it is a constructive avenue for developing an appreciation for and participation in educational research. The studies also indicate that action research does promote reflective teaching practices.

METHODOLOGY

Subjects and Setting

The participants in this study were 13 students enrolled in the middle level MAT program at EKU. All students began their program in spring or summer of 2002. The MAT program is designed for *highly qualified* candidates with a bachelor's degree. To be considered highly qualified, candidates must have earned a minimum 3.0 grade point average (GPA) in their undergraduate program (or 3.0 in the last 60 hours), score at least 350 on both verbal and quantitative sections of the graduate records examination, and present evidence that they have the dispositions to be a successful classroom teacher. Table 6.1 shows the frequency of candidates in the various certification emphasis areas. The participants were fairly evenly divided by gender with seven females and six males. All were Caucasian. After taking the two introductory foundations in education classes, students in the MAT program are eligible for temporary provisional certification (TPC). Consequently, they can teach full time while completing this program. Ten of the participants were teaching full time with this type of certification.

EKU is a medium sized, state supported regional institution located in the south central portion of the state. Its service region includes 20 counties in the surrounding area, which are mostly rural communities located in or near the Appalachian Mountains. Students complete their student

Table 6.1.   Numbers of Students in Middle Grades Master of Arts in Teaching by Emphasis Areas

Emphasis Areas	Number of MAT Candidates
English/social studies	6
English/math	1
Math/science	2
Math/social studies	1
Science/social studies	3
Total	13

teaching/teaching experiences in a variety of school settings, including two in urban schools in nearby Lexington.

Procedures

The action research project was introduced, developed, revised, and completed in four courses throughout the program. During the first semester of their program, students were enrolled in two courses concurrently: (1) EGC 820, Professional Studies I: Teachers, School & Society, and (2) EGC 830, Professional Studies II: Learners/Teachers & Action Research. In EGC 820, students read and discussed *A Short Guide to Action Research*, a brief text that introduces the action research process (Johnson, 2002). In EGC 830, students chose an action research topic and prepared a five to seven page proposal that included the research focus and main questions, a short literature review, a description of the proposed methodology, and the expected results and conclusions. In the second semester of the program, students participated in a special teaching methods course that combines specific methods for providing instruction in the four major content areas of language arts, math, science, and social studies. Students heard presentations by experts in each content methods area and reviewed and practiced methods specific to their fields. During this course, students submitted their proposals to their instructor as well as content specialists for suggestions for needed revisions. Finally, while completing the student teaching semester in spring 2003, the candidates participated in a Web-supported seminar in which they made weekly reports on the status of their action research and then summarized findings in an informal, face-to-face class meeting. Throughout this seminar, the instructor was available to provide advice and technical assistance.

The MAT students completed a student teaching internship during the third semester of the program. As previously noted, 10 of the students were provisionally certified and teaching full-time in their own classrooms. The remainder of the students completed a traditional student teaching internship in each of their emphasis areas, under the supervision of two certified teachers. During this semester, the students actually conducted their research (see Appendix A for a selection of the action research topics).

During the final capstone seminar course, students were guided through the final process of analyzing data and writing the final action research paper. As a part of this course, students read and critiqued published action research and conducted peer reviews of their classmates' work. Finally, students made multimedia presentations that summarized their research and findings to peers and professors. These presentations also served as the oral examinations for the master's degree. At the end of this course, students were asked to complete a summative program evaluation.

Data Collection and Analysis

Due to the nature of our question, we administered a post-project questionnaire based on the program objectives (Appendix B) to gather both quantitative and qualitative data. The participants completed the questionnaire during the fall of 2003 while all of them were employed in regular full time teaching positions in middle schools. The questionnaire utilized a Likert scale with questions addressing each of the alternative certification MAT program objectives along with six open-ended questions that were designed to address issues not targeted by the program objectives or to gather in-depth knowledge of these objectives. The specific question used to answer our research questions was, *How valuable did you find the action research project to be for your professional development? Please explain.* Responses to this question determined if students (1) understood the value of educational research, and (2) found action research to be a significant avenue of reflection.

RESULTS

Responses to the Likert-style questions of the MAT program assessment (Appendix B) are summarized in Figure 6.1. No statistical analyses were conducted due to the small sample size. Many of these items deal more specifically with the program as a whole, and helped us identify strengths as well as areas for improvement. However, the relatively high mean responses to items 14, *Evaluating my professional strengths and needs and selecting appropriate experiences for continued professional growth*, and 15, *Identifying how academic and professional development affect my teaching/learning practices and my understanding of the academic, emotional, and social growth of students*, speak to the success of the action research project.

Eight of the program participants responded to the question, *How valuable did you find the action research project to be to your professional development? Please explain.* We then categorized the responses as positive or negative.

Middle Grades MAT Candidate Survey

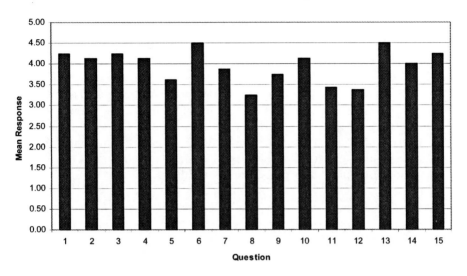

Figure 6.1.   Mean responses to Questions 1-15 on MAT candidate survey.

Positive Responses

- I had never conducted action research before and I found that very difficult because I was never sure if I was getting all of the right information. Looking back now, I think it was helpful to my success as a teacher and hopefully future leaders in the school district, which gave me an avenue to figure out how students learn.
- I found the research experience extremely beneficial. To take journal research, formulate an in class application, document and analyze results, and modify my own teaching methods to better teach my students, was awesome. Even should I never write a professional journal article, I am sure to use what I learned to improve my students' learning experiences.
- Very valuable. I utilize components of my project on a regular basis.
- It motivated me to work harder at involving families in their children's education.
- I looked at material I may not have used before this experiment. I overcame a process I've never enjoyed before. I think that I enjoyed this more because it was more realistic.
- I learned that there are many factors that influence behavior and achievement.

- Little things influence students' attitudes about homework and the content in general.

Negative Responses

- The action research would have been more valuable if classroom experience had guided the selection of the research. I could do a better job of implementing a project now that I have a year of experience in the classroom. As it was, because of the timing and the presentation, I think it hindered more than it helped. I could have used the time better preparing for students.

While these comments do not represent 100% of the participants, the success of the multimedia presentations along with more informal discussions with the participants during the capstone seminar class led us to conclude that action research is a valuable component of the MAT program.

When we evaluated the secondary MAT students' ($n = 42$) responses to the same question, we found a surprising trend. A higher percentage of those candidates who were under the TPC and teaching full time (54%) viewed the action research process as positive when compared to the traditional graduate students (38%). This trend was not observed with the middle level certification students. In looking at their projects, it seems that the secondary student teachers were more likely to have planned complex, time consuming projects requiring multiple points of data collection. The three middle level students who completed traditional student teaching had planned relatively simple projects that did not require so much data collection from the children. Many of the secondary students encountered problems in conducting their action research in their student teaching placements. However, that was not the case with the three middle level student teachers. Also, Kentucky public schools were cancelled for a record number of days due to snow, ice, and flooding during the 2003 spring semester. These factors were more likely to impact those projects that required multiple points of data collection and time intensive instructional methods.

Other problems noted by the candidates in more informal communications include: (1) a lack of coordination among the different instructors regarding requirements, presentation, and formatting of the project itself; (2) instruction and assistance in research design and data analysis was provided too late in the program; and, (3) students were extremely pressed for time during the student teaching semester and the capstone seminar. Ten of the middle level students were still teaching at the time of the seminar and were forced to juggle end of the school year responsibilities, data analysis, multimedia presentation development as well as writing the paper. The seminar course also required additional readings, class meetings, and assignments that the students considered unproductive.

DISCUSSION

Researchers at EKU conducted this study of 13 alternative certification middle grades MAT students to determine if the required action research project promotes (1) the understanding and use of action research, and (2) reflective teaching practices. Based on the qualitative data, we concluded that action research appears to fulfill both of our goals. A majority (eight positive and one negative) of both the provisionally certified students and traditional graduate students noted that action research did contribute to their professional development. The one negative response reflected time demands and stress issues. Overall, students viewed the action research process itself as a valuable problem-solving process, but were negative about the program requirements or time demands of the project.

Interestingly, a higher percentage (54%) of the secondary students who held the TPC viewed the action research process as positive when compared to the secondary traditional graduate students (38%). These data confirm the research of DeCorse (1997) who proposes that there may be a magic window (p. 14), that of moderately experienced, for involving inservice teachers in action research. The secondary TPC students did indeed seem to see the experience as more beneficial. However, when looking just at the middle grades MAT students' comments, eight out of nine agreed that action research contributed to their professional development. This evidence reinforces the research of Ravid (1997) who cautions that action research in graduate MAT programs may be problematic when the participants do not have their own classrooms. The cooperating teacher may not be supportive of the research, changes in the school's schedule may interrupt the research plan, and the pressures of preparation for high-stakes testing may cause conflicts.

Many of our students encountered problems in conducting their action research in their student teaching placements. Kentucky public schools were also cancelled for a record number of days during the 2003 spring semester, which caused numerous problems in the research plans for our students. These last two factors could be considered limitations of our study.

PLAN OF ACTION

Based on our findings, several improvements have already been made or are planned for the program. All of the instructors involved in teaching the different courses now meet regularly to plan and share information about the students' progress toward completion of the action research project. There is considerable team teaching and collaboration within the program to ensure that all faculty have similar expectations. In an effort to provide in-depth instruction in research techniques and American Psychological Association style as well as guide students in choosing a pertinent topic, students are now required to write a short research paper on a current issue in education in the first required course, EGC 820. More specific lessons on the research techniques and critiquing published literature are also included at this point. In order to help students better visualize the final goal of action research, students read and critique published action research in the first semester of the program, rather than the final semester.

To address student concerns about their topic, the literature review, and working on their project throughout the program, we developed more detailed guidelines for the second semester of the program. During the special methods course, the instructor provides more specific guidance as well. Now, students are required to complete additional readings on their proposed topic and further refine their literature review by increasing the number of sources from the 8-10 required for the proposal to15-20. The students are also required to share their proposal and summarize the literature for their fellow classmates in the form of a Power-Point presentation. Additionally, the candidates should have their first three chapters of the action research paper as well as the beginning of their multimedia presentation completed prior to beginning the student teaching semester.

Many students indicated issues that were pertinent to the third semester of the program (data gathering, getting help, and adapting the project as needed). To address these concerns, we plan to better structure the Web-supported seminar during the student teaching internship semester. We will reinforce lessons on gathering and analyzing qualitative and quantitative data as well as provide advice, guidance, and an opportunity for peer support during the research process. To provide students with a clear outline of the research and writing expectations, we plan to give the final scoring guide early in the student teaching semester, rather than waiting until the capstone seminar course.

Finally, to avoid conflicts and improve project planning for traditional student teaching graduate students, we will establish the student teaching placement and cooperating teachers during the fall semester, instead of waiting until the spring. This will allow the MAT candidates to collabora-tively plan the project with the cooperating teacher, and possibly even begin their research prior to student teaching.

CONCLUSIONS

As many colleges and universities across the country are planning and instituting graduate alternative certification programs, the challenge of including an appropriate research component while educating these stu-dents for all their professional responsibilities continues to be a dilemma. Based on our findings, it appears that action research is an effective way to meet this challenge. The action research process engages alternative certification students in significant educational research that fosters a life-long reflective teaching ability. Despite the extra workload, action research appears to be especially meaningful to students who are teaching full-time while completing their program. Those developing such pro-grams should be cautioned to schedule and coordinate carefully the instruction these students need in designing, planning, and conducting their projects. Candidates who will be completing traditional student teaching internships should be paired with a classroom teacher mentor early in their program to ensure a successful action research plan.

APPENDIX A:
SAMPLE ACTION RESEARCH PROJECT TOPICS

- A study of the effects of parent communications on student achieve-ment found that increased parent communications yields improved student performance.
- A study of the relationship between athletic participation and GPA found that the average GPA for middle school student athletes was higher than the average GPA for nonathletes. Also, students' GPAs were higher while they were actually participating in the sport.
- The effects of an after school girls' science club on girls' attitudes towards science found that the membership of the girls' science club increase throughout the school year. Girls who participated in the club demonstrated more positive attitudes toward their science class.
- The use of simple songs as a means to improve use of action verbs in writing found that, even though middle school students were

able to sing a song that listed passive verbs, they still did not decrease the use of those verbs in their writings.

• The effects of cooperative learning groups on student achievement was unable to statistically show that the group work was a contributing factor to student achievement, but informal observations and student comments suggested that the students liked the group work more.

• The effects of the use of an exercise break on student achievement in a middle school classroom showed no improvement in academic performance, but did show improved behavior and participation.

• The use of comic strips showed some increase student understanding of historical events.

• Providing middle school students with book choices that correspond to their personal interests can increase these students' interest in reading for pleasure.

APPENDIX B:
MAT PROGRAM ASSESSMENT

In order to effectively evaluate the success of the MAT program, your input is essential. Please answer the following questions. On the first 15 questions, you will use a Likert scale from one to five to indicate your opinion. 1 = Strongly Disagree and 5 = Strongly Agree. The last four questions are open-ended to allow you to address additional problems or issues. Please note that these questions *do not pertain* to the temporary 2-year provisional certification but rather the coursework and experiences required to complete the MAT program.

After completing the MAT program, I feel competent in	Strongly Disagree				Strongly Agree
1. Using appropriate educational research methods.	1	2	3	4	5
2. Using appropriate educational information technology.	1	2	3	4	5
3. Using appropriate educational instructional resources.	1	2	3	4	5
4. Demonstrating my knowledge of the curriculum.	1	2	3	4	5
5. Demonstrating ways to integrate across the curriculum.	1	2	3	4	5

6. Demonstrating ways to collaborate with col-   1   2   3   4   5
    leagues.

7. Facilitating student learning by utilizing   1   2   3   4   5
    appropriate theories and principles of human
    growth and development.

8. Citing factors which influence and affect   1   2   3   4   5
    change in the total curriculum.

9. Citing factors, which influence and affect   1   2   3   4   5
    change in my content areas.

10. Identifying and describing current reform ini- 1   2   3   4   5
    tiatives including KY Education Reform com-
    ponents (CATS, block scheduling, etc.).

11. Identifying and using current reform initia-   1   2   3   4   5
    tives, which are relevant and appropriate in
    specific instructional situations.

12. Identifying appropriate learning experiences   1   2   3   4   5
    for stude at all academic levels from different
    ethnic, social, and cultural backgrounds.

13. Demonstrating advanced knowledge in my   1   2   3   4   5
    subject.

14. Demonstrating ways to integrate across the   1   2   3   4   5
    curriculum professional growth.

15. Identifying how academic and professional   1   2   3   4   5
    development affect my teaching/learning
    practices and my understanding of the aca-
    demic, emotional, and social growth of stu-
    dents.

16. Do you feel well prepared as a beginning
    teacher? Explain.

17. What are the major advantages to a program
    like the MAT?

18. What are the major disadvantages to a pro-
    gram like the MAT?

19. Did you receive your temporary 2-year provi-
    sional certification?

    If yes, explain how that impacted your prepa-
    ration (completion of program, etc.)

20. How valuable did you find the action research
    project to be to your professional develop-
    ment? Please explain.

21. Other concerns or remarks?

REFERENCES

Bennett, C. K. (1994). Promoting teacher reflection through action research: What do teachers think? *Journal of Staff Development, 15,* 34-38.

Daniels, D. C. (2002). Becoming a reflective practitioner. *Middle School Journal, 33*(5), 52-56.

DeCorse, C. (1997, March). *I'm a good teacher, therefore I'm a good researcher: Changing perceptions of expert and novice teachers about doing research.* Paper presented at the meeting of the American Educational Research Association, Chicago.

Dolbec, A., & Savoie-Zajc, L. (1995, April). *Problems emerging from the practicing of action research in graduate programs in education.* Paper presented at the meeting of the International Conference on Teacher Research, Davis, CA.

Feldman, A., Alibrandi, M., Capifali, E., Floyd, D., Gabriel, J., Mera, M., Henriques, B., & Lucey, J. (1996, April). *Looking at ourselves look at ourselves: An action research self-study of doctoral students' roles in teacher education programs.* Paper presented at the meeting of the American Educational Research Association, New York.

Fullan, M., & Hargreaves, A. (1992). *Teacher development and educational change.* London: Falmer Press.

Hussar, W. (1999). *Predicting the need for newly hired teachers in the United States to 2008-09.* National Council on Education Statistics. Retrieved November 11, 2003, from http://nces.ed.gov/pubsearch/pubsinfo.asp?pubid=1999026

Ingersoll, R. M. (1999). The problem of under-qualified teachers in American secondary schools. *Educational Researcher, 28*(2), 26-37.

Johnson, A. (2002). *A short guide to action research.* Boston: Allyn & Bacon.

National Council for the Accreditation of Teacher Education. (2002). *Unit standards.* Retrieved July 25, 2004, from http://www.ncate.org/standard/unit_stnds_ch2.htm

National Middle School Association. (2001). *Middle level teacher preparation standards.* Retrieved July 25, 2004, from http://www/nmsa.org

National Middle School Association. (2003). *This we believe: Successful schools for young adolescents.* Westerville, OH: Author.

Ravid, R. (1997, October). *Research component in graduate teacher education programs: Asking the stakeholders.* Paper presented at the meeting of the Mid-Western Educational Research Association, Chicago.

Sparapani, E., Abel, F., Easton, S., Edwards, P., & Herbster, D. (1996, February). *Action research: A strategy for bridging the gap between theory and practice.* Paper presented at the meeting of the Association of Teacher Educators, St. Louis, MO.

CHAPTER 7

USING ACTION RESEARCH FOR ASPIRING MIDDLE LEVEL ADMINISTRATORS

Going Beyond the Traditional Practicum Experience

Sue C. Thompson, Larry Gregg, and Loyce Caruthers

ABSTRACT

Professional organizations, school district personnel, and policymakers want universities to produce graduates who are equipped to reculture schools in order to support teaching and learning, and the healthy development of young people. The practicum is an opportunity for students concluding their master's program in educational administration to integrate theory and practice in a middle level school. The aspiring middle level administrators in the Urban Leadership and Policy Studies in Education (ULAPSIE) program at the University of Missouri, Kansas City (UMKC) conduct action research projects to better understand and meet the developmental and academic needs of young adolescents. This chapter highlights three of those action research projects.

Making a Difference: Action Research in Middle Level Education, 125–145
Copyright © 2005 by Information Age Publishing
All rights of reproduction in any form reserved.

125

This chapter focuses on using action research to improve the rigor and relevance of the practicum experience for aspiring middle level administrators in the ULAPSIE division at UMKC. As university professors, we are strongly connected to middle level schools because these are the spaces in which we have forged life-long projects as teachers, administrators, staff developers, and program evaluators. We became excited about our aspiring middle level administrators using problem-based action research as a way to turn theory into practice and, subsequently, expand opportunities for student learning for university level students, practicing administrators, and middle level students.

Action research is grounded in the work of Kurt Lewin. According to Schein (1985):

> As Lewin (1952) noted long ago, if one wants to understand a system, one should try to change it. The spirit of that dictum underlies action research and diagnostic activities in all human systems and is especially relevant to the diagnosis of cultural elements. (p. 135)

Lewin actually coined the term *action research* to reflect that the investigation of school problems were not separate from the action needed to solve problems (Patterson, Santa, Short, & Smith, 1993).

Extant literature on action research indicates that action research:

- Creates a system-wide mindset for school improvement—a professional problem-solving ethos;
- Enhances decision-making—builds greater feelings of competence in solving problems and making instructional decisions;
- Instills a commitment to continuous improvement;
- Creates a more positive school climate in which teaching and learning is a foremost concern;
- Impacts directly on practice; and
- Empowers those who participate in the process. Educational leaders who undertake action research may no longer, for instance, uncritically accept theories, innovations, and programs at face value (Glanz, 1999, pp. 22-23).

The value of action research correlates strongly with ULAPSIE's conceptual framework, which is grounded in the theory of constructivism. The program faculty works from the following assumptions and strives to:

1. Create meaningful educational processes and experiences;
2. Promote diversity, equity, and social justice;

3. Develop constructivist leaders;
4. Create democratic classrooms and schools;
5. Create learning organizations;
6. Emphasize the significance of relationships;
7. Use technology to enhance educational experiences;
8. Demonstrate reflective practice; and
9. Focus on school change and reculturing.

Missouri is one of only seven states with middle level principal licensure. Consequently, all aspiring middle level administrators in the state of Missouri must take a middle level administration course, as well as a course in adolescent development. In the middle level administration course at UMKC, an emphasis is placed on the latest theory, research, and best practice in middle level education, as well as leadership theory and practices necessary to create and sustain a high-performing middle level school. Students study the research and recommendations in *Turning Points 2000* (Jackson & Davis, 2000) and the characteristics of highly successful middle schools in *This We Believe: Successful Schools for Young Adolescents* (National Middle School Association, NMSA, 2003). The professor who teaches this course is also a member of the National Forum to Accelerate Middle Grades Education (1999) and uses its vision statement and leadership modules as course material. Students understand the power of the principal that Jackson and Davis (2000) talk about when they assert that "no single individual is more important than the school principal" (p. 157).

Much dialogue occurs related to the recommendation in *This We Believe: Successful Schools for Young Adolescents* (NMSA, 2003) for courageous, collaborative leadership and what this looks like in a middle level school. Course work is centered in the role of the principal in creating, with all stakeholders, a middle level school that is high performing by being academically excellent, developmentally responsive, and socially equitable. The students create a learning organization in their university classroom and use many of the collaborative professional development practices necessary to create a learning organization in a middle level school. Students also read *Developing Teacher Leaders: The Principal's Role* (Thompson, 2004) in order to better understand distributive and collaborative leadership.

When these students are ready to complete their one semester practicum course, they are well aware of the needs, issues, and problems in their own middle level school. They are already teacher leaders in their respective schools and have credibility with their administrators/mentors and their fellow teachers. Using action research in the middle level administrative practicum creates a more meaningful educational process and experience because practicum students must identify collaboratively with their mentor a real problem that is challenging their school and has an impact on school improvement. Through the action research project, the practicum student must provide a viable solution to that problem. The problem's focus on school improvement requires the candidate to reflect upon and understand the school culture with the realization that change always takes place in the context of school culture. This action research project also provides an authentic platform for the aspiring middle school administrator to demonstrate competency in many of the areas upon which the ULAPSIE framework is built, especially democratic schools, learning organizations, relationships, reflective practice, school change, and reculturing.

In order to address the preparation of school leaders, The National Policy Board for Educational Administration (NPBEA) is comprised of 10 national associations who work collaboratively to develop standards for the improvement of educational administration programs. These 10 organizations are The American Association of Colleges for Teacher Education, American Association of School Administrators, Association of School Business Officials, Association for Supervision and Curriculum Development, Council of Chief State School Officers, National Association of Elementary School Principals (NAESP), National Association of Secondary School Principals (NASSP), National Council of Professors of Educational Administration, National School Boards Association, and University Council for Educational Administration. The Educational Leadership Constituent Council (ELCC) standards reflect a move from a traditional transformational or visionary leadership model to a more constructivist model of leadership where instructional improvement as the focus of leadership is absolutely essential. The ELCC standards promote the development of a body of ideas and concepts that define school administration as an applied field where the profession is linked to valued outcomes. Action research projects are another way to assess the level of knowledge, skills and dispositions reflected in the ELCC standards.

ELCC standard 7 on the internship states that

> The internship provides significant opportunities for candidates to synthesize and apply the knowledge and practice and develop the skills identified in standards 1-6 through substantial, sustained, standards-based work in real settings, planned and guided cooperatively by the institution and school district personnel for graduate credit. (The National Policy Board for Educational Administration, NPBEA, 2002, pp. 16-18)

Action research provides a platform for practicum students to exhibit an understanding, through real life application, of all of the assumptions upon which the ULAPSIE program is built. Educational administration programs that have a problem-solving focus and emphasis on the concrete offer real promise to the profession (Murphy, 1992). Aspiring principals in a middle level practicum experience have an opportunity to grapple with the issue of instructional improvement and actually produce a product that will improve teaching and learning in his/her middle school. Action research provides aspiring administrators an opportunity to develop what Gardner (1993) defines as intelligence, "the ability to solve problems or to fashion products that are values in one or more cultural or community settings" (p. 7). Making action research a part of the middle level practicum experience provides this opportunity for students.

As acknowledged by the work of the NPBEA, traditional educational administration programs are under attack (2002). Williamson and Galletti (2003) state that preparation programs for school leaders are struggling to reculture the experiences of their students in order to assure that graduates are fully prepared for the complexity and challenges of today's schools. School leadership is more demanding than ever because of accountability, the No Child Left Behind Act legislation, strained budgets and schools that are impacted by societal and economic shortcomings. Critics of educational administration programs are saying that principals are not prepared for the challenges of the position (Murphy, 1992, 1993).

In addition to the belief that leaders are under prepared for the rigors of the position, there is also a critical shortage of educational leaders. Fenwick (2000) states in *The Principal Shortage: Who Will Lead?* that the data supports this shortage. "The U.S. Department of Labor estimates that 40 percent of the nation's 93,200 principals are nearing retirement and that the need for school administrators throughout the year 2005 will increase 10 percent to 20 percent" (pp. 9-10). The NAESP and NASSP surveys conducted in 1998 found that:

> The top three barriers to acquiring a sufficient quality and quantity of principals were compensation insufficient compared to responsibilities, job generally too stressful, and too much time required. In all, the report points to four primary solutions for resolving the principal shortage: (1) improve the rigor and relevance of graduate training programs/preparation, (2) increase pay, (3) improve working conditions, and (4) provide more professional support for aspiring and appointed principals, particularly via mentoring programs in school districts. (Fenwick, 2000, p. 10-11)

As an educational administration preparation program, ULAPSIE can have an impact on one barrier by improving the rigor and relevance of our graduate training and preparation program by requiring practicum students to use action research as a culmination of their program. In turn, when administrators know how to solve problems successfully, working conditions can improve. Problem-based action research calls for the learner, in this case the middle level practicum student, to encounter the dilemmas of real-world school problematic situations and to address the concern with empathy (Fogarty, 1998). Middle level practicum students are asked to identify a sometimes *fuzzy* or *messy* situation or problem that is facing their middle school and to investigate ways of solving or improving the situation. The practicum student has a choice in determining the problem on which he/she will work. Then problem-based learning is about understanding the circumstances and the subsequent consequences of action taken (Fogarty, 1998).

The design of the problem-based action research strategy relies heavily upon brain-based motivational theory. A person's brain is motivated to attempt something new and to continue the practice when a person has some choice and control over their actions and when they are actively engaged in work that is significant and related closely to the real world. A person also needs to receive specific and timely feedback and to see positive results from their efforts (Hart, 1983). Problem-based action research meets these requirements.

Once a commitment to investigate a problem is decided with input from the supervising mentor, usually the principal or assistant principal, and the professor, then the practicum student is asked to conduct action research around the problem. Many researchers suggest that one way to promote professional growth in our schools is to involve teachers in researching within their own classroom. Our beliefs are that aspiring administrators and administrators can and should use action research to look at their school, groups of students and teachers, or one student or teacher, to improve both the culture of their school and student learning. Many of our middle level practicum students, who are now teachers, have not used action research in their own classrooms. If principals are going to ask teachers to use action research as one way to encourage job-embedded professional development, principals must understand the concept and have participated in action research themselves. A value added benefit of the action research requirement is the exposure of practicing administrators to action research. Thus, ULAPSIE is also providing more professional support for appointed principals through their involvement with the practicum student and university professor concerning the action research occurring in their school.

At a time when school leadership is recognized as one of the most important, if not the most important, element of successful school reform, programs preparing tomorrow's principals must provide more authentic experiences for their students. These experiences must give these aspiring leaders the confidence to move into leadership positions because they have the skills, knowledge, and strategies to work collaboratively with other staff members to investigate problems and find solutions to problems in the real world of school, not just through case studies.

A systematic approach of identifying a problem that the practicum student feels is important to his/her school, reviewing the literature regarding the educational theory involved, developing advocated solutions for solving the problem, developing and implementing a plan for the school's implementation, collecting and analyzing data, reflecting upon the results, all the while with feedback and support from peers, administrators, and university professors, may assist practicum students in improving their understanding of systemic reform, school culture and student and adult learning.

The professors in ULAPSIE use the following action research prototype for the practicum students.

1. Describe the setting, including background information about the community, the school, and the researcher.
2. Identification of problem that the middle school is facing. Clearly describe the problem and why it is important to you and your school.
3. Review of the literature.
4. Advocated solutions/interventions, including target aspect of the problem and why a particular solution/intervention was chosen.
5. Implementation plan for action research project, including measurable goals and procedures to achieve the goals.
6. Actual or expected outcomes, determined by the length of the action research project.

Below are abbreviated examples of the action research conducted by three middle level educators in the ULAPSIE program.

School A: The Effectiveness of Implementing a Character Education Program

1. Background: This administrative candidate teaches at an urban profile middle school. ULAPSIE identifies urban profile schools as schools that are located in the first tier of districts outside the urban center of the city. The schools have many of the characteristics of urban schools, including a significant number of students of color and students on free or reduced lunch. In School A, there are approximately 650 students and 75 staff members, 44 of the staff

members are certified teachers. Because of the opening of a second middle school and moving sixth graders into the middle schools, 52% of the staff is new to the building. The student population is 52% African Americans, 45% White, and 3% other. There are 26,000 single families with an average income of $42,000 but more than 50% of the families make less than $34,000 a year. Only 29% of the community members have a bachelor degree or higher. This is the forth year of teaching for the practicum student. She teaches seventh grade science, coaches volleyball and cheerleading, and directs the school plays.

2.   Identification of problem and problem statement: The problem that this practicum student is investigating is the effectiveness of the school's character education program. During the 1999-2000 school year, this student's interdisciplinary team received a grant to implement character education at School A. The team decided to start with a pilot program on their team. At the end of the year, the team brought the results of their program to the board of education (BOE) and asked for the school mission to be rewritten to include character education and for the character education initiative to be adopted for the entire system, K-12. The BOE approved the policy to adopt character education district wide. At the beginning of the 2000-2001 school year, an in-service day was devoted to character education at School A, with the team that had implemented the program providing the professional development for the staff. The school now has a 25-minute period 4 times a week to teach character education, as well as teachable moments being used within the regular day for reinforcement. School A also has a character education committee that has been, according to the practicum student, slow in getting started but is now in place. There is also a district-wide character education committee that meets monthly. The practicum student wants to determine if the procedures that are being used at school A for teaching positive character behaviors are effective. She wants to know if the program is working at her school, and if not, what possible changes need to be made. This is an important topic to investigate because 25 minutes a day 4 times a week is being devoted to the program and time is extremely valuable.

3.   Abbreviated review of the literature: Highlights of the review were several significant studies related to character education. One study that was particularly helpful was *Elementary School Teachers' Sense of Efficacy for Character Education* (Milson & Mehlig, 2002). This study had an extensive review of the literature and the character education efficacy belief instrument, developed and validated

by the authors, and completed by a sample of 254 elementary school teachers in a large Midwestern suburban school district. Combining these studies with the middle level literature that supports the need for schools that provide for the emotional and social well-being of young adolescents, the practicum student built a solid case for the need for the advisement program at her school. The practicum student said that she has a much better understanding of the history of character education after completing the literature review for the action research project.

4. Advocated solutions/interventions: This middle school tried to implement an advisement program many years earlier with little or no success. This program had been called Prime Time. Prime Time was restructured and supported through the development of a character education curriculum. This action has been taken to assure that the same language concerning character education is used throughout the building. The curriculum for Prime Time gives teachers a variety of activities to choose from that fit their teaching style and the learning style of their students. These activities have been chosen because of the belief that positive character traits can be taught to young adolescents. The following interventions were used:

   • Reinforcing the use of teachable moments to reinforce positive character traits. The target aspect of the problem is that positive behavior that is only focused on during Prime Time does not reinforce the importance of exhibiting positive character traits as a natural part of one's behavior. This solution/intervention has been chosen because there needs to be constant reinforcement of positive behavior.

   • Creation of character education committee. This solution/intervention has been chosen because efforts to implement character education in the building has been isolated. The solution/intervention gives character education a central focus in the school.

   • Implementation of community service projects. This solution targets the importance of making positive behaviors a part of life, not just what is expected of young adolescents in school. This activity gives students an opportunity to experience the effects of helping others.

5. The measurable goals for this action research project were:

- Is the Prime Time character education program effective?
- Are teachable moments being used effectively?
- Is the character education committee working effectively in order to centralize efforts and improve the positive behavior of students?
- Is the use of community service having a positive effect on students' feelings toward helping others?

To achieve the goals, the practicum student developed and conducted a variety of surveys to determine the opinions of staff, parents, and students for each of the goals (see Appendix for examples of surveys). Also, the practicum student looked at office referrals to see if there was any change related to the number of referrals related to negative behavior such as disrespect toward staff and other students.

6. Expected outcomes relation to the above mentioned goals:

- Staff currently using the curriculum is seeing positive results.
- Teachable moments are being used in the classroom to reinforce character education and are effective in the classroom, but teachable moments are not being used outside the classroom.
- The character education committee is not working effectively.
- Those staff members who are using community service on their interdisciplinary teams have felt positive effects, but many teams have chosen not to participate in community service projects.

The practicum student had her beliefs about the effectiveness of the character education program validated through the survey results. Although solutions/interventions had been developed to implement the program, much more work needed to be done with the whole staff before this program could become part of the school culture.

The exit interview between the practicum student and the professor involves deconstruction of the action research and how the experience increased and broadened the understanding of the student regarding school leadership. The professor and the practicum student talked about possible ways that the actual outcomes of the project could be improved through the use of different leadership strategies. In School A, the practicum student realized that the character education program was flawed from the beginning because of the lack of involvement of all stakeholders who had the responsibility to implement the character education program. She determined that faced with another opportunity to implement a new program, a different set of experiences would have to be planned in order to avoid the resistance she and the character education program faced in her school.

School B: Improving Middle School Students' Interest in Science

1. Background. School B is one of two middle schools in an urban profile district in the Midwest. Over 80% of the students are on a free or reduced lunch program. The student population is 43% Hispanic, 36% African American, 16% White, 4% Asian, and less than 1% American Indian. Approximately 10 % of the population receives special education services. There are 82 staff members at School B, including two counselors, a librarian, a security guard, a truancy specialist, a principal, and two assistant principals. The practicum student is the science teacher on one of the three eighth grade interdisciplinary teams. In visiting with science teachers on the other eighth grade teams, he found that the other science teachers, as well as he, believed that many students did not have an interest in science and, consequently, were doing poorly in science class. The eighth grade science teachers and the principal wanted to find out if they changed the way they were teaching science, would they see an improvement in a desire to learn science, a motivation to complete work, and an improvement in test scores.

2. Identification of problem and problem statement. Each of the eighth grade science teachers, including the researcher, have been working at School B over 5 years teaching eighth grade science. They have been teaching their students virtually the same way and wanted to do action research using conceptual learning as a process for improving student engagement with learning that would improve attitudes toward science and result in higher grades. The practicum student said that it was frightening to see so many of their students with such poor performance. The practicum student's goal is to evaluate the teaching strategies being used to see if the teaching practices are at fault. The middle level practicum student wanted to determine if changing instruction in science would improve students' attitude towards science and increase test scores.

3. Abbreviated review of the literature: The practicum student focused his review of the literature on conceptual learning, which

promoted engaging students in more active learning. While conceptual learning was not new to the teachers, they had relied on what they described as *book-based* learning, which was based on the belief that it was more appropriate for students needing remediation. According to Delisle (1997), students need to discover the role science plays in everyday life and they need to know that science is not something just found in book. The research confirmed that young adolescents learn best when they are *doing* science, rather than just reading about science. Middle school students need to know how scientific information or technique can be connected to real life and teachers needed to connect learning to prior knowledge. Brain research was investigated in the student's review of the literature. One of the most important findings discussed by the science teachers and principal was that by teaching to the test, they were actually depriving students of the opportunity for meaningful learning. According to Caine and Caine (1994):

> Testing and performance objectives have their place. Generally, however, they fail to capitalize on the brain's capacity to make connections. By intelligently using what we call *active processing*, we give students many more opportunities to show what they know without circumscribing what they are capable of learning. Testing and evaluation will have to accommodate creativity and open-endedness, as well as measure requisite and specific performance. (p. 8)

This kind of information and other brain based research has important implications for administrators and their responsibility for student learning. The practicum student discovered that the research confirmed that the importance of endorphins to one's mental state is related to a rich learning environment. Sylwester (1995) reports that "doing worksheets in school prepares a student emotionally to do worksheets in life" (p. 77). Conceptual learning expands students' independence and ability to learn and solve problems on their own. The literature showed that some middle school science teachers in urban settings found that students tune the teacher out when he/she stands at the front of the board lecturing, but they actively participate when given an experiment to conduct or a problem to solve. Kovalik (1997) says that brain-compatible curriculum is constructed and expressed in terms of concepts. These middle school science teachers viewed conceptual learning as an opportunity to connect with the experiences and backgrounds of their students.

4. Advocated solutions/interventions and measurable goals: Prior to implementing the new strategy of conceptual learning, the practi-

cum student conducted a random survey of 60 of the eighth grade students, 20 from each team. The surveys indicated that the majority of students liked working in small groups, saw studying science as somewhat important, and were dissatisfied with their grade in science and that their grade should improve. The practicum student found that most of the eighth grade students did not like doing worksheets as a form of instruction. In order to obtain a more realistic view of the science teachers teaching, the practicum student also asked students to respond to a customized questionnaire. The science teachers wanted a more thorough evaluation of themselves from the students' perceptions, contending that they had to evaluate themselves to see if their teaching practices were at fault. An analysis of the survey suggested that students did not feel that these three teachers made connections with students' background knowledge and experiences and that they were less likely to try to find out what students did not learn about a lesson and to teach concepts differently. Moreover, students felt that the teachers could do a better job in giving them feedback about their work and showing an interest in their learning.

The teachers set up a series of lessons from which the students could choose that covered major concepts in the eighth grade science curriculum. Students had an outline of procedures to follow for organizing their work, setting up portfolios, incorporating technology, making presentations, and using a scoring rubric. The students worked at their own pace with teachers serving as *guides on the side*.

5. Expected and actual outcomes: The practicum student, along with his fellow eighth grade science teachers and the principal believed that through participation in the conceptual teaching of eighth grade science, students (a) would improve their attitude about science and (b) improve their grades in science. Value added benefits of conceptual learning were that students would improve their communication, speaking, and writing skills through sharing their discoveries with others; collaborate more with their peers and teachers; and act on the knowledge acquired through designing and organize their personal approaches to problem solving and using technology to solve problems.

According to the practicum student, "In general, I would have to say that we were successful in most respects. We certainly had some "glitches" and some "hick-ups" along the way, but changing the way one teaches is hard work" (personal communication, May, 2003). The science teachers' perceptions were that through their participation in the conceptual teaching of eighth grade science, students were more enthusiastic about science. Moreover, they saw improvement in the grades that the students were receiving. Conceptual learning, according to the practicum student, had proven to be successful. With additional training and support from their administrator these instructors are going to continue to refine their science teaching to be more active and engaging. The teachers concluded that they were glad that they became adventuresome and *just did it.*

The exit interview with the middle school practicum student showed that he understood curriculum and instruction better and the challenges of changing teaching in order to better meet the needs of students. He certainly felt that this experience would help him be a better administrator someday because he would have a stronger knowledge base in teaching and learning and understand how difficult it is for people to change their teaching practice.

School C: The Effectiveness of Looping

1. Background information: This middle school seventh grade social studies teacher works at a suburban middle school that is experiencing changing demographics as more children from low-income families move into the district. The enrollment at the school has topped the 1,000 student threshold, marking a new high in the recent trend of increasing numbers of students. To serve those students, the school has approximately 55 certified staff members and another 30 administrative, support, and paraprofessional staff. Class sizes range from 23 to 26 for sixth grade classes, 25 to 27 for seventh grade classes, and 30 or over for eighth grade classes. The elementary schools that feed into School C report higher enrollments as well, indicating a continuing trend. Twenty-four percent of the population has a post-high school degree. Census data indicates that approximately 20% of the African American population is served by the district, with 78% of the population being White. Demographics for this particular school indicates that White students make up 65% of the enrollment and 33% of the enrollment is composed of African Americans. The remainder of the population is composed of American Indians, Asian, Hispanic, or Other.

2. Identification of problem and problem statement. This practicum student wants to determine if looping helps enhance the teacher-student relationship and results in higher levels of student learning. Students are already organized into teams in a school-within-

a-school model and progress to a new team of teachers each year. However, strict adherence to the standard model is not observed as students are readily *cross-teamed* as deemed fit due to other considerations. The practicum student teaches on the *short team*, having only two classes of seventh graders and two classes of eighth graders assigned to their team. Three of the four of the teachers on this team, teach an additional class of crossed-team eighth graders: social studies, algebra, and science. The language arts teacher teaches seventh grade reading. The cross-over classes mean that these team teachers' teach five periods, like the other teams. They teach a new class of seventh grade students each year, keeping the eighth grade students for another year. This is the only interdisciplinary team in the building with this mixed grade teaming. The practicum student wants to determine if the team is realizing any benefits from the practice of looping, which is occurring on their team. Questions include:

- Is looping effective for increasing student learning and improving relationships between teachers and students?
- Is student learning higher for the eighth grade students who have stayed with the same teachers for 2 years? If so, why might this is occurring? If not, why not?
- What changes need to be made to increase learning?

3. Review of the literature: The practicum student gained much knowledge from his literature review. He learned that looping is a term that is used to describe a classroom where a teacher or groups of teachers develop a partnership with a group of students in contiguous grades for 2 or more years. For example, sixth grade teachers may progress on with their students to the seventh grade or even eighth grade. A teacher moves with his or her students to the next grade rather than turning them over to another teacher or another group of teachers. Some loops may be for 2 consecutive years while others may have a longer duration (Burke, 1997). University of Maine education professor Edward Brazee (1997) states that "Looping 'holds a ton of promise' to address what he considers public education's greatest failure—its lack of continuity" (p. 15).

    The literature indicated that there were several benefits to the implementation of a looping program in middle schools. First, gains in learning time were reported. Second, strengthening of relationships between teachers, students, and parents were commonly cited. The stability of the teacher-student relationships seemed to be of major interest. Finally, changes in the attitudes of students, teachers, and parents were documented. There were downsides that the literature discussed, particularly pressures placed on new students arriving during the looping period and overloading a looped team with many special needs students. These students were not just those labeled special education, but those with behavior or other academic problems. Overall, the research that the practicum student reviewed was overwhelmingly in favor of looping. Since there is no need to start from scratch, learning new names, personalities, and expectations, teachers estimated that a month of learning time was gained at the start of the second year (Gaustad, 1998).

Burke (1997) found that the additional month of learning at the beginning of the year was one of the most important benefits of looping. Time was saved in skill assessment. Teachers were able to provide instructional activities over the longer period of time that is needed to master certain basic skills. Teachers came to know the students' learning styles, preferences, and interests.

The literature is replete with evidence regarding the positive benefits to the relationships that are important to student learning. There is a stability in the relationship between the student and the teacher that the student can use as a basis for his or her ability to be successful in school. The teacher and student are able to establish a working relationship that the young adolescent can count on.

According to Haberman (1995), looping was especially important for students who have grown up in poverty. These students have often become suspicious of adults and have developed a lack of trust in authority figures, such as teachers. When teachers take the initiative to empower students, believe in students, treat them with respect and courtesy, it helps to establish a safe learning environment and reduces anxiety and fear in the student.

4. Advocated solutions/interventions: The practicum student's goal was to gain the support of the administration to expand all teams to full teams with a core teacher for each subject and a special education/inclusion teacher. This goal was to target large class sizes due to increased enrollment in the school. The purpose of the intervention is to maintain the *school-within-a-school* interdisciplinary team model that was implemented 5 years ago. Also, the invention would reduce or eliminate the cross-teaming that now occurs. The second goal was to designate one core team as a looping team, sixth grade through eighth grade. The target aspect of this intervention is to improve relationships and learning for students. The practicum student decided to examine past data on the

state testing results for the students on his team. Additionally, surveys of the attitudes of teachers, students, and parents on this team would provide additional insight into the relationship component of this problem.

5. Expected outcomes: The practicum student expects to find the following: Teachers will report that they see substantial growth in the intellectual, social, and emotional growth during the 2-year loop. Teachers see the need to build relationships with the students and feel that the extra time is of benefit to difficult students. Teachers will report that they feel that students with the most severe behavior issues are directed to their looped team. Students will report positive benefits from the looping process. However, the practicum student believes that some of the students will indicate dissatisfaction. These students will probably be the ones who face academic or behavior challenges because their methods to disguise their difficulties or lack of effort will not get a *grace period* the second year. Those with behavior issues will not get a grace period either.

Parents will report greater satisfaction with the looping process than with previous non looping school experiences. Past anecdotal experiences by the practicum student and fellow teachers reflect that parents see positive results from the long-term relationship that is built between students, teachers, and parents. The team has been successful with a number of students with behavior and academic issues that are not resolved the first year they are on the team as seventh grade students. Progress is definitely made their second year on the team. The team has also been successful in achieving positive relationships with parents with whom initial relations were less than satisfactory for everyone concerned.

Finally, this student expected to find that the state test data showed mixed results at best. He believed there were several reasons for this. First, no data was available to show how much progress each student had made individually. Second, students have been so readily cross-teamed that results may not be reflective of the effectiveness or ineffectiveness of looping. Third, only 50 to 55 students on this team were tested their 8th grade year. There are over 300 students on the other two eighth grade teams. Consequently, validity may be an issue.

Some actual outcomes, determined by the length of the action research project, were that a healthy dialogue took place in the school concerning pure teams and looping. The administrative team did consider the proposal that resulted from this action research and a pure team was established for the next school year that would loop students from sixth through eighth grade. The administrative team and staff were not able to find a way to not cross-team on other teams because of the number of teachers that were assigned to the school for the following school year.

CONCLUSION

These abbreviated examples of the three action research projects show that action research has a legitimate place in an educational administration program. All three examples clearly provided the practicum student an opportunity to use leadership skills, knowledge, and dispositions to make significant and meaningful changes in their middle level schools. They learned more about themselves in a leadership position, the importance of building relationships, and the challenges of reculturing schools. Traditional educational administration programs must also be recultured in order to develop constructivist cross-cultural leaders who truly understand their students, student learning, and school culture.

Traditional research has not necessarily been valued by many practitioners. According to Patterson, Santa, Short, and Smith (1993), "Teacher researchers seek to understand the particular individuals, actions, policies, and events that make up their work and work environment in order to make professional decisions" (pp. 8-9). If aspiring administrators are going to change their practice, then reflection and inquiry through action research must become a part of the school's culture and infrastructure. Then and only then will teachers and leaders, both formal and informal, provide the kinds of learning experiences that will improve student learning through democratic classrooms and school wide practices.

APPENDIX

Examples of Surveys

Prime Time Curriculum Survey for Staff

1. Do you use the Prime Time Curriculum?

   __ Usually   __ Sometimes   __ Seldom   __ Never

2. If you use the Prime Time Curriculum, do you believe that the activities are effective in teaching positive character traits to our students?

   __ Very effective   __ Somewhat effective   __ Not very effective

In the space provided below, please make any comments that are relevant to the character education program at School A. If you have any suggestions on how to improve the program, please include those in your answer.

Teaching Moments Survey for Staff

1. Do you use teachable moments in your classroom to reinforce positive character traits?

   __ Usually   __ Sometimes   __ Seldom   __ Never

2. Do you use teachable moments outside of your classroom to reinforce positive character traits?

   __ Usually   __ Sometimes   __ Seldom   __ Never

3. If you use teachable moments, how effective do you feel the use of teachable moments in your classroom is in helping your students exhibit positive character traits?

   __ Very effective   __ Somewhat effective   __ Not very effective

4. If you use teachable moments outside of your classroom, how effective do you feel the use of teachable moments is in helping our students exhibit positive character traits?

   __ Very effective   __ Somewhat effective   __ Not very effective

5. In the space provided below, please provide any comments and/or suggestions regarding teachable moments.

Community Service Survey

1. Have you or your team done any community service projects this year?

   __ yes, individually   __ yes, team
   __ no, individually   __ no, team

2. If you answered yes, either for individual or team community service projects, what projects have you done?

3. How effective do you believe these projects were in actually providing a service to the community?

    __ Very effective   __ Somewhat effective   __ Not very effective

4. How effective do you believe these projects were in helping students internalize the importance of helping others?

    __ Very effective   __ Somewhat effective   __ Not very effective

5. In the space provided below, please share any suggestions you have that you would like to see implemented concerning the use of community service projects?

REFERENCES

Brazee, E. (1997). In the loop. *Middle Ground, 1*(1), 15.

Burke, D. (1997). Looping: Adding time, strengthening relationships. *ERIC Digest*. Retrieved November 4, 2002, from http://ericeece.org/pubs/digests/1997/burke97.html

Caine, R. N., & Caine, G. (1994). *Making connections: Teaching and the human brain.* Menlo Park, CA: Addison-Wesley.

Delisle, R. (1997). *How to use problem-based learning in the classroom.* Alexandria, VA: Association of Supervision and Curriculum Development.

Fenwick, L. (2000). *The principal shortage: Who will lead?* Cambridge, MA: The Principal's Center.

Fogarty, R. (1998). *Problem-based learning: A collection of articles.* Arlington Heights, IL: SkyLight.

Gardner, H. (1993). *Multiple intelligences: The theory in practice.* New York: Basic Books.

Gaustad. J. (1998). Implementing looping. *ERIC Digest.* Retrieved on November 9, 2002, from http://eric.uoregon.edu/publications/digests/digest 123.html

Glanz, J. (1999). Action research. *Journal of Staff Development, 20*(3), 22-23.

Haberman, M. (1995). *Star teachers of children in poverty.* Indianapolis, IN: Kappa Delta Pi.

Hart, L. (1983). *Human brain and human learning.* Village of Oak Creek, AZ: Books for Educators.

Jackson, A. W., & Davis, G. A. (2000). *Turning points 2000: Educating adolescents in the 21st century.* New York: Teachers College Press.

Kovalik, S. (1994). *ITT: The model—integrated thematic instruction.* Kent, WA: Books for Educators.

Lewin, K. (1952). Group decisions and social change. In G. E. Swamson, T. N. Newcomb, & E. L. Hartley (Eds.), *Readings in social psychology* (Rev. ed., pp. 330-344). New York: Holt, Rinehart & Winston.

Milson, A., & Mehlig, L. (2002). Elementary school teachers' sense of efficacy for character education. *Journal of Educational Research, 96*(1), 47-53.

Murphy, J. (1992). *The landscape of leadership preparation: Reframing the education of school administrators.* Newbury Park, CA: Corwin/Sage.

Murphy, J. (1993). Restructuring schooling: The equity infrastructure. *School Effectiveness and School Improvement, 4*(2), 111-130.

National Forum to Accelerate Middle-Grades Reform. (1999). *Our vision statement.* Retrieved August 16, 2004, from http://www.mgforum.org/about/vision.asp

National Policy Board for Education Administration. (2002). *National policy board for educational administration: Standards for advanced programs in educational leadership for principals, superintendents, curriculum directors and supervisors.* Retrieved August 16, 2004, from http://www.npbea.org

National Middle School Association. (2003). *This we believe: Successful schools for young adolescents.* Westerville, OH: Author.

National Policy Board for Education Administration. (2002). *National policy board for educational administration: Standards for advanced programs in educational leadership for principals, superintendents, curriculum directors and supervisors.* Retrieved August 16, 2004, from http://www.npbea.org

Patterson, L., Santa, C., Short, K., & Smith, K. (Eds.). (1993). *Teachers are researchers: Reflection and action.* Newark, DE: International Reading Association.

Schein, E. (1985). *Organizational culture and leadership: A dynamic view.* San Francisco: Jossey-Bass.

Sylwester, R. (1995). *A celebration of neurons: An educator's guide to the human brain.* Alexandria, VA: Association for Supervision and Curriculum Development.

Thompson, S. (2004). *Developing teacher leaders: The principal's role.* Westerville, OH: National Middle School Association.

Williamson, R., & Galleti, S. (2003). Leadership for results. In P. G. Andrews & V. Anfara, Jr. (Eds.), *Leaders for a movement: Professional preparation and development of middle level teachers and administrators* (pp. 271-298). Greenwich, CT: Information Age.

CHAPTER 8

SELECTING MASTER TEACHERS IN A PROFESSIONAL DEVELOPMENT SCHOOL

Inquiry and Action Using Peer Evaluation

Holly J. Thornton

ABSTRACT

This selection describes how teachers involved in a middle level professional development partnership (PDS) questioned traditional means of choosing supervising teachers to work with student teachers. It examines the steps they took as researchers into their own and other's conceptions and performance of best practices. It describes how they developed, implemented, and refined a selection process using the National Board for Professional Teaching Standards, including a peer observation and rating, and an interview process. The study examines the impact on teachers, apprentices, and schools involved. It delineates challenges, benefits, and conditions, which sustain this teacher driven focus on teacher quality within the PDS.

Making a Difference: Action Research in Middle Level Education, 147–168
Copyright © 2005 by Information Age Publishing
All rights of reproduction in any form reserved.

CONNECTING THEORY AND PRACTICE IN THE
PROFESSIONAL DEVELOPMENT SCHOOL

One of the challenges of teacher preparation is providing opportunities for preservice teachers to engage in real life teaching situations that support the development of philosophies and practices they learn within their preparation programs. Making the connection between theory and practice while developing a repertoire of best practices is imperative for these novice teachers. The supervising teacher must serve as a model of instruction and a source of sound feedback and evaluation in order for this to occur (Shantz & Brown, 1999).

Far too often preservice teachers report that rather than seeing a connection between their experiences at the university and their related field experiences, they see a gap between two sometimes oppositional realities. Preservice teachers work in classrooms with supervising teachers who may or may not model effective teaching practices. This is of particular concern in the latter case, as students then begin to emulate the practices of their supervising teachers (McIntyre, 1984). By the end of student teaching many preservice teachers shift from the progressive attitudes they developed at the university to the more traditional attitudes of their supervising teachers (Ziechner, 1980). Their coursework is viewed as disconnected from the real world of school. This disconnect reinforces the notion that theory and practice are not interwoven and mutually supportive, often leading to a filtering away of skills and knowledge gained at the university.

Professional development schools (PDS) emphasize collaborative planning, teaching, and decision making in a variety of ways that redefines the teaching at both institutions (Darling-Hammond, 1994). If the goal of co-reform, improving both teacher preparation and education in P-12 schools, is integral to the partnership, such filtering runs counter to this purpose. Schools of education may change, but unless they do so in collaborative partnership with school colleagues committed to a shared vision of school improvement little else will change.

Action research collaboratively conducted with teacher partners in the schools is a powerful means to cultivate this vision and put it into action. As classroom teachers become involved in the education of preservice teachers and are able to share their stories with other professionals, they discover their own knowledge base growing, and their teaching becomes more grounded in theory (Darling-Hammond, 1994). According to Paul, Epanchin, Rosselli, and Duchnowski (1996) this type of collective inquiry involves risking vulnerability, negotiating paradigm differences, and ownership of the research process. Teacher leaders representing each of six middle school PDSs took the risk of engaging in collaborative action research to examine school improvement at its very core. They grappled with and examined the question of how to select high quality supervising teachers (master teachers) within their schools.

THE STUDY

The Context: Developing a Model of Coherence

A small urban university comprised of primarily nontraditional students embarked on developing a PDS network with schools from the surrounding four districts. Twenty-six schools were in the partnership, six of them middle schools. The six middle schools involved in the study represented urban, rural, and suburban contexts and were representative of the ethnic and socioeconomic diversity of the area. University faculty has typically designed teacher education programs and PDS with the partnership encouraging school-based faculty to propose ideas and assume key roles in implementation of teacher education in the field (Barnhart et al, 1995). In contrast to this, the initial focus of this collaborative work was to develop coherence across the many elements of teacher preparation including course work, program requirements, and field experiences. Involving teachers in the decision making process regarding all aspects of school life is a key feature of the professional development school (Nelson, 1998). Revision of the teacher preparation program, establishment of PDS sites, revision of evaluation tools, and alignment with standards for practice had all been part of the work. Such ground up collaboration lead to joint ownership in redefining the middle level teacher preparation program and empowerment of teachers in the PDS sites. A teacher leadership group of six building coordinators (classroom teachers at each school) and two university middle level faculty members took on the challenge of establishing coherence and developing a link between theory and practice within field experiences, in particular the culminating full time, semester long field placement, termed apprenticeship.

The apprenticeship model differed significantly from the student teaching model previously employed. The responsibility and opportunity to provide the student teacher, or apprentice, with further learning and evaluative feedback was the role of the supervising, field-based, master teacher. With university faculty, these master teachers worked to codevelop new evaluation tools for feedback, goal setting, evaluation, reflection and demonstration of candidate proficiency. Traditionally, faculty observations of student teachers tend to be intermittent, infrequent and limited in their follow up to the observation, thus calling into question the potential for change and improvement of the preservice teachers' instruction based on such a traditional model (Bedient & Fox, 1999). A beneficial shift can be made where the college supervisor moves from a focus on observing and evaluating preservice teachers, to consulting with their field-based colleagues who take on this role (Rickard, 1990). Such a shift was made within these six middle level PDSs.

Full-time faculty members acting as university coordinators facilitated regular biweekly meetings with groups of master teachers in the building to discuss professional practice and alternately facilitated groups of apprentices at the school to engage in dialogue, reflection, and problem solving.

The apprenticeship model utilized a coaching, coteaching model that was diagnostic, dialogic, developmental, and critical in nature. The focus was on authentic evaluation, reflection, and goal setting. The apprentice and the master teacher jointly determined needs as the apprentices demonstrated their competence against the Interstate New Teacher Assessment and Support Consortium (INTASC) standards of practice for beginning teachers. Apprentice competence was evidenced within a culminating portfolio leading to a 2-year guarantee of the graduate.

This new definition of student teaching had direct implications for master teachers who worked as coaches and mentors, as well as the evaluators of these beginning professionals. How teachers measured up to these new requirements became the focus of dialogue among the teacher PDS leaders in the building (building coordinators) and an action plan to identify and cultivate high quality master teachers to work with apprentices resulted. These six middle level building coordinators worked to develop a peer selection process to identify and cultivate high quality teachers to work as master teachers within the site.

The building coordinators at each school met regularly to discuss the quality of master teachers who were working with apprentices. These conversations lead these teachers to ask, "What are best practices, what are students learning at the university, and how does this fit with their experiences and opportunities and teachers in our schools?" Because these teachers and many of their colleagues had a hand in redesigning the field experiences and courses, they were well aware of what the university students were learning and the standards that guided their coursework. Based on this, the building coordinators decided that not everyone was qualified to be a master teacher and that a better way of selecting teachers to serve in this role needed to be developed. The principal would still be a part of the process, but the process needed to become standards based and grounded in evidence related to two aspects: the teachers' professional practice and their ability and desire to serve in the role of coach and mentor.

Master Teacher Selection as Action Research

In essence, as they worked on the selection process, the university faculty and teacher participants engaged in action research to examine how to define and select quality teachers to serve as mentors of novice teachers. A qualitative participatory research method gathered data from teacher interviews and on going focus groups. The types of questions investigated via the development of the master teacher selection process and tool were as follows:

- What are the issues inherent to the process?
- How does such a process serve as professional development for teachers? What are the potential benefits of a teacher-led peer evaluation process situated within a university/school partnership?
- Is the learning of students ultimately impacted?
- What conditions support or inhibit such a process?

Building coordinators expressed concern about the effect of the process on the pool of master teacher applicants. They asked:

- Can such a process help teacher partners (building coordinators) to articulate concerns they had about the teaching and mentoring abilities of their peers?
- Can such a process help to more objectively identify teachers who exhibit these, concerns, in relation to standards of practice?
- How does such a selection process affect the pool of applicants in terms of numbers and quality?

The six middle level building coordinators worked to develop the selection process using both an observation and interview process. Action research focused on gathering data to describe the nature of the process and the intent and meaning the participants made of it. The artifacts designed and used by the teachers were one source of data. Other sources were field notes taken at regular meetings of the building coordinators as they developed observation and interview tools for selection, planned for the use of the tools, and engaged in the selection process after observation and interviews were conducted. Further, feedback from those engaged in the selection process was part of the data set, and member checks with the building coordinators were present across the study, as identified issues emerged. The data were coded to identify these and provide their description. Themes that emerged were: issues in the process, the need for professional development, reported benefits of the process, the need to examine the impact on students in the schools, and the reported conditions that were necessary for the process to emerge.

FINDINGS

Issues in the Selection Process

Several issues emerged while designing, implementing, and evaluating the selection process. One issue was how to address teachers who were not selected especially during the first year when teachers currently in the pool had to reapply. As letters of congratulations and acceptance were sent out to teachers who had been selected, the university and building coordinators sent a letter of *nonselection* to teachers who had not met the standards. Even though 2 years had been spent cultivating relationships and building trust with master teachers in the PDS sites, this step led to a set back in many of the schools. The letter was basic and thanked the applicants for trying, but did not give enough feedback and explanation to those involved. As a result, many of the not selected teachers decided to no longer work with any students from the university or participate in other PDS work at the schools. In these cases, the university coordinator and building coordinator met with teachers individually to provide more information and to offer support and extend an invitation to serve in the PDS in other capacities. The university and building coordinators revised the nonselection process for the second year of implementation, framing it in terms of a mismatch between the teacher's practices and philosophies and those of the PDS teacher preparation program. It also offered teachers direct feedback in need areas and opportunities for professional growth and support to work toward obtaining those goals for reapplication.

Another issue was the need for increased communication about the PDS and master teacher role before the selection process. This would also allow interested schools to engage in mini in-service sessions with the building and university coordinator throughout the school year to gain a better understanding of the standards of practice. Some teachers were no longer interested when they realized what the standards actually meant. Some did not agree with the standards or the middle school philosophy and they opted out before engaging in the process. The need for clearly communicated standards and criteria for master teachers in advance of the observations and interviews became a central part of the PDS work, which was subsequently addressed in master teacher workshops led by veteran master teachers and coordinators.

Meeting the Need for Professional Development

Most professional development schools emphasize the benefits to pre-service teacher preparation but rarely focus on the professional development opportunities for the practicing, experienced teachers at the site (Clark, 1999). As the standards reflected in the master teacher selection process became central to the PDS, a need for professional growth and development for the teachers within the PDS sites emerged. The professional growth agenda, which grew from ensuing dialogue, included many initiatives designed by the master teachers working closely with their university counterparts. Workshops for master teachers about best practices and the new role of the master teachers were held. Courses focused on best practices in the middle level were designed with and for master teachers, including one focusing on integrated instruction, and another on effective teaming. A group of 13 master teachers and two university faculty decided to design and implement a *true middle school* for at-risk students over a period of 2 years. They worked together to develop their knowledge base, curriculum, instruction, and authentic assessment measures. This initiative also served an inquiry project related to student achievement and teacher leadership. The concept of standards-based practice continues to lead to the development of collaborative growth opportunities for all of the PDS participants.

As these professional development initiatives emerged, the focus was at times in conflict with the existing culture and political context of the schools and districts. As the teachers' collective knowledge grew, they worked to form a vision of schooling based on student-centered instruction, integrated curriculum, meaningful learning, active engagement of students, inquiry and problem-based instruction, student ownership, and democratic decision-making. Teachers often shared feelings of opposition to this vision within their schools and districts. Within this context, learning centered on accountability and standardized tests. The tests often dictated the curriculum and instructional strategies as some schools employed prepackaged teacher proof programs for instruction in the basics. Teachers felt they had little say in instructional strategies and felt a time crunch to cover material for testing purposes. Students had even less say over daily decisions in school.

Open communication with district and building level administrators and teacher partners was vital to continue to support the work of the teachers involved. When issues surfaced related to the incongruence between required practices in the school and the standards-based practices of the PDS, frank discussions were held to work toward coming up with workable solutions to address current concerns and to make plans for change in the future. The cultivation of teacher leadership within the schools and teacher dialogue with administrators around central issues of instruction, assessment, and best practices did allow some small changes to begin to occur. The next step for these emerging PDS sites is gaining permission and support from the district level to be identified as uniquely different from their non-PDS counterparts, affording them unique opportunities for crafting their identities as schools. This may provide more autonomy over time for the professionals in these schools to pursue research-based practices in innovative ways, which still ensure student achievement and success.

Benefits of Master Teacher Selection

The master teacher selection process has benefited directly the two primary participants in the apprenticeship, the apprentice and the master teacher. The apprentice can now walk into a setting for apprenticeship where the supervising teacher has an understanding of the teacher preparation program, best practices, and a shared commitment to the establishment of a classroom learning environment that is conducive to learning for all.

Critical feedback and dialogue about practice, which is key to the development of the apprentice teacher, increased since the use of the selection process. This is evidenced through interviews with apprentices, and in the use of the apprenticeship evaluation tools, which have become increasingly focused on feedback related to standards, goal setting, and authentic assessment of the apprentice. Prior to this process, supervising teachers would often give students higher scores and less feedback related to improvement. The tools were often viewed as an accountability or paperwork issue, rather than a formative process of feedback and growth. Both apprentices and master teachers reported a better *goodness of fit* between the apprentice and master teacher after the selection process was employed. This was documented in the master teacher matching forms completed by both parties, both before and after the change in teacher selection and via ongoing meetings with each group. An increase in reporting by apprentices of opportunity and support to take risks to implement innovative practices during apprenticeship was documented, in comparison to the apprenticeships prior to the selection process. Master teachers reported that they were more open to this, since it was a better match with their own beliefs, knowledge base, and practices than it was for the prior pool of master teachers. Another benefit reported by both apprentices and master teachers was an increased sense of belonging on the part of the apprentices and an increased view of the apprentice as a true member of the teaching team, who acted more as a colleague than a student.

Participants reported benefits to the new cadre of master teachers. Master teachers, who were involved in the selection process, reported more of a sense of professionalism and identity as master teachers, as the new process articulated more clearly what that status meant. The new processes also lead them to report that they had demonstrated their expertise as teachers who were qualified to act as the professionals responsible for the culminating experience in teacher preparation. This is similar to a study conducted by Seinty (1997), which revealed that as teachers became more intimately involved in true collaboration and role shifts within the PDS model, they reported a positive response to the changing roles and an increased sense of accomplishment in the process that prepares future teachers.

Those involved in developing and using the evaluation process reported an increased sense of ownership in the PDS and an increased level of trust, as the university turned this important task primarily over to their professional judgment. This process caused the issues of best practices and teaching standards for veteran teachers to come to the fore of dialogue, professional development, and inquiry. This was documented through the subsequent professional development initiatives developed and undertaken by the master teachers including master teacher-led workshops on teaching standards, building-based sessions on the selection process, and a standards-based middle level summer academy. The once *touchy* subject of the quality of teaching and learning in the schools became a part of the dialogue about school improvement and teachers forged a path to work on this together via professional development and inquiry.

Impacting Student Learning

The ultimate goal of this increased focus on quality teaching and best practices is to increase the learning and achievement of students in the partner middle schools. A process to document the impact on student learning via engaging in and developing standards-based practices in the PDS is being developed with the teachers, university faculty, and preservice teachers. A work sample methodology is being employed, where preservice teachers gather student work samples, analyze the data, and reflect upon how their teaching affected learners. They then focus on how to make changes to increase student learning. A database is being developed to track these data. Impacting student learning lessons, artifacts, and reflections are an integral part of the apprentice's culminating standards-based teaching portfolio. This work is ongoing and the master teachers are integral partners in the process of investigating and documenting how the PDS work affects middle level students.

The professional development and inquiry, which have resulted from the focus on best practices, have led to a continued dialogue about school improvement and positively impacting middle school student learning. Daane and Latham (1998) indicated that as cooperating teachers increased their professional development opportunities to explore and learn effective instructional strategies, they were more likely to model those strategies and allow the preservice students to use them in the classroom setting. The professional development initiatives that have resulted from this work have become central to school improvement plans and the professional development within the schools.

Master teachers are taking ownership of the standards for practice in their schools. They are partners in making the critical decisions involved in who works with novice teachers and in contributing to the expectations and components of all field-based experiences. They make the decisions about who is selected to become a master teacher, and which preservice teachers are ready to become a part of the profession. They set the direction for future professional development and inquiry. The teachers are central to the development of a shared vision and continuous reflection upon and improvement in the joint venture of preparing new teachers and continuing professional development as colleagues shaping their profession together.

Necessary Conditions

It was essential that the development of the master teacher selection process came from the teachers themselves. University coordinators documented the issues which surfaced related to working with apprentices during the weekly meetings with master teachers at each school site and brought them to master teachers and building coordinators for discussion. The realization that *not everyone is cut out to be a master teacher* and that *being a good teacher isn't necessarily enough to be a master teacher,* and that *principals don't always have the best handle on what goes on inside of a teacher's classroom* came from the teachers. The abundance of teachers in the selection pool was a direct result of the prior work of empowering and involving teachers as true partners in the PDS. A struggle just to find enough willing teachers to accept preservice teachers may be an indicator that the collaborative needs to work on issues of ownership, and make the work of master teachers in the schools more central to the culture of the school. Further, it must be embedded and supported as part of the role of a high quality teacher in the PDS. The work of the university coordinator became facilitating the dialogue and working with teachers to problem solve. If university faculty or the district administrators had developed the same selection process, it would not have been as successful. The ownership of the process by the teachers involved is paramount to the development of the process itself.

Support from university and school-based administrators is also important. This support is most crucial at the building level and at the department chair level at the university. Those administrators most intimately involved in the PDS and most directly involved with the teachers can provide support in the form of time, money, recognition, and connecting the work of the teachers to the broader goals of the program. Inclusion of district level administrators is important if the process is to be moved along and not challenged at a higher level. Regular meetings to update and inform administrators, and to gain their input, were built into the development of the teacher selection process.

Support of the teachers' work was not secured wholly at every level in every case; therefore, an element of risk was always involved in moving the plan foreword. Openness to risk taking, involvement in continued evaluation and revisions as well as flexibility and tolerance of ambiguity are also central elements to the process. The building coordinators wanted to move ahead with the process. These teachers were responsible for conducting the observations and taking on the major decision making role in the selection process. This was a big risk to take, venturing outside of the traditional teacher role. The old processes and roles were no longer there as safety nets. Since the process was emergent it was by nature ambiguous, allowing teachers to decide what standards and procedures to commit to, embrace, and refine.

All of this must occur within a context of trust. Prior to the development and implementation of the selection process, the relationships among partners, which sustain this work, had begun and were continuing to form. Building-based weekly and biweekly meetings, semiannual cross PDS professional development conferences helped communication and input from all master teachers to occur. School and university-based teachers learned to talk openly and directly with one another. They learned to rely on each other. They learned that the knowledge, vision, and power they collectively possessed were far greater than that which they possessed alone. They learned that when they worked together, they could make a difference. This sense of efficacy coupled with trust continues to be the driving force of this team of educators.

THE MASTER TEACHER SELECTION PROCESS AND TOOLS

Initially, an application was the primary means of making a determination as to who would be selected as a master teacher. The application included basic information such as grade level and subjects taught, certification held, prior teaching experiences, educational background, leadership experiences, and experience with teacher supervision or training. The application included a two-page narrative where the teacher described his or her philosophy and practice related to INTASC criteria. It contained three reference letters to be completed on required forms where the applicant was rated in terms of teacher quality. For the first year of the apprenticeship model, university faculty reviewed the applications and eliminated those of major concern. The applications were then *approved* by the principal and virtually all applicants became part of the master teacher pool. This approach did not meet the needs of apprentices nor reflect the kinds of pedagogy the building coordinators valued.

The building coordinators decided that a master teacher's pedagogy needed to mirror a belief in, understanding of and commitment to research-based and professionally recognized standards of practice. The entire teacher preparation program including coursework, assessments, field experiences, and the compilation of a comprehensive portfolio had been designed to reflect the INTASC standards for beginning teachers. Middle school philosophy and practices grounded in National Middle School Association standards as articulated in *This We Believe* (1995) were also an integral part of the preparation program. These two pieces were both reflected in the National Board for Professional Teaching Standards (NBPTS) Early Adolescence Generalist standards of practices, which were more appropriate for accomplished teachers. After several meetings the group collectively decided that these NBPTS would serve as the framework for developing the master teacher selection process. The group decided that evidence related to these standards would be gathered and scored based on an observation of practice and an interview process.

The Observation

The building coordinators kept the application process, but decided to develop an observation process and tool (Appendix A) to enable them to engage in peer evaluation. The teachers rejected a perfected, prepackaged rubric, in favor of a grounded tool developed and used by the teachers in a way that made sense to them. The tool development, predicated on the fact that the tool requires the professional judgment of the teachers completing the evaluation, mirrored the beliefs and commitments of the NBPTS to this concept, and acknowledged the ability and right of teachers to monitor and set the standards for their own profession. A second commitment was to design a tool that was holistic, usable, and descriptive of practice.

The decision can then be made as to whether the information that is desired from the evaluation can best be acquired through the use of an analytic or holistic scoring rubric. If an analytic scoring rubric is created, then each criterion is considered separately as the descriptions of the different score levels are developed. This process results in separate descriptive scoring schemes for each evaluation factor. For holistic scoring rubrics, the collection of criteria is considered throughout the construction of each level of the scoring rubric and the result is a single descriptive scoring scheme. (Moskal, 2000, p. 1)

The tool was not developed to gather research data, but rather to articulate the standards of practices the building coordinators felt master teachers should demonstrate; it tells what those standards *look like* in practice. Danielson's (1996) framework for professional practice was adapted to align with the NBPTS early adolescence generalist standards. A benefit of this rubric is that utilized language understood by teachers, thus enabling it to be used as a professional development tool. The building coordinators agreed upon a holistic 1-4 scaled scoring. It was determined that a master teacher candidate would need to score an average of 3 to be selected.

The teachers involved used a holistic approach for several reasons. Occasionally, it was not possible to separate an evaluation into independent factors. Teachers found this to be the case when they worked on descriptors for classroom practice. They viewed teaching as a complex set of interdependent, overlapping variables, rather than discrete behaviors. When such an overlap exists between the criteria set for the evaluation of different factors, a holistic scoring rubric may be preferable to an analytic scoring rubric (Moskal, 2000). A holistic scoring rubric, considers criteria in combination on a single descriptive scale (Brookhart, 1999). A holistic rubric supports broader judgments concerning the quality of the process or the product (Moskal, 2000).

The master teacher selection rubric describes only the highest and lowest levels of practice, following a typical pattern of thinking in rubric development. The first step in developing a scoring rubric is to clearly identify the qualities that need to be displayed to demonstrate proficient performance (Brookhart, 1999). According to Moskal (2000) the identified qualities form the top level of scoring criteria for the rubric. After defining the criteria for the top level of performance, the evaluators then defines the criteria for lowest level of performance. The contrast between levels is likely to suggest criteria that may be used to create score levels that fall between the existing score levels (Moskal, 2000). If meaningful distinctions between the score categories cannot be made, then additional score categories should not be created (Brookhart, 1999).

The teachers agreed upon a holistic 1-4 scaled scoring, and discussed thoroughly what these numerical ratings indicated. In order to receive a score the applicant must consistently demonstrate the described level throughout the observation. The teachers decided on the following:

4 = exemplary level—level of excellence/mastery
3 = proficient level—level of proficiency
2 = in progress level—approaching proficiency
1 = unsatisfactory level—not proficient at this time
N/O = not observed

It was determined that a master teacher candidate would need a score of at least 3 (proficient) on each standard to be selected.

The building coordinators decided to conduct the observations and evaluate their peers. The teachers felt that it would be more objective if building coordinators did not conduct observations in their own buildings. This would not only give an outside view of the teachers observed, but also would help to avoid problems that a building coordinator might incur if a fellow teacher was not selected. After the rubric development, a schedule was set for the building coordinators to conduct observations. The building coordinators contacted each other, arranged times for observations, made teachers aware of the times and dates, and secured release time from their building principals to observe and evaluate. Once the observations were complete, the building and university coordinators met to discuss scores and make selections for principal approval.

Building coordinators crafted several iterations of the observation tool over a period of 3 years, based on feedback from the master teachers being observed and the building coordinators using the tools. N/O was added for those behaviors not observed/applicable. This helped to address standards 9 and 10, which centered on reflective practice and collaboration that were often hard to determine during the observation of a class period. During the third year of selection, those applying were given the descriptors and professional development sessions about the standards and expectations. In this manner, the evaluation became a means of professional dialogue and growth. Teachers observed also had the option of completing and turning in a reflection sheet to be considered during the selection process. If there were special circumstances, or information applicants wanted to share, the open-ended reflection sheet allowed them to do so.

The Interview

A companion to the observation process was an interview. The building coordinators decided that the university coordinators would conduct these. Together, both parties designed interview questions (Appendix B) focused on the NBPTS elements of professional practice such as instructional resources, learning environment, meaningful learning, students' social needs, and collaboration with families, communities and colleagues. The interview protocol also included questions directed at gaining information about the applicant's conceptions of middle school and the mentoring/coaching aspect of the master teacher role. University coordinators took field notes during the interview process and rated the response to each of the 10 questions using the same 1-4 scaled scoring. Building and university coordinators reviewed both the interview responses and observations at a meeting that led to master teacher recommendation for principal approval.

Data from the Selection Process

Basic data in the form of mean score trends were gathered as related to each category/standard during the second year of the selection process to begin look at basic patterns across the NBPTS standards. One standard that was often difficult to determine was standard 10, which focuses on collaboration. Overall, the highest scores were received in standard category *knowledge of subject matter*, and standard category *learning environment*. The lowest ratings consistently occurred in standard category, *multiple paths to knowledge*, and *assessment*. Generally, teachers receiving unsatisfactory ratings of 2 or below exhibited a consistent pattern of low scores across each of the 10 NBPTS early adolescence standards.

The new processes impacted the number of teachers eligible to act as master teachers. The initial pool of applicants who became master teachers through the principals' appointment included 94 teachers. After the first year of full PDS implementation, the building coordinators determined that all master teachers who had been previously selected based on application only needed to reapply and complete the observation and interview processes. Any new applicants would complete the same procedures. Some previously identified master teachers chose not to apply. Others did and were successful in the observation and interview process; some were not. The new selection process lead to 37 master teachers successfully completing the process and being chosen to become master teachers. Those that had been of concern to the building coordinators did not make the cut score to remain master teachers, when evaluated by a peer from another PDS building, thus providing very *loose* inner-rater reliability for the process. In the second year of the selection process the number of new applicants for the six middle schools was 33. The number of applicants was lower than anticipated, but the expectations for the role and the requirements to be selected were clearer and building coordinators reported that those who did apply were better prepared and qualified. The total number of master teachers in the pool after this 2-year process was 55. Once selected by this new process, master teachers would not need to reapply.

Professional development "cannot be imposed, but must reflect the needs of the practicing teachers" (Michelli, 1993, p. 4). These initial results guided the focus for professional development within the PDS sites and launched yet another action research project. This time the focus would be beyond understanding the process of developing a peer master teacher selection process. It would center on how to make sense of the evaluation data resulting from the process in determining the next layer of inquiry and how both process and evaluative data can be used to continue to increase the quality of master teachers in the PDS. The building coordinators continue on the iterative path of action research.

CONCLUSION

The lack of explicit and intentional connections between theory and practice, university-based and field-based learning, and standards of practice and predominate practices in the schools, is problematic for teacher preparation and overall improvement in the quality of teaching. The establishment of the PDS model is a means to address this problem, but even within the PDS such connections are not a given. The often taboo topic of the quality of teaching practices in the field is politically volatile and charged with tension and challenges. If a new institution is invented, consisting of the best of what the university and public schools can offer, anxieties about change must be overcome (Dixon & Ishler, 1992). If change related to issues of teacher quality are not addressed as a central part of our collective work within the PDS structure, then we may be merely giving lip service to standards of practice and missing the opportunity to develop best practices within our programs and partner schools. An environment of trust and ownership, inculcated by true collaboration with and empowerment of teachers allowed this question of teacher quality to be raised, owned, examined and addressed by teachers and university colleagues. What is most important is not the perfection of the process, and the *objectivity* of the selection, but the value of teachers' professional ownership of the problem, dedication to grapple with it, and power to define what teacher standards look like in the classroom. It recognizes and honors their right and need to exercise their professional judgment as peer evaluators to select master teachers and to provide professional development and support for all who want to get there. A result of this work is an increased focus on assessing and documenting the impact of the apprentice teacher on the learning of middle level students. Ultimately, the work of the PDS is one of coreform where both the teacher preparation program and the public schools benefit from sustained collaborative dialogue, research, inquiry, and innovation. Allowing teachers to take the lead in centering on issues of best practices provides a more authentic path to such coreform.

APPENDIX A

Master Teacher Observation

Teacher Name _____

Building _____

Grade level _____

Subject areas _____

Based on the following descriptor, rate the Master Teacher applicant you have observed on a scale of 1-4. Please indicate N/A for those standards which you could not observe/determine.

NBPTS 1 knowledge of students: _____

NBPTS 2 knowledge of subject matter: _____

NBPTS 3 instructional resources: _____

NBPTS 4 learning environment: _____

NBPTS 5 meaningful learning: _____

NBPTS 6 multiple paths to learning: _____

NBPTS 7 social development: _____

NBPTS 8 assessment: _____

NBPTS 9 reflective practice: _____

NBPTS 10 collaboration: _____

Observation descriptors

NBPTS standard: Rating 4	Rating 1
Instruction based on knowledge of students: Teacher displays understanding of typical developmental characteristics of the age group as well as exceptions. Teacher displays a variety of approaches to learning based on students' developmental needs intellectually, socially and personally. Teacher recognizes the knowledge and skill students bring, and builds upon this.	Instruction based on knowledge of students: Teacher displays a consistent lack of understanding of developmental characteristics of the age group. Approaches to learning are not based on students' needs. No attempt is made to build upon knowledge and skills students bring to learning. Inquiry and the disciplines.

2. Knowledge of subject matter within and across disciplines:

Teacher displays solid content knowledge and makes connections across the disciplines. Teacher's plans and practices show an understanding of relationships among topics and concepts. Investigation and inquiry related to concepts and topics are present as the teacher links students' knowledge and experience to content learning. Teacher engages students in lessons that require higher level thinking and application of concepts and topics while students are cognitively engaged in activities and projects to enhance understanding of content learning. Appropriate resources are used to support content learning. Teacher develops long-and short-range curriculum goals which show a well-developed understanding of the content and interconnections within the discipline. Teacher understands the learning strengths and weaknesses of the students and uses this understanding to fashion a variety of learning activities. Teacher is familiar with the community's demographics and resources. Teacher uses the QCCs and national standards when planning.

2. Knowledge of subject matter within and across disciplines:

Teacher makes frequent content errors or does not correct errors students make. Teacher displays no knowledge of connections across the disciplines. Teacher displays a lack of understanding of relationships between concepts and topics and a lack of prerequisite knowledge important to student learning of the content. Teaching is didactic and requires little to no inquiry on the part of students, who act in a passive role. Resources are limited to the continuous use of the text as the primary source of instruction. Teacher fails to make coherent lesson plans or makes plans that have activities with no links to curriculum goals. Teacher consistently makes mistakes in content. Teacher fails to make connections within the discipline (e.g., biology with chemistry, grammar with writing). Teacher has no understanding of QCCs or national standards and how they relate to the classroom curriculum.

3. Use of rich and varied instructional resources:

Teacher communicates clearly and accurately. Teacher uses questioning and discussion techniques based on primary sources of knowledge. Students conduct research using a variety of resources, including technology. A variety of resources are used beyond the text. Teacher and students use technology as a tool for learning.

3. Use of rich and varied instructional resources:

Teacher's instruction and directions are unclear or confusing. Teacher uses lecture/direct instruction as predominant means of instruction. Available technology is seldom used. The text and seatwork are the primary resources for instruction.

4. Learning Environment:

Teacher demonstrates caring and respect for students. Students demonstrate through active participation enthusiasm for learning. Students demonstrate self-motivation and pride in work. The classroom conveys high expectations for student learning. Teacher is alert to student behavior and encourages student ownership of behavior and problem solving when issues arise. Teacher response to student behavior is appropriate and based on student's needs while respecting student dignity. Responses to behavior problems are appropriate and successful.

4. Learning environment:

Students are confused as to what standards of behavior are. Student behavior is not monitored and teacher is unaware of what students are doing. Students depend on the teacher and extrinsic factors such as grades, reward or punishment for motivation for learning and positive behavior. Teacher response to misbehavior is inconsistent, overly repressive or does not respect student dignity. Teacher is rude or sarcastic to students and students are rude or sarcastic with each other.

5. Meaningful Learning:

Teacher asks questions which require students to formulate multiple answers. Students are engaged in true discussion and have the opportunity to make unsolicited contributions. Teacher plans and implements lessons which require students to use critical and creative thinking. Teacher engages students in problem solving activities. Teacher links student prior skills, knowledge and understanding to thinking skills development to foster understanding. Assessment requires student performance of knowledge and understanding and feedback is consistently given to students. The lesson is coherent and allows time for student reflection.

6. Multiple paths to knowledge:

Teacher uses the variety of approaches students bring to learning within planning and instruction. Teacher displays flexibility and responsiveness to the diverse needs of learners. Teacher displays the ability to plan, implement or adapt instruction to meet a variety of students learning styles, abilities or other needs. Teacher displays knowledge of the interests or cultural heritage of groups of students and recognizes the value of this knowledge.

7. Social development of students:

Teacher creates an environment of respect and rapport. Students collaborate with each other while engaged in a variety of learning experiences. Student interactions are positive and built into instruction. There is a sense of community, collaboration and belonging for students.

8. Assessment:

Teacher uses a variety of assessments, choosing the type most appropriate for each instructional activity. Teacher develops evaluation plans/rubrics which both teacher and students can use for assessment. Assessment is authentic and guides further learning. Teacher uses authentic assessment strategies which simulate real world experience and focus on learning outcomes for students, intellectually, socially and physically. Teach-

5. Meaningful Learning:

Teacher directions, procedures and questions are confusing to students. Interaction between students and teacher is predominantly recitation style; with the teacher mediating all questions and answers. Questions are focused on one correct answer. Few students participate in the discussion. Students are not actively and cognitively engaged in learning. Feedback related to learning is limited or nonexistent. The lesson has no clearly defined structure and makes no linkages to students' prior knowledge or skills.

6. Multiple Paths to knowledge:

Teacher adheres rigidly to an instructional plan, even when change will clearly improve a lesson. Teacher ignores student interests or questions, or blames students for lack of success. Teacher is unfamiliar with different approaches students bring to learning such as learning styles or modalities. Teacher displays little attention to students' interests or cultural heritage and does not see this as valuable.

7. Social development of Students:

Students rarely communicate with each other about learning. Student interactions are very limited and not encouraged. Student interaction is limited to free time or break time and not viewed as part of the learning process.

8. Assessment:

Teacher uses primarily objective tests that do not measure higher-level thinking skills. Teacher has a mismatch between learning and testing (e.g., uses true/false questions to test higher-level thinking skills, uses essay tests to test instruction that was mainly drill and practice). Teacher uses primarily drill and practice to teach state testing objectives without relating the skills to real-world examples.

ers and students assess how well student's work together to achieve learning goals. Teacher understands state testing requirements and integrates the objectives into the larger goals of classroom instructional activities.

9. Reflective practice:
Teacher reflects on instructional activities and evaluates their effect on student learning. Teacher thinks of alternative strategies when something has not worked well. Teacher considers student needs, parent concerns, and best practices when planning and evaluating instructional goals and activities. Teacher reads professional journals and attends conferences whenever possible.

10. Collaboration:
Teacher develops and maintains a collegial relationship with other teachers. Teacher seeks ideas from colleagues. Teacher uses community resources to enhance student learning. Teacher communicates with parents in various ways. Teacher takes responsibility for all students on the campus.

9. Reflective practice:
Teacher consistently uses activities that aren't effective. Teacher cannot explain what went wrong with an activity and how to correct the problem. Teacher seldom seeks input from other teachers or from journals or other resources. Teacher fails to consider how parents or the community might react to an activity. Teacher is unable to explain more than one way of teaching a concept.

10. Collaboration:
Teacher is consistently critical of peers and parents. Teacher does not collaborate with peers. Teacher does not communicate with parents. Teacher fails to use community resources. Teacher is concerned only with students in his/her classes.

Name _____

School _____

Grade level/subjects taught _____

How would you evaluate the lesson you taught?

_____

_____

_____

_____

How did this lesson reflect a *typical* lesson with these students?

_____

_____

_____

_____

What changes would you make and why?

_____

_____

_____

_____

APPENDIX B

Master Teacher Interview Guide

(Rate on 1-4 scale and write supporting comments)
Name_____
School_____
Concentrations_____ Grade_____

1. How do you plan and implement instruction to address adolescent needs/characteristics?

2. What instructional resources do you use?

3. What is the *ideal* learning environment in your classroom and what strategies do you employ to work toward that ideal?

4. How do you work toward meaningful learning with all students?

5. How do you address students' social needs within your instruction?

6. How do you assess student learning?

7. In what ways do you collaborate with families, communities, and colleagues?

8. What one thing would you change about middle school?

9. What skills or characteristics do you have that would serve you well in a mentoring/coteaching role?

10. Why do you want to be a master teacher?

REFERENCES

Barnhart, M., Cole, D., Hansell, S., Mathies, B., Smith, W., & Black, S. (1995). Strengthening teacher education. In R. T. Osguthorpe (Ed.), *Partnership schools* (pp. 45-71). San Francisco: Jossey-Bass.

Bedient, D., & Fox, J. (1999). Drama: A tool for supervising student teachers. *Contemporary Education*, 70(4), 11-12.

Brookhart, S. M. (2000). The art and science of classroom assessment: The missing part of pedagogy. *ERIC Digest*. (ERIC Document Reproduction No. ED. 432 938). Washington, DC: ERIC Clearinghouse on Higher Education.

Clark, D. (1999). *Effective professional development schools*. San Francisco: Jossey-Bass.

Darling-Hammond, L. (Ed.). (1994). *Professional development schools: School for developing a profession*. New York: Teachers College Press.

Dixon, P., & Ishler, R. (1992). Professional development schools: Stages in collaboration. *Journal of Teacher Education, 43*(1), 28-34.

Daane, C., & Latham, D. (1998). Helping supervising teachers stay abreast of effective instructional strategies. *Contemporary Education, 69*(3), 141-142.

Danielson, C. (1996). *Enhancing professional practice: A framework for teaching*. Alexandria, VA: Association for Supervision and Curriculum Development.

McIntyre, J. D. (1984). A response to critics of field experience supervision. *Journal of Teacher Education, 35*(3), 42-45

Michelli, N. (1993). *The agenda for teacher education in a democratic project: Summary of New Jersey policy recommendations*. Upper Montclair, NJ: School of Professional Studies, Montclair State College.

Moskal, B. M. (2000). Scoring rubrics: What, when and how? *Practical Assessment, Research & Evaluation, 7*(3). Retrieved May 11, 2003, from http://PAREonline.net/getvn.asp?v=7&n=3

National Middle School Association. (1995). *This we believe: Developmentally responsive middle level schools*. Columbus, OH: Author.

Nelson, M. (1998). Professional development schools: An implementation model. *NASSP Bulletin, 82*, 93-100.

Paul, J., Epanchin, B., Rosselli, H., & Duchnowski, A. (1996). The transformation of teacher education and special education. *Remedial and Special Education, 17*(5), 310-322.

Rikard, G. L. (1990). Student teaching supervision—A dyadic approach. *Journal of Physical Education, Recreation and Dance, 61*(4), 85-86.

Shantz, D., & Brown, M. (1999). Developing a positive relationship: The most significant role of the supervising teacher. *Teacher Education, 119*(4), 693-694.

Sienty, S. F. (1997). The changing roles of student teacher supervisors. *Education, 117*, 506-10.

Ziechner, K. (1980). Myths and realities of field-based experiences in preservice teacher education. *Journal of Teacher Education, 31*(6), 45-55.

CHAPTER 9

CREATING EFFECTIVE MIDDLE SCHOOLS THROUGH INQUIRY

Conversations with Practitioners

Heidi Bulmahn Barker and Carole Basile

ABSTRACT

Historically, professional development schools have centered around four functions: teacher preparation, professional development, student learning, and inquiry. Because inquiry is explicitly named, professional development schools often have in place structures that provide the impetus for conducting action research, research aimed at improving professional practice. We will tell the stories of how inquiry has played itself out in four middle schools that are professional development schools, and how that inquiry has become a part of the culture of the schools. We will also discuss how the structures of their partnerships with university support action research and how those structures could be generalized to other middle schools.

The nature of a middle school is much like the community of adolescents it serves. Middle schools are places where staff and students are constantly trying to find identities. Because of middle school reform efforts, much of that school identity has been defined more clearly. But as Jackson and

Making a Difference: Action Research in Middle Level Education, 169–183

Davis (2000) point out in *Turning Points 2000: Educating Adolescents for the 21st Century*, more work needs to be done to improve our teaching practice as it impacts young adolescents. Lounsbury (2003) states,

> No other age level is of more important to the future of individuals, and, literally, to that of society: because these are the years when youngsters crystallize their beliefs about themselves and firm up their self-concepts, their philosophies of life and their values—the things that are the ultimate determinants of their behaviors. (p. 2)

For this reason, Kinney (2003) concludes that it is time for middle level proponents to step up to the plate and become serious advocates for middle level students. One way to advocate for students and for student learning is through the process of inquiry. This chapter reflects on how middle school practitioners are creating a school culture of inquiry and reflective practice in order to meet the needs of students and to create social and educational equity.

INQUIRY AND THE PRACTICE OF SCHOOL

Teacher inquiry, also known as action research or practitioner research, is a form of research designed by practitioners who seek to improve issues related to teaching and learning and solutions to daily classroom or school dilemmas (Stringer, 1999). Teacher inquiry helps practitioners in the field of education investigate their own practice systematically and intentionally (Ayers, 1993; Cochran-Smith & Lytle, 1999; Schön, 1983).

Teacher research is connected to the early work of Dewey (1916/1997) and Lewin (1948) who both argued that the primary aims of practitioner research were to enhance understanding and to improve learning and teaching. Some perceive that practitioner research is beneath the scholarship of academics in universities; others view practitioner research as a form of *local knowledge* (Cochran-Smith, 1997) that may lead to change within particular classrooms and schools but is not claimed as being generalizable.

However, Zeichner, and Noffke (2001) claim that practitioner research should not be judged with the same criteria as research conducted by outsiders. Anderson, Herr, and Nihlen (1999) suggest that validity might be better accomplished in practitioner research with a variety of criteria, with each appropriate to the specificity of each inquiry. This helps school practitioners individualize the inquiry to meet the school's needs and provide initial insight into the complexities of specific problems in the school.

In this chapter, we will tell stories of how inquiry has played itself out in four middle schools, middle schools that have been professional development schools for more than 5 years, and how that inquiry has become a part of the culture of these schools.

INQUIRY AND THE PROFESSIONAL DEVELOPMENT SCHOOL

At the University of Colorado at Denver, university educators partner with 28 schools in six Denver metropolitan districts that serve large populations of low-income and/or minority students, students for whom English is a second language, and students with special needs. Each partner school hosts between 12-15 teacher candidates each semester. A site professor from the university supports learning at the school one day per week as does a full-time master teacher, or site coordinator, a teacher on special assignment.

Historically, professional development schools have centered around four functions: teacher preparation, professional development, student learning, and inquiry (Goodlad, 1994; Osguthorpe, Harris, Harris, & Black, 1995; Teitel, 2003). Because inquiry is included as a main component, professional development schools often have structures in place that provide the impetus for conducting practitioner research, research aimed at improving professional practice. Practitioner research can give schools and university partners an individualistic way of looking at the partnership within a school context and provides them with information that informs their practice and their constituencies.

Therefore, in the spirit of a fully functioning professional development school model, inquiry has always been a part of our partnership culture. Students have taken inquiry classes and have conducted projects in professional development schools since the beginning of the program 11 years ago. Students are also responsible for *legacy projects*, service projects for the school community, many of which are inquiries that inform practice related to student learning. Students complete eight performance-based assessments, several of which are rooted in an inquiry stance. The university facilitated leadership academies to guide professional development schools through processes of practitioner research, secured a number of grants for the intended purpose of providing resources to our professional development schools for practitioner research, and for 7 years, hosted a conference for practitioners, students, and faculty from several universities and school districts as a venue for the presentation of practitioner research projects.

We believe that when teachers participate with other practitioners and university faculty to investigate important dilemmas, they increase the possibility of developing a richer understanding of their students and themselves as well as improving students' learning and informing their own teaching practice.

CONVERSATIONS WITH SITE COORDINATORS

Researchers have emphasized the uniqueness of the middle school curriculum and the special challenges and opportunities middle school educators confront in shaping and reshaping their curricular leadership cultures (Brown, Claudet, & Olivarez, 2002). Within our professional development school structure, there is the unique distributed leadership culture that includes a master teacher we call a site coordinator or teacher on special assignment. This master teacher assumes an important role in the implementation of school-university partnerships. The position also enables them to take a very important leadership role in the school relative to inquiry. Essentially, the site coordinator walks in two worlds, allowing them to hear the voices of both school and university faculty (Utley, Basile, & Rhodes, 2003). In the sections that follow, conversation excerpts represent dialogue among four site coordinators who have been part of the university partnership and their reflections about the culture of their schools as places for inquiry.[1]

Each site coordinator represents schools in four different school districts[2] with a diverse student population. The first school, Denver Middle School, has been serving the Southwest Denver community since 1959. The neighborhood serves predominantly low to middle income families. The current student population is 885, grades 6-8. Approximately 88% of the students receive free or reduced lunches. Their English language acquisition program serves over 200 students, and also serves 125 students with special needs. The second school, County Middle School, is in the heart of an industrial area in northeast Denver. The current student population is 702, grades 6-8. Approximately 67% of the students receive free or reduced lunch and 60% of the students are English language acquisition students. Third, Creek Middle School, serves a population of 927 students in grades 6-8, predominantly white (53%) and Hispanic (35%) with 50% receiving free or reduced lunch. The majority of Creek's families live in mobile homes. The fourth school, Choice School, is a preK-12 alternative public school of choice in the largest school district in the state. This middle school serves approximately 107 students grades 7 and 8. Approximately 21% of the population receives free or reduced lunch. We share these demographic descriptions to show that each of these schools has its own set of issues and complexities. Yet, they also share common threads; each has been a professional development school for over 5 years, each is committed to the four partner functions, and each is committed to being an effective middle school.

Getting Started With Inquiry

Three years ago, Denver Middle School was an inner city school that was rated *unsatisfactory* on the state school accountability report card. Teacher turnover was high; twelve alternatively licensed teachers worked in the school, and morale was quite low. Their story of inquiry and what inquiry has done for the teachers and students in the school demonstrates the critical nature of inquiry and how it can change a school's climate and culture and impact student learning.

In this school, inquiry is a distributed process across teachers. Study groups were formed to stop the isolation of teachers and allow them to share practices and data among each other and the entire school community. The site coordinator at Denver Middle School told us their story:

> For years, others kept saying to us that the expertise lies within our building. We need to capture it and use it to our advantage, and it wasn't until we switched the focus of our work as a site professor and site coordinator from the teacher candidates to the clinical teachers did we realize that indeed, there is tremendous knowledge in the building that has been isolated and not utilized. We also felt that inquiry might be a way to harness the energy and knowledge and share it among the teachers in the school. Unfortunately, we also knew that long time staff members at our school had gone through sort of a frightful experience years ago when the idea of inquiry was forced upon them, and they rebelled. And so, we knew we had to do a real soft sell with them. How we approached teachers was going to be critical if we wanted the project to be successful. It couldn't come across as top-down or mandatory … so we started by just throwing out the idea and letting them come up with the logistics. It was also voluntary; some of the initial teachers who came to the meeting opted out, some of those have come back later.
>
> First, we called the group a "study group" which gave it more of a professional development feel rather than inquiry or research. In the study groups, we started with the idea of teacher talk in the classroom and the impact that has on students and developed an entire taxonomy on what we think teacher talk is. From that, we decided to narrow in looking specifically at teacher response and the student response to the teacher's response. And, so we bought a video camera, and we were able to release clinical teachers while the teacher candidate delivered instruction. The clinical teacher was then able to go, not only to view the lesson, but videotape another study group member and bring some of that "data" back to the study group.

And the funny thing was, through the video, teachers realized that what we originally thought was good practice, wasn't as good as they thought or at least wasn't done in a critical way. Through this process, teachers really developed and have been able to take that information back to teacher candidates, and that's making an impact on lots of people around the school.

Our greatest success has been with a real quiet introverted teacher who I think had lots of confidence in himself, but wasn't ready to show that to other people for fear of someone being critical. He was also someone who always participated on the periphery of any meeting. So, by being somewhat nosy and pushy, I was able to get into his classroom and videotape his instruction. And so when we watched him bloom after showing the tape of him in the classroom and allowing him to discuss what it was that he was doing and why he was doing it, he took on a whole new role and now has decided that, "Ok, I'm real thoughtful about what I'm going to do in the classroom and I want you to come in and tape me while I'm doing this because I want to learn more about what I'm doing, and I think that my colleagues will learn from me as well."

It's also been interesting to me as we develop our site seminars with teacher candidates, the growing number of staff members that keep doing this and saying, "Hey, I think I have something I think I can share with your teacher candidates." And these are people who are not necessarily clinical teachers but they want to share this information with teacher candidates just because they feel like it's good for both of them. Another thing that has happened is teacher candidates come to meetings and say, my clinical teacher came back to the classroom today and said they were going to try something because they heard how it works in someone else's classroom.

Now, when I do go in and coach teacher candidates, the clinical teacher is right there. We discuss instruction together and it's reinforcing the work of the study groups. The most interesting thing is when the clinical teacher ends up saying, "You know what, I don't do that. It's my fault, and that's the reason why the teacher candidate didn't do it either."

I have to commend all of these clinical teachers for volunteering and seeing the value of what is going on. Because they're coming back and saying, "Yes, this is fantastic." It's giving them the reassurance that these are having significant changes for students in their learning as well. So, it is fantastic. These study groups have really changed how teachers approach this idea of professional development through inquiry, although after a year of this, we still haven't said that what they're doing is inquiry.

In this second year, teachers are all conducting mini-experiments (and they do call them "experiments"). Each person is at a different point in their experiment. And we help each other with what comes next. Some people are collecting data, some are analyzing data. It has been baby steps…but when teachers report back on their findings we hear how it's impacting students, individually and as a group.

In a middle school everyone needs to be a profound instructor, and it all comes from each other, analyzing what's happening, and getting feedback based on data. The varying expertise level lends itself to this continual learning environment. A mixed group of novice and experienced teachers ... novice teachers who bring "new" knowledge and experienced teachers who bring "experienced" knowledge. They respect each other and that is good for kids. We know we have a long way to go with inquiry, but this has been a huge start. There are currently 15 teachers in the group and as the word gets out about the successes we're having, we hope more will join us. Our goal is to institutionalize the processes so that it's just a way of life at our school.

The Effective Middle School and Inquiry

The story at Denver Middle School, told above by the site coordinator, shows that inquiry is a journey, and that at different points along that journey the idea of inquiry becomes embedded within particular aspects of the school's culture if teachers feel ownership of the idea. We found similar stories as we talked with the site coordinators in each of the schools. In our conversations with the four site coordinators about inquiry in their respective middle schools, all told stories connected to the particular context of their own buildings and communities in which they work, but they also held together with some common themes.

We found the themes related to inquiry matched those related to effective middle school reform. Morocco, Clark-Chiarelli, Aquilar, and Brigham (2002) discuss factors that contribute to effective middle schools, including leadership, organization and structure, approaches to curriculum and teaching, and internal and external relationships. The following sections represent the voices of the four site coordinators and the pieces of the conversations that fit within each theme. These excerpts are not exclusive and certainly cross the boundaries of each factor, but we placed them where we felt they best exemplified a particular factor.

Leadership

Effective schools research states that school leaders can make a difference in the effectiveness of schools (Brown, Claudet, & Olivarez, 2002). Related to inquiry, each of the four site coordinators felt that without a strong leadership base, a culture of inquiry would not exist. The site coordinator at Creek Middle School described how leadership has encouraged teachers to ask questions and search for answers through the use of data.

I've been in at this school for 16 years. In the beginning, we did our job, taught kids, and went home; we didn't ask any questions let alone collect or analyze data to inform our practice. Over the last 4 to 5 years the school has experienced a tremendous amount of renewal mostly because of our principal. He has made relationships with teachers that have made the teachers feel like professionals. He has created an atmosphere of collaboration and cooperation where inquiry can occur. The staff has an attitude of learning and people feel safe asking questions and providing data that will give us answers. There are so many young teachers in the building who don't know how good they have it.

The Choice School site coordinator pointed out how leadership can impede the culture of inquiry.

> Leadership is key to a culture of inquiry. When we had the good leadership, inquiry thrived in the staff and with students; in our current situation with interim leadership, focused inquiry has certainly taken a backseat. However, even good leadership has to be sensitive to who's asking the questions, who's asking for data, and to what end.

Both of these excerpts from our conversations show that having leadership that creates a climate that values inquiry is important. Teachers need to know that they can ask questions, have support in collecting data and use that data to inform the teaching and learning in their middle school context. Leadership is key to providing that support.

Organization and Structure

Another component of effective schools has to do with organization and structure. How is time organized? Who is encouraged to collaborate? How are meetings and planning times spent? What is the focus of staff development? What conceptual and concrete structures are in place for supporting inquiry? The four site coordinators each talked about the structures and systems that have been put in place that foster inquiry in their schools and keep inquiry at the forefront of renewal and an impetus for change. County Middle School's site coordinator gave an example of how a culture of inquiry was institutionalized through the meeting structure in his middle school.

> Inquiry for us is an informal process not a formal process. It started with a grant through the partnership with the university that formed building level teams (BLT). What was unique about this BLT was that the focus of the team was to be instructional issues not administrative issues and that all decisions were to be based in research. So now, all decisions that are instructional are made by this team but only after research has been brought forward. Questions are brought to the table; a task force is formed to examine the question and determine what data is needed to answer the question. When the data is collected it's brought back to the BLT for discussion. With this process, decisions are not based on personal experience but on the findings of the group. Changes are made to bring our practice into line with the inquiry.

What's been most remarkable is that this system has trickled down to department teams and to individual teachers. Everyone in the school thinks about the process of inquiry because the leadership team constantly models its use. So over the last 4-5 years, it's moved from leadership to teacher teams to individual practice. Now teachers own work because they are generating their own data.

The Denver Middle School site coordinator gave the example of how the position of site coordinator itself has become a structure that promotes inquiry.

Teachers often say, 'I don't know about this process, but where do I go for information?' In the position of site coordinator, I have the time to help them find resources…an article or a website. I've become part of the structure for promoting inquiry. Teachers need that help and resource.

The site coordinator at County Middle School related the process of inquiry to the isolation of teaching. "Inquiry changes the structure of the school. Middle schools can be big and unwieldy, teachers can feel isolated, inquiry brings people together to discuss and reflect." Collaboration in the form of discussion and reflection is not always an easy process. At Choice School, the process of inquiry brought out the difficulties of collaboration. Through the structure of protocols that promote inquiry by looking at student work, more collaboration is possible as the data helps inform their teaching decisions.

At our school there are only six middle school teachers.[3] They want to do a good job together but thinking collectively requires trust and time and there may be a fear that having a real collective conversation that explores answers to real problems might conflict with individual beliefs. We don't know how to deal with conflict because we want to protect what we've created. The organization and structures that we've put in place through critical friends has helped us have those conversations in healthy ways.

Another example of teachers using collective time for learning together came from the site coordinator at Creek Middle School.

We have a staff development team of 4-5 teachers who plan our early release time. It is not unusual for that time to be spent thinking about the questions we have, reading and conversing about how to find the answers and change our practice.

In each of the previous excerpts, teachers have become involved in the process of inquiry and were supported by the structures in place at their schools. Those structures include being a part of planning committees, having teacher planning time to look at data from students work and have conversations, voicing their questions as part of the process of setting up collective professional development, and looking at the site coordinator as a resource. These structures seem to give teachers a voice and also the space to make that voice heard as they are invested in the process of research about their practice.

Approaches to Curriculum and Teaching

Each site coordinator was asked to provide examples of inquiry projects and talk about the impact each has had on student learning. The following selected quotes exemplify those that we thought were particularly significant with regard to curriculum and teaching. They each show how a process of inquiry has impacted decisions regarding curriculum and instruction. The County Middle School site coordinator talked about a question teachers at this middle school investigated. Their inquiry was about practices related to retention.

> A number of years ago our school board policy required the retention of children who did not master certain subjects. The leadership team decided to do an intensive search of the literature related to retention of kids. After the review, they decided that retention was not a good thing and did more harm than good. So with that as a foundation, we began to ask, what is mastery, can we ask students to repeat the material the same way, what can we do to prevent retention, how do we change our practices with regards to retention? Again, we went to the literature for answers and collected data about our practices that we felt contributed to the problem. As a result, we changed our practices in a number of ways and our retention rate dropped significantly. Inquiry is just the way we think about our practice. We work very hard to isolate and refine the question to get to answers that help kids.

He gave another example showing the influences of inquiry and decisions made about the math curriculum.

> We've been looking at the issue of positive deviance, a topic that has become prevalent in the staff development literature. We have two math teachers that out produce other teachers in student learning. So we asked, "What are these teachers doing that is different and transferable?" Now we are doing an analysis protocol to look for what these teachers are doing in the classroom and once we get a handle on the things that work, we hope others will start doing the same things.

This example, from Creek Middle School, addressed the language arts curriculum.

The English teachers in our school realized that they weren't defining "proficient" the same way in terms of student work. They have pulled together to not only discuss the issue and create a common language, and as a result they have created curriculum. They have common assessments that allow for interrater reliability and that [further focus] the definition of "proficient." This has also allowed them to use state test scores to analyze change.

Some inquiries created a space for teachers and middle school students to work together. The following example, again from Creek Middle School, highlighted an ongoing science project where inquiry formed the basis of the content.

The Endangered Lake Fish project really got us started in thinking about inquiry. We were part of a national team studying these fish and it involved everyone in the school ... students, teachers in other disciplines besides science, teacher candidates, everyone. It opened our eyes to the possibilities, especially the possibilities of doing inquiry that included students. It informed our practice by seeing how excited kids got about their results and sharing those results with other kids and teachers across the country. This project has continued for over 6 years, it's really been amazing and contagious.

The site coordinator from Creek also told that the process of doing inquiry creates the conversation that indirectly leads to curriculum or instructional examination.

Inquiry for us isn't always about collecting data, sometimes it's just collectively reading a book and having continued conversation about what we do in relation to the ideas presented. We just finished a two and half year study of Ruby Payne's work on *Framework for Poverty* and we've read *Who Moved the Cheese* by Alan Spencer. One thing just leads to another and it impacts what we do and how we think about student learning.

Teachers at these four middle schools have seen the process of inquiry impact teaching and learning decisions in a variety of areas of curriculum. The process has given them a space to examine instructional policies (e.g. retention issues), instructional strategies (e.g. looking at math classes), approaches to teaching (e.g. involving students in inquiry), and ideas about learning (e.g. reading groups). Questions raised were directly related to examining the ways that teaching and learning are enacted within middle school classrooms.

Internal and External Relationships
The conversations we had with site coordinators gave us insight regarding the culture of inquiry and its impact on promoting relationships both

internally and externally. Every example that the site coordinators gave to us included ways that teachers had come together to collaborate about *real* issues. Every day, teachers go into their classrooms, close the door, and teach. There is little time to converse with others, discuss their practice, their concerns, or their ideas. In a school that promotes inquiry, teachers begin to open the doors and literally and figuratively allow others to come inside. The structures and systems examples discussed earlier represent ways that relationships can be fostered. The following are examples that show more specifically the power of collaborative relationships. These sound bites from a variety of the site coordinators reflect how inquiry promotes deep relationships.

- Inquiry has allowed every department to meet with each other; admittedly we spent an hour just chatting. (Creek Middle School)
- Just talking about what they do … and how to do it … why we do it. (Denver Middle School)
- We have a really, really healthy building … inquiry adds to the health of the building. (Creek Middle School)
- By building relationships internally, externally, building better processes … it stops the isolation. (County Middle School)
- Inquiry makes a difference on how we deal with kids … people are happy in their job … free to go to other people to get help! (Denver Middle School)
- Inquiry promotes collaboration; it is contagious in the school; it has become an expectation. (Choice Middle School)

THE IMPORTANCE OF INQUIRY AT THE MIDDLE SCHOOL LEVEL

Talking to these site coordinators makes creating a culture of inquiry seem simple, but we know it is not. As part of the leadership teams in their schools, they have worked very hard to help teachers see that inquiry can be a positive experience and particularly in a middle school, a necessary practice. Because of the developmental needs of middle school aged students, and the need for communication between the teachers that work to meet those needs, a culture of inquiry is a positive influence in finding ways to make teaching and learning more productive. As the County Middle School site coordinator stated,

This age group is so dynamic socially and emotionally that it's easy for kids to slip through the cracks, for learning not to happen because of that dynamic. Teachers have to keep thinking and inquiring so they can be dynamic and diagnose potential problems before they occur.

As professional development schools, each of these middle schools has had some impetus for changing toward a culture of inquiry, but the university does not get all the credit. In fact, the university has to be very careful that it does not overshadow what the school wants to know. The importance of a balance between the university's agenda and the school's needs is evident to us. The importance of this balance can present dissonance for university faculty or it can provide incredible opportunities to look at the ways in which those closest to students think about their impact on student learning. At one point in our conversations, these site coordinators talked about the influence of the university partnership. They provided examples of how the university helped them with organization and structure for inquiry or brought resources or processes for healthy inquiry conversations. They also gave examples of faculty who imposed their own research and created a schism between the school and university. The importance of the university collaborating with the school and working with the teachers and their ideas cannot be overstated. The influences of inquiry, as shown throughout the chapter, are powerful because they are practitioner research. The research, or inquiry, projects were directly related to needs that teachers and students owned in their particular school setting.

What we see in each of these schools is the appreciation for inquiry and the recognition that inquiry can play a critical role in creating and developing effective middle schools. Their school improvement plans, partnerships, curriculum design, instructional practice, professional development, governance, and community all revolve around inquiry. It is what makes the school healthy. The Choice School site coordinator summed it up this way:

> By placing inquiry into the organizational structure of the school provides for an inquiry mentality. It forces everyone to ask what are we doing that causes problems, what can we do better, how can we help kids. Students at the middle level are emotionally and socially volatile, so it requires teachers who are dynamic, flexible, and accepting. The only way to be that way is by having an inquiry stance.

ACKNOWLEDGMENT

Special thanks to Kelli Varney, Phil Sorenson, Flo Olson, and Jennifer Weese for their time and thoughtful leadership.

NOTES

1. The four site coordinators interviewed represent all of the middle schools within our partnership who have been partners with our university for 5 or more years. One other middles school joined this year. The interviews were semistructured. Site coordinators also read the manuscript and gave feedback on their stories.
2. All of our partner schools have their own site coordinator. Some site coordinators work between two schools, some are also instructional coaches, and some are also assistant principals in the schools. These configurations depend on funding available to support the position. The site coordinators interviewed for this chapter each represent different districts in our metro area, but each only works with one middle school in that district. The names of each of the schools have been changed.
3. This quote came from our conversation with the site coordinator at the PK-12 school. The middle school part of Choice School has only six faculty members.

REFERENCES

Anderson, G., Herr, K., & Nihlen, A. (1999). The new paradigm wars: Is there room for rigorous practitioner knowledge in schools and universities? *Educational Researcher, 28*(5), 12-21.

Ayers, W. (1993). *To teach: The journey of a teacher.* New York: Teachers College Press.

Brown, S. R., Claudet, J. G., & Olivarez, A. (2002). Investigating organizational dimensions of middle school curricular leadership: Linkages to school effectiveness. *Research in Middle Level Education Online, 26*(1). Retrieved July 22, 2004, from http://www.nmsa.org/research/rmle/rmle_fall/rmle_fall_art5.htm

Cochran-Smith, M. (1997). Knowledge, skills, and experiences for teaching culturally diverse learners: A perspective for practicing teachers. In J. J. Irvine (Ed.), *Critical knowledge for diverse teachers and learners* (pp. 27-88). Washington DC: American Association of Colleges for Teacher Education.

Cochran-Smith, M., & Lytle, S. L. (1999). The teacher research movement: A decade later. *Educational Researcher, 28*(7), 15-25.

Dewey, J. [1916] (1997). *Democracy and education: An introduction to the philosophy of education.* New York: Free Press.

Goodlad, J. (1994). *Educational renewal: Better teachers, better schools.* San Francisco: Jossey-Bass.

Jackson, A. W., & Davis, G. A. (2000). *Turning points 2000: Educating adolescents in the 21st century.* New York: Teachers College Press.

Kinney, P. (2003). *Advocacy is imperative.* Retrieved July 22, 2004, from http://www.nassp.org/publications/pl/pl_advocacy_imperative_1203.cfm

Lewin, K. (1948). *Resolving social conflict: Selected papers on group dynamics.* New York: Harper.

Lounsbury, J. (2003). *Understanding and appreciating the wonder years.* Retrieved July 22, 2004, from http://www.nmsa.org/moya/new2002/pk_related_ understanding.html

Morocco, C. C., Clark-Chiarelli, N., Auilar, C. M., & Brigham, N. (2002). Cultures of excellence and belonging in urban middle schools. *Research in Middle Level Education Online, 25*(2). Retrieved July 22, 2004, from http://www.nmsa.org/ research/rmle/rmle/article4_april2002.html

Osguthorpe, R. T., Harris, R. C., Harris, M. F., & Black, S. (1995). *Partner schools: Centers for educational renewal.* San Francisco: Jossey-Bass.

Schön, D. (1983). *The reflective practitioner.* New York: Basic Books.

Stringer, E. T. (1999). *Action research* (2nd ed.). Thousand Oaks, CA: Sage.

Teitle, L. (2003). *The professional development schools handbook: Starting, sustaining, and assessing partnerships that improve student learning.* Thousand Oaks, CA: Corwin.

Utley, B. L., Basile, C. G., & Rhodes, L. K. (2003). Walking in two worlds: Master teachers serving as site coordinators in partner schools. *Teaching and Teacher Education, 19,* 515-528.

Zeichner, K. M., & Noffke, S. E. (2001). Practitioner research. In V. Richardson (Ed.), *Handbook of research on teaching* (4th ed., pp. 298-330). Washington, DC: American Educational Research Association.

CHAPTER 10

"JUST PRETENDING TO READ"

Teaching Middle School Students to be Strategic Readers

Penny A. Bishop, Nicholas Boke, Susanna W. Pflaum, and Ned Kirsch

ABSTRACT

This chapter describes the design and findings of an action research project conducted by teachers, the principal, a literacy consultant, university researchers, and students at a suburban middle school. The research team formed an inquiry community (Cochran-Smith, 2002) and employed an action research cycle to address the question, how can teachers help students become strategic readers? Data included student and teacher surveys, student drawings, standardized test scores, and monthly literacy team reports. The importance of local knowledge and of cumulative content-rich reading instruction emerged as central to school-wide change.

Making a Difference: Action Research in Middle Level Education, 185–213
Copyright © 2005 by Information Age Publishing

INTRODUCTION

Ivey and Broaddus (2001) asserted, "Middle school reading instruction is full of mixed messages and inconsistency" (p. 350), when describing the findings of their recent survey of middle school students' reading motivation. In Vermont, students' scores on the English language arts New Standards Reference Exam (NSRE) mirrored a national trend of the downward spiral for students' reading comprehension after Grade 3 (Boke, 2002). Concomitantly, Cochran-Smith urged the educational community to "turn swords into ploughshares," to move away from the violent metaphors of the reading wars, the science wars, the testing wars and the research wars, and toward the goal of building shared local knowledge. Local knowledge is the result of direct experience, concepts, and the perspectives through which the locals see. It is generated when educators systematically investigate questions that emerge from local sites, make the questions accessible to others' critique, and do so in the service of learning (Cochran-Smith, 2002). In response to concerns regarding students' low reading skills, Essex Town Middle School has developed over the past 2 years into an *inquiry community* (Cochran-Smith, 2002), one that is dedicated to generating local knowledge regarding teachers' reading comprehension instruction and their students' reading comprehension strategies through ongoing action research. Specifically, the purpose of this action research was to examine how to teach middle level students to become strategic readers. Strategic readers actively and consciously apply cognitive strategies, such as rereading, analyzing text structure, making connections, exploring inferences, summarizing, and synthesizing (Appendix A).

REVIEW OF THE LITERATURE

Two recent reports demonstrate the need for improved instruction in reading comprehension (National Reading Panel, 2002; Snow et al., 2002). Many children who read at the third grade level in Grade 3 are not automatically proficient in later grades. Statewide test scores revealed that in Vermont, as elsewhere, student reading achievement drops significantly between Grades 2 and 4 with an even steeper plummet for low-income schools (Lipson, Mosenthal, & Russ, 2002). Therefore, teachers must teach reading comprehension explicitly, beginning in the primary grades and continuing through high school (Lipson, Mosenthal, & Russ, 2002).

Research has demonstrated that a teacher's expertise makes a big difference in teaching comprehension; yet few teachers receive adequate preservice preparation or ongoing professional development focused on reading comprehension (Snow et al., 2002). While there is relatively little research on supporting teachers to teach reading comprehension, there is some indication that teachers spend little time actually teaching comprehension (Snow et al., 2002). While school reform efforts continue to center on teacher professional development as a means toward improving reading comprehension, it is also clear that student comprehension is strongly related to student reading engagement (Baker, Dreher, & Guthrie, 2000; Guthrie & Alvermann, 1999).

Reading Engagement

Engaged reading is "strategic and conceptual as well as motivated and intentional" (Guthrie & Wigfield, 2000, p. 404). When students are engaged in reading, they actively apply strategies and are deliberate in their approach. Students show increased motivation and engagement under conditions with teacher support, student choice, interesting texts, productive strategies, and peer collaboration (Baker, Dreher, & Guthrie, 2000; Guthrie & Alvermann, 1999). These studies primarily relied upon utilize paper and pencil response, strategy application, and formal observation. Students seldom are consulted directly, however, in identifying factors that contribute to or inhibit their engagement or success, as the student experience of schooling is rarely placed at the center of research (Cook-Sather, 2002; Erickson & Schultz, 1992).

Cognitive Strategies

Baumann asserted, "There is ample extant research supporting the efficacy of cognitive strategy training during reading as a means to enhance students' comprehension" (1992, p. 162). Cognitive strategy training is the overt teaching of strategies readers can employ when faced with challenging text. While more research is needed, including in whether strategies are more appropriate at certain ages and with different kinds of students, ages, achievement levels, or with different kinds of texts (National Reading Panel, 2002), clearly instruction should not end in the primary grades, and reading comprehension strategies need to be taught explicitly. This awareness and rising concern for the skill of Vermont's young adolescent readers brought Essex Middle School (EMS), as a part of the Vermont Strategic Reading Initiative (VSRI), to grow into an inquiry community; the action research cycle that has ensued is the focus of this chapter.

METHODOLOGY

Theoretical Underpinnings

Action research is often aligned with the interpretive paradigm, which is predicated on a belief that the social world is an emergent social process, coconstructed by those who inhabit it (Patton, 2001). Action research relies considerably on the interpretive paradigm's related qualitative methodologies, including participant observation, interview, and document review. However, some researchers feel that the interpretive paradigm is an insufficient epistemology in which to classify action research (Lather, 1986). Rather, a paradigm of praxis is seen as where its main affinities lie, in which the researcher acts upon certain conditions with the express purpose of changing them. As such, three theoretical perspectives informed the methodology of this study: action research, students as knowers, and reflective practitioners.

Action Research

Several characteristics distinguish action research from other types of research. First is action research's overt focus on including participants as researchers, based on a belief that locals hold and generate valuable knowledge. Participants join as researchers in identifying their own questions and in gathering and analyzing data. This is in contrast to the positivist paradigm, which asserts phenomena can and must be studied objectively and experimentally (Guba, 1990). In action research, the initiating researchers, unlike in other disciplines, make no claims of objectivity, but rather acknowledge their biases to the participant researcher, and view local knowledge as valuable to understanding the phenomenon under study.

Second, action researchers aim to understand explicitly a phenomenon or context in order to improve it. "Participatory action research is aware of its inevitable intervention in the social situations within which it operates and seeks to turn these to consciously applied effect" (Wadsworth, 1988, p. 6). While conventional science often views the change as contamination or bias, action researchers seek such change as the desired outcome, therefore making data collection, analysis, and action often cyclical and integrated, as is discussed within this paper.

Over the years, action researchers have proposed many cycles as a means to capture and convey the cyclical and iterative nature of this type of research. Common to most cycles, and to our process in this study, is the sequence of planning, acting, observing, reflecting, and taking subsequent action. Also central is the integrated nature of the data collection and analysis. For these reasons, we present the collection and analysis of multiple forms of data together within this chapter.

Students as Underrepresented Knowers

Historically, educational researchers have undervalued student perception (Cook-Sather, 2002; Erickson & Schultz, 1992; Shultz & Cook-Sather, 2001). To understand student experience, researchers often infer through adult responses to surveys or engaged adult observers in formal observation (Erickson & Schultz, 1992) with little regard for the student as a valuable source of information about schools and learning. While there are, of course, exceptions (e.g. Cook-Sather, 2002; Mee, 1997), only recently have researchers viewed students as informants into the experience of schooling in a way that invites the critical examination of curriculum and surrounding structures. "Because of who they are, what they know, and how they are positioned, students must be recognized as having knowledge essential to the development of sound educational policies and practices" (Cook-Sather, 2002, p. 10).

Reflective Practitioner

The role of reflection in teaching and learning is attracting increasing interest in recent years. A neo-Vygotskian understanding of the teaching/learning cycle, for example, emphasizes the importance of learners watching themselves learn in order to support the move from reliance on knowledgeable others to the internalization of skills and knowledge. In order for the self-directed speech of stage two of the zone of proximal development to take effect, the learner must develop the ability to watch, understand, and respond to him or herself as learner. The learner must, in other words, learn to reflect productively on his or her own thinking and behavior (Tharp & Gallimore, 1988).

Insofar as reflection applies to the acquisition of reading comprehension strategies, the focus has been on the role of metacognition, or thinking about one's own thinking. Such thoughts can be about what one knows (metacognitive knowledge), about what one is doing (metacognitive skills) or about one's current affective or cognitive state is (metacognitive experience) (Flavell, 1979). Metacognition is most obviously manifested in students' abilities to monitor their own comprehension-quite literally by asking themselves whether they comprehend what they are reading, and then deciding what strategies might help them improve that comprehension (Snow et al., 2002). Reading specifically and learning in general need to be viewed as problem-solving activities requiring teachers to reflect not only on the reading and instruction immediately at hand, but also on their larger instructional goals, and then to draw the students into that process of reflection (Jacobs, 2002).

Furthermore, this recognition of reflection's importance plays a central role in some efforts to teach teachers how to integrate reading comprehension instruction into their content area instruction. The goal, for example, of the WestEd's Strategic Literacy Initiative is to create classrooms dominated by metacognitive conversation, in which

> teacher and students discuss their personal relationships to reading in the discipline, the cognitive strategies they use to solve comprehension problems, the structure and language of particular texts, and the kinds of knowledge required to make sense of reading materials. (Schoenbach, Braunger, Greenleaf, & Litman, 2003, p.135)

However, creating such classrooms is accomplished by first providing teachers with opportunities to become more metacognitive about their own reading and learning, and thereby more reflective on their own larger pedagogy (Schoenbach, Greenleaf, Cziko, & Hurwitz, 1999).

The VSRI has shared from its inception this vision of the role of reflection both in improving students' reading comprehension and in transforming teachers' goal setting, planning, and classroom practice. Originally named the Reflective Reading Project, the VSRI initiates its work with teachers by providing them opportunities to reflect on the reading comprehension strategies they themselves use; on their students' understanding of and ability to use reading comprehension strategies; and on the implications of both for integrating reading comprehension strategies use into upper elementary, middle, and high school content area classrooms (Boke, 2002).

Site and Participants

The VSRI is present now in over 40 schools in our rural state to varying degrees. For the purposes of this chapter, we highlight one middle school in particular, which moved beyond mere professional development to engage in action research: EMS. EMS is situated in a suburban community with a wide range of socioeconomic diversity and, characteristic of Vermont overall, relatively little ethnic and racial diversity. A bedroom community to the neighboring city of Burlington (population 40,000), Essex is home to approximately 19,000 people, many of whom are white-collar professionals employed by IBM, the state's largest private employer. Other nearby employers include the nearby university, hospital, many small businesses, and increasingly fewer family farms. The Essex town community has a median household income of $58,000.

EMS is one of two middle schools serving the community. It houses 550 students in Grades 6 through 8, has one interdisciplinary team of four teachers, seven partner teams of two or three teachers, and a total faculty of 53. All teams are either multigrade or looping, enabling the establishment of multiyear relationships between and among teachers and students. The middle school building is well resourced with a rich array of technology available, as well as many opportunities for arts, music, and sports exploration. EMS has a reputation for academic strength and a history of community support. Yet, like many Vermont schools, EMS has recently endured fiscal challenges, with its school budget being voted down for the first time in many years.

EMS was one of six schools accepted in the spring of 2001 to take part in the most intensive strand of the newly established VSRI. Like all middle schools in the state, EMS annually administered the eighth grade NSRE, which is a national, standards-based, test. Concerned that student reading abilities as represented on the exam were declining, the principal and district curriculum coordinator assembled a team of teachers willing to attend a week-long summer institute and then to work with a VSRI-supplied reading consultant on a weekly basis to support the integration of reading comprehension work into content area instruction throughout the school. This literacy team consisted of a math-science teacher, an English language arts teacher, a special educator, the district curriculum coordinator, and the principal. This group, joined by the VSRI reading consultant and two university researchers, gradually became the team for the action research project described here. As the project grew, so did this team, as described later in the chapter.

Methods of Verification

Action research is often questioned with regard to its trustworthiness, because one of action research's primary goals is change. To help ensure the dependability (Lincoln & Guba, 1985) or trustworthiness (Glesne, 1998) of our data, we employed several techniques. We relied upon multiple researchers with various research backgrounds and paradigms to the same end. The inclusive nature of action research whereby participants are themselves involved in the data collection, analysis, and action provided avenues for ongoing member checking. The use of multiple, varied data sources enabled us to triangulate our methods, thus strengthening the trustworthiness of the data. The primary limitation of the study is typically associated with action research methodology; the findings here are not generalizable to other settings. Rather, the local knowledge is generated in service to the local community.

CONTEXT: THE CREATION OF THE VSRI

Just as low NSRE scores prompted EMS to participate in the VSRI, so was the VSRI created in the previous year in response to statewide NSRE scores. These showed fourth graders performing adequately on both the *basic understanding* and the *analysis and interpretation* parts of the assessment, followed by noticeably weaker performances among eighth graders, and dismal performances among 10th graders, with fewer than one third of the latter meeting the standard on analysis and interpretation. A series of symposia to determine appropriate actions to take to deal with the status of adolescent literacy in Vermont and the rest of the country was held in 1999 and 2000. With the blessing of the Vermont State Board of Education, the VSRI spent its first year creating the *Nine Strategies for Reading Comprehension* document (Appendix A) that framed its work. The VSRI also conceived the three approaches it would take: Strand 1, including a school team and weekly visits by the reading consultant; Strand 2 supporting the work of local literacy leaders through regional meetings and online discussions; and Strand 3, entailing ad hoc professional development work in schools and districts.

As the VSRI shaped its approach to improving reading beyond Grade 3, the International Reading Association's (IRA) *Adolescent Literacy: A Position Statement for the Commission on Adolescent Literacy of the International Reading Association* (Moore, Bean, Birdyshaw, & Rycik, 1999) played a central role. The IRA's position statement, as well as the findings of the National Research Council, draft findings of the RAND Reading Study Group, and practitioners' insights such as those found in *Mosaic of Thought* (Keene & Zimmerman, 1997) and *Reading for Understanding* (Schoenbach, Greenleaf, Cziko, & Hurwitz, 1999) informed the program. Using *Nine Strategies* as a starting point and drawing upon current literature about reading beyond Grade 3, the VSRI developed a tripartite theoretical framework that highlighted what research says about good readers, about teachers who foster good readers, and about schools that create good readers.

The following eight premises about effective teachers' understandings and behavior, related to reading beyond Grade 3, guided the VSRI's work.

1. They encourage students to read a variety of genres both fiction and nonfiction and help them find ways to become engaged in the reading;

2. They understand that reading has affective, cognitive, and meta-cognitive elements and take this into account as they teach;

3. They provide opportunities for students to talk and write about what they read, emphasizing higher-order interactions rather than recitation;

4. They understand that reading strategies can be taught, and integrate this instruction into their content instruction in a holistic fashion, rather than as a stand-alone exercise;

5. They understand the importance of vocabulary knowledge for successful reading, using effective instructional techniques to support vocabulary acquisition and use;

6. They understand the importance of matching reader to reading level to the extent possible, and can support independent-level reading as well as instructional-level reading

7. They are knowledgeable about discipline-specific discourse features and text structure that influence the way their subject matter is presented, and have techniques for helping students use this knowledge to improve their comprehension;

8. They understand that their job is to provide students with the skills they need to learn independently (Vermont Strategic Reading Initiative, 2002).

Teachers as Readers

Framing the entire effort was the essential belief that to transform teaching around reading comprehension, the project had to systematically incorporate opportunities and support for reflection among participating faculty. The first VSRI activity with teachers required that they read difficult text, reflect on their own strategy use, and consider what their students need to approach difficult text. This act-reflect-plan paradigm lay at the heart of the initiative. Engaged in the act of challenging reading themselves, teachers came to understand the challenges and frustrations felt by their students, often eliciting strong emotional responses. Through this common experience, the participants of the VSRI gained realization of the importance of explicit reading instruction and momentum for the action that ensued.

Perhaps most importantly, the VSRI held the broad goal of transforming the way teachers and students viewed the place of books and reading in the learning experience. The ideal transformation was described in a commentary by one of the VSRI codirectors about the program published in *Education Week*:

If the Vermont Strategic Reading Initiative succeeds, several years from now our upper-elementary, middle, and high school classrooms will be very different places from what many of them are today. Teachers will help their students learn how to learn from the materials they ask them to read. As a result, students will become more capable of learning through independent reading in all subject areas. And, as a final result, a heck of a lot more learning will take place in a heck of a lot of classrooms. All because the classrooms will be filled with students who know how to read a book. (Boke, 2002, p. 38)

Initial Goal Setting

EMS was among the six schools included in the VSRI's Strand 1, its most intensive work. EMS sent its five-member literacy team to the weeklong summer institute, working with a reading consultant who would join their team and visit the school weekly. The team committed to a 3-year-long process, designed to gradually bring the full faculty into the fold of integrating reading comprehension instruction into content instruction. The team developed goals at the summer institute that were periodically reviewed. The team determined it would focus first on four of the nine reading strategies: (1) Analyze structure; (2) Determine important ideas and themes; (3) Evaluate, summarize, synthesize; and (4) Make connections. Additionally, the team acknowledged the importance of gathering more information about where the school's students needed most assistance in reading.

DATA COLLECTION, ANALYSIS, AND ACTION: THE FEEDBACK-LOOP PREMISE

The work at EMS, as at other VSRI schools, reflected the cycle of action research: the literacy team established plans, took action, observed, reflected on the outcome, and made new plans. Data informing action served as an ongoing feedback loop. The team met with the reading consultant at least once a month over the course of the school year, and worked with the full faculty through faculty meetings and other vehicles. The consultant helped the team implement the goals and reach other faculty members on a weekly basis. Literacy team members also attended two follow-up meetings per year with teams from other schools, and posted weekly reports on the VSRI Web site. The Web site activity and the follow-up meetings provided participants with new information and enabled participant contact across the schools in the VSRI.

Although the team had established at the summer institute instructional goals pertaining to the teaching of reading comprehension, team members also desired to base these decisions on more information. In order to gather these data, and to better examine how to teach their students to become strategic readers, the literacy team began to collect data that responded to three research subquestions, which follow.

Where Do EMS Students Need the Most Assistance in Strategic Reading?

In order to uncover where the students at EMS required the most assistance in strategic reading, the literacy team used several data sources. Members of the team, led by the VSRI reading consultant, examined the results of the NSRE at the eighth grade level. They did the same with the Terra Nova Standardized Test at the seventh grade level. Further, teachers shared formal and informal observations of their students' reading approaches. At full faculty meetings, they discussed the implications of these data.

Examination of the standardized test scores revealed low student skills in summarizing and determining important ideas and themes, in particular. The results of the NSRE provided a synopsis of implications for instruction, which further underscored this need. These, coupled with teachers' observations and anecdotal evidence, informed the focus of action for the next step in the action research cycle: to act upon this knowledge by incorporating explicit instruction pertaining to summarizing and paraphrasing.

What do EMS Students Identify as Strategies They Use?

To address this question, the team did not, however, rely solely on standardized measures and teacher observation. Instead, the team also engaged students as knowers and informants about their schooling experience. In addition to class discussion of the reading comprehension strategies, students provided their perceptions in two more formal arenas: through surveys and in drawings.

All students in the middle school completed a reading strategy self assessment developed by the literacy team (Appendix B), which totaled approximately 550 student surveys. The team compiled the survey results by grade level. Additionally, some of the teaching teams compiled the results for team level data. Discussions ensued between students and teachers, followed by examination of the results by the literacy team, and further discussion by grade level faculty and teammates.

Additionally, 60 seventh grade students illustrated their strategies, thoughts, and emotions when encountering difficult reading (see Appendix C for sample). Responding to the prompt, "Please draw what you do when you are faced with challenging reading," students drew between one and six depictions of responses and strategies. A total of 200 drawings were collected and analyzed first by the university researchers, followed by other members of the literacy team, and finally by the other teachers at a school-wide faculty meeting.

The use of drawing as a data collection technique offered three methodological strengths. First, its open-ended nature did not suggest experiences or strategies as surveys can, allowing participant perspective to be paramount. Second, the middle schoolers were able to present a particular moment in their schooling history, enabling a helpful level of specificity in the data. Third, it offered students the opportunity to represent their approaches in a nonverbal manner, an alternative at a time when most schools continue to value and cater to verbal ability (Gardner, 1991), and when the topic itself is so verbal in nature.

Examination of student drawings and surveys revealed a primary reliance on rudimentary strategies such as asking for help, looking up words in a dictionary, reading slowly, and rereading. There were substantially fewer examples of making connections and imagining as techniques, and even fewer reports of more sophisticated comprehension strategies such as analyzing text structure, summarizing, and synthesizing. Overall, the findings generated from the students' drawings and surveys confirmed and extended the literacy team's understanding of where to place instructional emphasis.

Which Reading Comprehension Strategies do EMS Teachers Currently Teach?

All of the teachers in the middle school also completed a survey in which they responded to 16 questions based on the nine reading strategies they use when teaching (see Appendix D), for a total of 53 completed surveys. The literacy team tallied the survey responses and determined the top four strategies explicitly taught in the building: (1) rereading; (2) looking for author's main point, idea or thesis; (3) using context to find meaning; and (4) reading more slowly for better understanding. The surveys and the subsequent results formed the basis of discussion on both teaching teams and in full faculty meetings, and participants considered the relationship between strategies reported taught, student skills revealed through assessment, and student-reported strategy use.

For each of these three research subquestions, data collection took multiple forms. There were several means of collecting information about student skills, teacher behavior and needs, and faculty feelings about the work. And, central to action research, the analysis was highly collaborative and ongoing. As the work unfolded, an image emerged that help explains how the system worked: action, informed by the ongoing data collection, was generated through a series of circles (Figure 10.1).

The center circle was comprised of the literacy team working in conjunction with the reading consultant. Together, they worked to carry out the team's initial actions. These included presenting information about reading comprehension strategies to the full faculty, discussing in subject-area meetings how strategies could apply to each field, and conducting surveys: the survey about strategy use among students and the comparable survey about explicit strategy instruction among faculty.

One role of this central circle was to extend its work to the rest of the faculty to the largest circle, which included everyone. A few teachers responded somewhat negatively to the initiative; by and large, however,

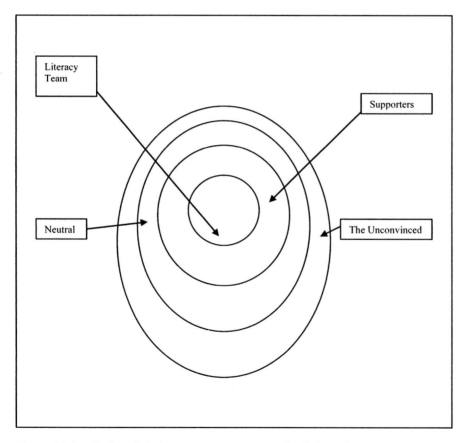

Figure 10.1.   Series of circles represent a system of collaboration among groups.

the response was at worst neutral and at best interested. By late October of the first year, three teachers who had not participated in the summer institute joined the literacy team: two science teachers and an English teacher. This meant that the team now had representation from more than half the school's teams, making the central circle larger and, more importantly, stronger because of its broader representation and the extended range of its voice.

Next, the school possessed a second circle surrounding the first; a group of people interested in, committed to, and willing to work on reading in the content areas beyond the *inner circle* of the literacy team; teachers who were generally supportive of the work. A very important step in this process of solidifying the second circle as a partner in the process was conducting the teacher and student surveys mentioned above, and the dissemination of the findings at full faculty meetings in the fall. About this effort, the principal wrote,

> In early October, we tabulated the surveys, made charts and graphs, and distributed the results to the faculty. Immediately, the storm winds began to blow. "The surveys aren't scientific," began one chorus. "The kids don't even know what these strategies that you're asking about are," chimed another. So, the literacy team broke the faculty into small groups and discussed both the results and the qualms teachers had about acting on the results.... As I listened to faculty concerns some of which were legitimate and significant, and some of which seemed smokescreens to prevent taking action I wondered exactly what kind of Pandora's box we had opened here. As I listened to the conversations that developed over the succeeding days, however, I realized that we had accomplished something important we had gotten people's attention. Whether, in fact, 58 percent of our sixth graders frequently "use my imagination to help me understand (e.g. webs, mental pictures)" versus only 38% of our seventh graders turned out to be beside the point. What our discussions of the surveys and of our concerns about the surveys did was to start the conversation in a way that previous presentations to the faculty, handing out VSRI's lively "Nine Reading Comprehension Strategies" posters and all the rest, hadn't really accomplished. Teachers began to look at their students and what they were asking them to read differently. (Kirsch, Picard & Boke, 2003, p. 46)

The public nature of the survey gave the reading consultant a focus for his conversations with nonteam members, drawing them into the second circle of support for reading comprehension instruction. His technique was multifaceted: greeting a teacher in the hallway might lead to a discussion of what the survey might indicate for his/her classroom; he responded to any request for materials immediately; he offered to visit and model or observe in classes. These interactions served two purposes: first, they showed that he was there to help, not enforce; second, they showed that he was most interested in finding what people wanted, not in telling them what they should be doing. Once this second circle came into being, new, ad hoc voices were added to the promotion of the project, and new possibilities came into being for directions the work might take.

By late November, EMS had four circles: The literacy team at the center, supporters of improving reading comprehension instruction within the second layer, teachers who remained neutral but not closed to the project, and, finally, the unconvinced, who were hoping the project would just go away. The literacy consultant served as the common thread to all the work. He met with, observed and modeled for individuals, both team members, and others; he met with the literacy team and helped shape their plans; he worked with the entire faculty to support the literacy team's work at faculty meetings.

FINDINGS AND DISCUSSION:
THE FEEDBACK LOOP GIVES FEEDBACK

Over the course of the year and a half, the literacy team went through several action research cycles, within an iterative, feedback process. In so doing, the team learned both about teaching reading comprehension and about generating local knowledge to inform school wide change efforts.

Local Knowledge Leads to Local Tools

As the work progressed, the team presented strategies to the full faculty, and the consultant worked with individuals. Teachers, particularly those closer to the center of the circle, came to view themselves as knowledgeable and to rely on themselves, their colleagues, and their students as important sources. Gradually teachers came to create their own tools for teaching reading strategies.

One science teacher, for example, working with the reading consultant, expressed concern that his students did not seem able to determine the main point of what they were reading, and the tools he had found for supporting this skill did not seem appropriate. Together they developed a tool for helping students find the main point, and determine the ways the author used evidence to support that point. The activity entailed coding the text *1* for the main point and *2* for the supporting evidence. When the students tried the activity, they found that there was other information, which then became *3*. A *3* represented information, such as examples and quotations, which elaborates on and clarifies the supporting evidence. The teacher and consultant refined the activity and the tool and circulated them among the faculty. Now the project had an additional resource to share with other faculty a homegrown, reading-strategy-enhancing tool.

In another case, the reading consultant worked with two new teams to support their efforts modifying previously developed materials about summarizing and finding the main point. In addition, he developed follow-up examples and instructional strategies based on his analyses of work done in the various classes. One teacher modified the 1, 2, 3 code; she and her students determined that some articles had *4s*, which were *fluff* that merely made the piece more readable. She and the consultant next met with her team members to report on their findings in preparation for creating a team-wide effort.

In yet another instance, a science teacher quickly ascertained that her students were not ready to summarize yet. By working with the consultant, she focused on helping them find the main point of what they were reading using science-related newspaper articles. In so doing, she realized that the students did not understand the difference between a fact and a concept. She decided that the way to tackle this was to focus on their responses to questions. So she developed an activity in which they worked first on *What?* questions, then on *How?* questions, and finally on *Why?* questions. While she was working on this, the English teacher on the same team was working with her students on finding the main point in expository works they were reading.

Meanwhile, collaboration between two literacy team members was highly productive. Starting with a day-long, in-service on the analysis of text structure, the English teacher and the librarian developed a tool for understanding the structure and evaluating the content of reference books, in preparation for some research the teacher planned for her class. This project followed a similar trajectory, as had the consultants' work with the two science teachers: a small collaboration around a particular project was extended to all other sixth grade classes. An unanticipated consequence of this work was that the librarian gained more insight into what teachers needed and felt she became more integrated into their thinking and their work. The classroom teacher found herself slowing down, concentrating on the *less is more* that makes for effective reading comprehension instruction.

Local Knowledge is Contagious

The foundation laid in creating the second circle paid off dramatically. The work of the project began to resonate with the four-person Phoenix team, and two of its four members joined the literacy team in the fall.

Phoenix teachers decided they wanted to work on the strategy of summarizing and synthesizing jointly in all four content areas. The reading consultant met with them and volunteered to develop a summarizing and synthesizing tool that enabled them to work on this across the subject-area board, including developing examples of its use for math and science. The team undertook the work, and found that not only were the majority of their students unskilled at summarizing, but many also struggled even to find the main point around which a summary could be built. This revelation about student inabilities to find main points and to summarize was borne out by the data examined in the NSRE. Second, when they all used the same tool, the Phoenix team teachers reported that their students' learning grew substantially, as measured by informal observation of comprehension, unit assessments, and quarterly progress reports.

This team's effort provoked excitement that proved contagious. Phoenix teachers presented their experiences to the full faculty at a spring meeting. In so doing, they promoted several things: the importance of determining student deficits and attempting to remedy them; the success of full-team comprehension strategy instruction; and the availability of the reading consultant to do work they might not otherwise have the expertise or the time to develop.

The two literacy team members who had taken part in the Phoenix venture were noticeably energized. The excitement that the Phoenix team's presentation generated made the literacy team bring that same enthusiasm to its own work, altering its bimonthly meetings. The literacy consultant suggested and the team members agreed that at least part of every team meeting be taken up with sharing what team members were learning about teaching reading comprehension. Thus, the second circle was strengthened. Additionally, the first circle was fortified as it responded to its own success by recommitting itself to the work.

Local Knowledge is Strengthened When Team-Wide

Furthermore, the feedback loop provided the team and consultant with new information. The momentum the Phoenix team's effort generated continued through the rest of the school year. This suggested to the literacy team the power of mutual, team-wide goals and action. At the end of the year, the principal met with all teams and instructed them to consider team-wide reading strategy work in their goals for the next year. The work the Phoenix team had voluntarily undertaken with the support of the reading consultant was powerful and persuasive; without complaint, teams constructed goals that reflected this request. At the following summer's weeklong literacy institute, the literacy team set new goals that focused less on presenting generic information about reading comprehension strategies and more on supporting team-wide efforts and generating team-specific knowledge and tools. Working together, the interdisciplinary and partner teams were able to provide consistency and depth in their teaching of reading comprehension, across subject areas.

Local Knowledge is Strengthened by Common Experience and Language

Throughout the first 2 years in this project, the importance of common, building-wide experiences quietly emerged as important to promoting a shared commitment and a common language. At the second, weeklong, summer literacy institute, some of the literacy team members took a long, systematic look at how their textbooks organize and present information. As a result, the team arranged for a school-wide August inservice that involved the entire faculty's going through a comparable process. The second year began, thus, with all teachers, building-wide, reflecting on how their students perceive and interact with what they read. As a full faculty, they continued a focus on finding the main point and summarizing, a need that had arisen as authentic and local, and which was borne out by the various forms of assessment data considered.

In order to share knowledge and experience across the building, the literacy team planned a subsequent full faculty meeting devoted to presentations about the ways individuals and groups were integrating reading strategies into their content instruction. In all, 10 teachers from seven teams made brief presentations about their recent efforts. This faculty meeting was more than a series of presentations, however. Only four of the presenters were members of the literacy team, and only two were members of the original team. The informal but articulate and enthusiastic presentations were clear evidence that paying attention to reading comprehension instruction was becoming an integral part of content instruction at EMS.

Other evidence of shared experience abounded. A biweekly after-school reading group read and discussed *Reading Don't Fix No Chevy's* (Smith & Wilhelm, 2002), a study of adolescent boys' literacy needs and preferences. The group began with 20 participants and attendance remained steady throughout the sessions. The group moved on to read and discuss *Strategies that Work* (Harvey & Goudvis, 2000). They chose this text in large part because the neighboring elementary school was using it for its after-school book discussions, and the EMS teachers acknowledged the importance of extending a common language and purpose across the school district.

Generating Local Knowledge is a Never-Ending Process

True to the cyclical nature of action research, the need to generate new local knowledge is ongoing. What lies ahead for the EMS inquiry community, focused so intently on reading comprehension? The literacy team is moving into the next stage of the VSRI plan, which entails peer observations and other vehicles for enabling EMS faculty to establish deeper and richer collegial support procedures and practices. The reading consultant is meeting with three new teams to help them coordinate their work, as well as continuing to collaborate with individual teachers and continuing to work with the teams with whom he had earlier established a relationship. Several teachers, who remained in *the unconvinced* circle of Figure 1, are talking with the consultant about work they had been attempting to do around summarizing; work set in motion by the foundations laid by the Phoenix team the previous spring. What does this do to the circles metaphor? The lines between the circles are being blurred or erased. There is no longer a clear distinction between those on the literacy team and those not on it regarding a commitment to working on reading comprehension. A new approach to the action research that emphasizes work with existing interdisciplinary teams now characterizes the project; an approach that reflects the centrality of the interdisciplinary or partner team in promoting building-based, middle school change.

IMPLICATIONS AND CONCLUDING DISCUSSION

Two incidents succinctly represent the implications of what can happen when teachers and students pay close attention to reading comprehension. First, a seventh grade student, who engaged in the data collection drawing activity described earlier, reflected on how using reading comprehension strategies had changed her. She explained succinctly, "Now I can really read instead of just pretending to read."

The second incident involves a math teacher. Thinking about her students' improved ability to learn on their own from text, she described, "I realized that the way I was doing it before was crippling my students— they were learning the math, but they weren't *learning to learn* the math." In each of these cases, student and teacher realized the distinction between their previous approaches and truly authentic learning. Authentic learning means internalizing; it means truly coming to know. As Duckworth (1996) posited, in order to understand, learners must arrive at a concept themselves. Learners, she asserted, come to understand by being placed in a situation where they *develop* that understanding, as opposed to being *told* what they ought to understand.

The past 2 years at EMS were rich with learning, both for its students and its faculty. Through their action research into the improvement of students' reading strategies, the literacy team at EMS, along with the consultants at the VSRI, came to four central understandings regarding the teaching of reading in this middle school.

Reading Instruction as Cumulative

First, the process of teaching students to read strategically is cumulative. It therefore takes time. Most students do not become strategic readers because their fourth grade teacher spent a semester showing them how a KWL (a teaching activity that elicits students' prior knowledge of the topic of the text and sets a purpose for reading) can help them predict what is coming next in the text. The fourth grade teacher needs to teach strategies explicitly, the fifth grade teacher needs to elaborate on them, and the sixth, and so on, right up to the twelveth grade advanced placement biology teacher. Accomplishing any one of these tasks takes a long time. It is not something one teaches on Monday, reviews on Wednesday, quizzes about on Friday, and assumes the students will be able to apply the strategy from then on. Students need multiple opportunities to practice, to reflect, and to apply the strategies in new contexts in order for them to become internalized.

Integration as Critical

Second, reading strategies become meaningful when integrated into the content instruction. The history teacher who guides students in finding the thesis of the subchapter provides them with the opportunity to make connections between an isolated technique and its actual application. Students learn the strategies through engagement with real content. Furthermore, integration across the content areas has an equally large impact. An interdisciplinary or partner middle grades team may first teach exploring inferences as a comprehension strategy with *Witness* (Hesse, 2003), and then go on to use the same strategy with a history text. Similarly, students who learn how their science book is structured can use the same skill to understand how their math book is structured and become better math students in the process.

Knowing Students as Learners

Third, teachers need to know their students as learners, as readers. They cannot assume their students have mastered certain strategies. They often set out to teach one strategy, only to find that their students do not have the basics that would allow them to use that strategy. One team at EMS planned to work on synthesizing, yet quickly found that its students were not able to summarize what they had read, which is a necessary first step to synthesizing. Other teachers who wanted to work on summarizing quickly determined that their students were not able to isolate the main idea of what they were reading. One science teacher, setting out to work on summarizing, realized she needed to help her students determine the main point of their reading. As she worked on this, she realized their misconceptions ran even deeper: "They don't know the difference between a fact and a concept," she explained, as she once again modified her lesson plans. In each case, the teachers realized the importance of teaching and reteaching the strategies and of paying close attention to what their students know.

Many teachers discover that the way they assess students causes them to arrive at incorrect assumptions about their students' comprehension skills. If teachers assess students' abilities to summarize information about ecosystems by asking that they memorize the summary that was provided, the students may not learn to summarize. Similarly, if teachers assess students' comprehension of inferences that might be drawn about the colonists' response to British tax policies by asking that they remember the inferences that they were told, they do not learn to infer from their reading.

Authentic Dialog about Text

America's classrooms are filled with *class discussion*. Absent from many classrooms, however, are conversations that involve the actual text: Classes read *Hatchet* (Paulson, 1999) and talk about going hunting with a courageous uncle; students read about the French Revolution and talk about the Three Musketeers. But fewer are the classrooms in which substantial time is spent actually examining what *Hatchet* says about courage, fear, and survival by quoting and discussing what the words might mean and how else the author might have made those same points. Similarly, not many students are asked to compare what one authority says about the reasons for Napoleon's rise with another by comparing texts, statement by statement. Teachers in this study came to recognize the importance of slowing down to ask, "And where in the reading did your thinking about that start? Has everybody found the place? Would you read aloud please?" Classrooms that support reading comprehension do not stop after asking how students feel about what they vaguely recall the authors having said. They enable students to extend text in meaningful ways, enriching their comprehension through dialog with others about what authors say.

The action research conducted at EMS, through the work of the VSRI, fosters real reading, and encourages teaching that helps students—as the catch phrase goes—read to learn. The action research at EMS continues, as the literacy team is poised to analyze once again teachers' instruction and students' use of reading strategies. Knowing one's students as learners; teaching reading strategies cumulatively, over time, and embedded within content instruction; and engaging students in authentic conversations about text can support the kind of metacognition that creates real, thinking readers. By talking, not only about what the authors wrote but also, about how we helped ourselves understand what they wrote, we help students quit pretending to read and begin to understand what reading really means: to make meaning, real meaning, from print.

APPENDIX A

Nine Strategies for Reading Comprehension from The Vermont Strategic Reading Initiative

The VSRI is a multifaceted statewide effort to help all Vermont students become good readers. Nine strategies have been shown to help readers *understand, analyze,* and *interpret* challenging text. Although use of these strategies is virtually automatic for proficient readers, other readers, especially struggling readers, are unaware of them. These strategies are especially useful in the content areas, where expository texts often seem daunting! To read is to construct meaning from print. Good readers read to gain information, to deepen their understanding, and for pleasure. Strategic reading requires that readers operate metacognitively, to think about their own thinking. They do this by asking themselves, "Am I getting it?" Metacognition enables readers to monitor their comprehension so they can determine when and why text is unclear, and then choose the strategy or strategies that will help them construct meaning. These strategies can be used before, during or after reading. Discussion and writing also support the construction of meaning, and supplement the benefits of strategic reading. Good readers are efficient, active learners. Good teachers share their enthusiasm for books and reading, teaching and continually reminding their students of the following strategies.

Strategic Readers:

Imagine, Using a Variety of Senses
(Standards 1.1 Reading Strategies, 1.3 Reading Comprehension, 5.13 Responding to Text)
This strategy includes visualizing a scene depicted in the writing, creating a graphic or three-dimensional representation of an abstract principle, imagining how a substance might feel, smell, or taste, etc.

Make Connections
(Standards 1.1 Reading Strategies, 2.2 Problem Solving)
This strategy includes drawing on prior knowledge to make text-to-self, text-to-text and text-to-world connections in order to clarify and extend understanding of the text.

Analyze Text Structure
(Standards 1.1 Reading Strategies, 1.4 Reading Range of Text, 5.13 Responding to Text)
This strategy includes using transition words, table of contents, subheads, bold print, and text patterns to help discriminate among fiction, nonfiction, comparative, explanatory and other text structures, as well as paying attention to other technical aspects of the author's craft.

Recognize Words and Understand Sentences
(Standards 1.1 Reading Strategies, 5.18 Structures)
The decoding of words and the comprehension of sentences provide the underpinning for successful reading. Strategic readers use: knowledge of sounds, syllables and letter patterns; a range of cueing systems; familiarity with vocabulary and word origins; contextual cues; knowledge of syntax; etc.

Explore Inferences
(Standard 1.1, Reading Strategies, 1.3 Reading Comprehension, 5.13 Responding to Text, 7.3 Theory)
This strategy involves various means of thinking about the text, including recognizing cause-and-effect relationships, making predictions, developing analogies, extending the logic of a piece of writing, and merging known and new information to develop new understanding.

Ask Questions
(Standard 1.7 Respond to Literature, 2.1 Ask a Variety of Questions, 5.13 Responding to Text)
The reader creates questions about the text, such as "What is the author

trying to say?" "How does this relate to my life?" or "Why did the author write in the way he or she did?"

Determine Important Ideas and Themes
(Standard 1.1 Reading Strategies, 6.3 Analyzing Knowledge)
Strategic readers focus on introductory material, topic sentences, and/or concluding material in order to identify important parts of text and to distinguish among subplots, examples, big ideas, and underlying themes.

Evaluate, Summarize, Synthesize
(Standards 1.1 Reading Strategies, 1.3 Reading Comprehension, 2.3 Types of Problems)
Strategic readers pause during or after reading to consider the main points, construct new ideas from two or more pieces of text, and reflect on the quality and relevance of the text.

Reread and Adjust Approaches to the Text
(Standards 1.1 Reading Strategies, 1.2 Reading Accuracy, 3.2 Learning Strategies)
In response to the differing demands of text, strategic readers modify the pace and rhythm with which they read, and take notes to clarify their understanding. As necessary, they also reread, read aloud, and/or underline the text, etc.

APPENDIX B

Checking Your Strategy Use

Directions: Think about what reading strategies you use as you analyze the text. Write the date at the top of a column and check the appropriate boxes as they apply.

Imagine Use all your senses while reading								
Make Connections Use what you already know. (T-S, T-T, T-W)								
Analyze Structure Figure out how text is organized.								
Recognize Words and Understand Sentences Think about meaning.								
Explore Inferences Think between the lines as your read.								
Ask Questions Ask yourself and others questions about what you are reading.								
Determine Important Ideas and Themes Figure out what is the most important.								
Evaluate, Summarize and Synthesize Consider main points, sum it up and reflect.								
Reread and Adjust Read it again, read it more slowly, read it aloud.								

APPENDIX C

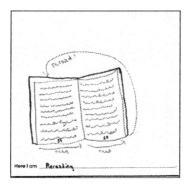

Student A, Picture 1

Student A, Picture 2

Student A, Picture 3

Student A, Picture 4

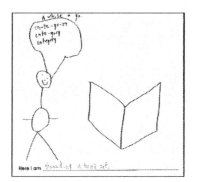

Student B, Picture 1

Student B, Picture 2

APPENDIX D

Reading Strategies Self-Assessment—Teacher Survey

Please answer questions based on strategies you use to support students in their reading

	Frequently	Sometimes	Never
1. I instruct to reread			
2. I teach to read more slowly			
3. I instruct to skim for main ideas and key phrases			
4. I instruct to read the topic sentence of paragraphs			
5. I instruct students to read confusing phrases and sentences out loud			
6. I instruct students to try and figure out the author's purpose			
7. I instruct to make predictions about what may come next			
8. I instruct to look for the author's main point			
9. I instruct students to ask themselves "what do I know so far?"			
10. I instruct to make connections with their own experiences			
11. I encourage students to talk with other readers			
12. I instruct students to pause and summarize what they have read			
13. I instruct students to try to figure out how the text is organized			
14. I instruct to take notes when they read			
15. I instruct how to tell that different texts are written in different ways			
16. I instruct students to use their imaginations to help them understand (e.g., webs, mental pictures)			

REFERENCES

Baker, L., Dreher, M. J., & Guthrie, J. T. (Eds.). (2000). *Engaging young readers: Promoting achievement and motivation.* New York: Guilford Press.

Baumann, J. F. (1992). Effect of think-aloud instruction on elementary students' comprehension monitoring abilities. *Journal of Reading Behavior, 24*(2), 143-172.

Boke, N. (2002). Reading to learn in Vermont. *Education Week, 21*(41), 35-38.

Cochran-Smith, M. (2002, February). *Swords into ploughshares.* Paper presented as the Judith Taack Lanier Lecture at the meeting of the Holmes Partnership, Washington, DC.

Cook-Sather, A. (2002). Authorizing students' perspectives: Toward trust, dialogue, and chance in education. *Educational Research, 31*(4), 3-14.

Duckworth, E. (1996). *The having of wonderful ideas* (2nd ed.). New York: Teachers College Press.

Erickson, F., & Schultz, J. (1992). Students' experience of the curriculum. In P. Jackson (Ed.), *Handbook of research on curriculum* (pp. 465-485). New York: MacMillan.

Flavell, J. H. (1979). Metacognition and cognitive monitoring: A new area of cognitive-developmental inquiry. *American Psychologist, 34*(10), 906-911.

Gardner, H. (1991). *The unschooled mind: How children think and how schools should teach.* New York: Basic Books.

Glesne, C. (1998). *Becoming qualitative researchers: An introduction.* Boston: Addison-Wesley.

Guba, E. (1990). *The paradigm dialog.* Thousand Oaks, CA: Sage.

Guthrie, J. T., & Alvermann, D. E. (Eds.). (1999). *Engaged reading: Processes, practices and policy implications.* New York: Teachers College Press.

Guthrie, J. T., & Wigfield, A. (2000). Engagement and motivation in reading. In M. Kamil, P. Mosenthal, P. Pearson, & R. Barr (Eds.), *Handbook of reading research,* (Vol. 3, pp. 403-422). Mahwah, NJ: Erlbaum.

Harvey, S., & Goudvis, A. (2000). *Strategies that work.* Portland, ME: Stenhouse.

Hesse, K. (2003). *Witness.* New York: Scholastic.

Ivey, G., & Broaddus, K. (2001). "Just plain reading": A survey of what makes students want to read in middle school classrooms. *Reading Research Quarterly, 36,* 350-377.

Jacobs, V. A. (2002). Reading, writing and understanding. *Educational Leadership, 60*(3), 58-61.

Keene, E. O., & Zimmerman, S. (1997). *Mosaic of thought: Teaching reading comprehension in a reader's workshop.* Portsmouth, NH: Heinemann.

Kirsch, N., Picard, W., & Boke, N. (2003). Creating a culture of readers. *Principal Leadership, 4*(3), 46.

Lather, P. (1986). Research as praxis. *Harvard Educational Review, 56*(3), 257-77.

Lincoln, Y., & Guba, E. (1985). *Naturalistic inquiry.* Beverly Hills, CA: Sage.

Lipson, M., Mosenthal, J., & Russ, B. (2002, October). *The Vermont reading project: Standards-based literacy in Vermont.* Paper presented at the Early Literacy Roundtables at the LAB at Brown University and The University of Vermont, Providence, RI.

Mee, C. (1997). *2000 voices: Young adolescents' perceptions and curriculum implications.* Westerville, OH: National Middle School Association.

Moore, D., Bean, T., Birdyshaw, D., & Rycik, J. (1999). Adolescent literacy: A position statement for the commission on adolescent literacy of the International Reading Association. *Journal of Adolescent and Adult Literacy,* 43(1), 97-112.

National Reading Panel. (2002). *Report of the national reading panel: Teaching children to read.* Rockville, MD: National Institute of Child Health and Human Development.

Patton, M. Q. (2001). *Qualitative research and evaluation methods.* Thousand Oaks, CA: Sage.

Paulson, G. (1999). *Hatchet.* New York: Simon Pulse.

Schoenbach, R., Braunger, J., Greenleaf, C., & Litman, C. (2003). Apprenticing adolescents to reading in subject-area classrooms. *Phi Delta Kappan, 85*(2), 133-138.

Schoenbach, R., Greenleaf, C., Cziko, C., & Hurwitz, L. (1999). *Reading for understanding: A guide to improving reading in middle and high school classrooms.* San Francisco: Jossey-Bass.

Shultz, J., & Cook-Sather, A. (Eds.). (2001). *In our own words: Students' perspectives on school.* Lanham, MD: Rowman & Littlefield.

Smith, M., & Wilhelm, J. (2002). *Reading don't fix no Chevy's.* Portsmouth, NH: Heinemann.

Snow, C. E., Alvermann, D., Dole, J., Fletcher, J., Garcia, G. E., Gaskins, I., Grasser, A., Guthrie, J. T., Kamil, M. L., Nagy, W., Palinczar, A. S., Strickland, D., Vellutino, L., & Williams, J. (2002). *Reading for understanding: Toward an r&d program in reading comprehension.* Santa Monica, CA: Rand Corporation.

Tharp, R. G., & Gallimore, R. (1988). *Rousing minds to life: Teaching, learning and schooling in a social context.* Cambridge: Cambridge University Press.

Vermont Strategic Reading Initiative. (2002). *Eight premises of effective reading teachers' behaviors and understandings.* Montpelier, VT: Author.

Wadsworth, Y. (1998). What is participatory action research? *Action Research International.* New South Wales, Australia: Institute of Workplace Research, Learning and Development, and Southern Cross University Press. Retrieved on July 13, 2004, from http://www.scu.edu.au/schools/gcm/ar/ari/p-ywadsworth98.html

CHAPTER 11

COLLABORATIVE TEAM ACTION RESEARCH IN THE MIDDLE GRADES

A Tool for Professional Development

Dan R. Saurino, Penelope L. Saurino, and Linda Crawford

ABSTRACT

The Institute for Educational Leadership stated that a first step toward improving our schools is increasing the professionalism of our teachers. With the enactment of the No Child Left Behind Elementary and Secondary Education Act, developing *highly qualified* teachers is an essential ingredient in meeting the needs of our middle grades students. In the middle school environment where many teachers are working in teams, one tool that might help their professional development is collaborative team action research (CTAR). This report presents our ongoing process of utilizing CTAR as an interesting and ongoing avenue of professional development for middle grades teachers.

Our form of action research is a methodology, a process of conducting research using a particular sequence of research techniques, strategies,

Making a Difference: Action Research in Middle Level Education, 215–237

215

and theoretical perspectives (McLaughlin, Earle, Hall, Miller, & Wheeler, 1995; Saurino & Saurino, 1996). The varieties of action research are as numerous as the topics addressed, and our variety is under the umbrella of collaborative action research. Although there are other forms, our collaborative action research is qualitative in nature, as we are interested in developing new insights concerning our interests, and discovering new approaches to solve problems, rather than addressing a particular hypothesis. The action research we utilize "is study conducted by colleagues in a school setting of the results of their activities to improve instruction" (Glickman, 1992, p. 17). Our research utilizes a particular sequence of steps that we will define as our model of CTAR, yet this paper is concerned with its use as one form of professional development. To that end, we will discuss the background of collaborative action research, the process of conducting CTAR, and reflections on its use as a tool for professional development.

Theoretical Undergirding

The concern we action researchers have for meaning is an important factor in the theoretical orientation of our approach. People use the word theory in many ways. Among action researchers in education its use is sometimes restricted to a systematically stated and testable set of propositions about the empirical world. The use of theory in the CTAR model is much more in line with its use in sociology and anthropology. Theory is more of a perspective, what we as collaborative researchers think of as a loose collection of logically held together assumptions, concepts, or propositions that orient our thinking and research. When we reflect on our *theoretical perspective*, we think about a way of looking at our world of teaching and learning, the assumptions we have about what is important, and what allows our middle school students to learn effectively. Our perspective is guided by a theoretical orientation that helps the data come together in meaningful ways, and enables the research to go beyond an aimless, unsystematic piling up of accounts. The theoretical perspective used in our study is *symbolic interactionism* and is based on a broader theoretical perspective called *phenomenology* (Blumer, 1969).

Most other research approaches trace their roots to positivism and the great social theorist, Auguste Comte. They emphasize facts and causes of behavior (Bogdan & Biklen, 1992). There are theoretical differences between qualitative approaches, even within single schools of thought (Gubrium, 1988), but most qualitative research reflects some sort of phenomenological perspective. Researchers in the phenomenological mode attempt to understand the meaning of events and interactions of ordinary people in particular situations such as teachers and students in a middle school classroom. Phenomenologists do not assume they know what things mean to the people they are studying (Douglas, 1976). Phenomenological inquiry begins with *silence* (Psathas, 1973) in an attempt to grasp what is being studied. What phenomenologists emphasize, then, is the subjective aspects of people's behavior. They attempt to gain entry into the conceptual world of their subjects (Geertz, 1975) in order to understand how and what meaning they construct around events in their daily lives.

Symbolic interactionism is compatible with the phenomenological perspective (Blumer, 1969, 1980), but is more specialized in attempting to understand the process of human interaction, especially the dynamics of group interaction. Symbolic interactionism narrows the scope of phenomenology by concentrating on the meanings, actions, and interpretations derived through social interaction. From the symbolic interactionist's perspective, interpretation is not an autonomous act, nor does any particular force, human or otherwise, determine it. Individuals interpret and learn through interaction and the construction of meaning, an important component in the teaching of middle level students (Saurino, 1998). Classrooms sharing experiences, problems, and background often develop *shared perspectives* constituting *shared definitions*, and these meanings are negotiated through the interactions of the participants. Through these symbolic perspectives we determine what students are learning and in turn the effectiveness of our teaching.

Rationale for the Study

On January 8, 2002, President George W. Bush signed into law the reauthorization of the Elementary and Secondary Education Act, also referred to as the No Child Left Behind Act. The implementation of the bill created new implications for education including controversial definitions of educational research, the potential for narrowing curriculum based on high stakes testing, and provisions that define highly qualified teachers (Cochran-Smith, 2002). An example of a repercussion for middle schools is the result of an emphasis of federal funding's goal of bringing all students reading proficiency to grade level by third grade (Moore, Bean, Birdyshaw, & Rycik, 1999). The government's tripled funding investment in reading requires teachers to use proven instructional methods toward that goal, methods that will need to be maintained at the middle grades level, and with which many reading specialists disagree (Allington, 2001, 2002; Coles, 2000; Garan, 2002). If the legislation succeeds in its ambitious mission, middle school teachers should spend less time and resources on remedial reading programs (George, 2002). However, it will be many years before that scenario can be realized, if ever. In addition, the bill's requirement for annual testing in reading and mathematics for students at grades 3 through 8, as well as administration of the National Assessment of Educational Progress to middle school students, underscores the need to continue to promote the reading and mathematics professional development of our middle school teachers. We believe the need translates to all content areas.

Meeting the Needs of Early Adolescents

The Institute for Educational Leadership (1986) states that a first step toward improving our schools is increasing the professionalism of our teachers. Thoughtful practice is at the heart of teacher professionalism. A defining characteristic of the teaching profession is its use of strategy-based techniques to solve problems and inform decision making. As new and improved techniques and methodologies are developed, teachers must often change their understanding of what teaching is and how teachers teach. One attempt to better understand and improve teacher thinking in recent years is the use of collaborative action research (Carr & Kemmis, 1983; McTaggart, 1991; Noffke & Zeichner, 1987). The next step in collaborative action research explores the concept of combining collaborative action research, used in examining teaching techniques and understandings, with group interactions, used to facilitate new ideas, reflect on understandings, and increase motivation (Saurino, 1998).

COLLABORATIVE TEAM ACTION RESEARCH (CTAR)

CTAR begins with a question of interest, originating often from classroom teachers, but may be an interest of school administrators or university researchers. The question can be general, but most often is specific and directs how the research will progress based on how the research team might go about answering the question. The object of the research is to answer the question or at least to work toward a laudable discernment of how the question might be answered. Therefore, the next step is to take action in an attempt to answer the research question. Reflection and interpretation of the results of the action is part of the data collected, preferably from a variety of sources and collectors to help triangulate the data. Reflection is used periodically to better define and understand how the research is progressing and to determine when the research question is satisfactorily answered. Next, data are analyzed and conclusions drawn, using qualitative techniques (Bogdan & Biklen, 1992). Finally, reflection is utilized again to better define what is learned during the research process and to more fully understand its implications. A written report might follow. After the initial sequence of steps, the research often continues by beginning the process again, and starts with either a new question or a modification of the old question based on what is learned during the first research sequence. In this way CTAR is an ongoing repetitive sequence, each completed series of research steps often referred to as a cycle of research, even though the term is a little misleading since the research never begins again at the same starting point, as an inquiry cycle might imply.

Defining CTAR

The addition of the word collaborative to action research implies that two or more researchers are working together, exchanging ideas and expertise, interacting as they conduct action research in an effort to be more productive than if they worked alone. They meet together regularly to plan, conduct, reflect, and write about the action research they are conducting. The collaborative action research referred to in this study involves groups or teams of researchers usually including teachers, university researchers, school administrators, and sometimes even students. The research is classroom based and is a means by which teachers can examine problems or questions associated with their own practice, and other researchers can learn from the experience. In addition, it helps teachers initiate strategies and techniques to attempt solutions to the problems or answers, and reflect on their results in an atmosphere that provides guidance and methodology. Additionally, current trends in middle level education often incorporate the use of the teaching team approach to educate groups of middle level students. Therefore, a research model designed specifically for educational teams is useful in conducting research, especially teacher research in middle schools.

At this time of strong public concern throughout the nation over quality education, it is significant to note the continued and widespread positive interest in middle level education. Efforts to provide an appropriate education of quality for young adolescents continue unabated with new middle schools springing up and efforts being made to implement the *middle school concept* (National Middle School Association, 1995, 2003) in existing middle schools. An important area of development in middle schools is the formation of teacher teams. By extending the methodology of collaborative action research to a team setting, CTAR is adapted specifically for use by middle grades teaching teams. However, we believe any educational group can benefit from the model. CTAR therefore is defined for this report as a team of educators working together collaboratively in an effort to conduct classroom-based and teacher-centered action research.

BACKGROUND

The original concept of action research came from the work of Lewin (1947) in his study of group dynamics where a change or action, an attempt to solve a problem existing in the group, was introduced by the group facilitator and the results of the change were noted. An important aspect of this work was the fact that interaction among the group created new ideas that often accounted for the eventual solution to the problem or the *results* of the change. Lewin defined his action research as a three-step process of (1) planning that involved reconnaissance; (2) taking action; and (3) fact-finding about the results of the action.

Since the early twentieth century, researchers identified developmental characteristics of young adolescents, and educators have sought to structure schools, curriculum, and instruction to meet the needs of these middle level students. Despite these efforts, the Task Force on Education of Young Adolescents from the Carnegie Council on Adolescent Development (1989) determined that middle schools are still failing many of our young adolescent students (see also Jackson & Davis, 2000). The Task Force concluded:

> Middle grades schools (junior high, intermediate, and middle schools) are potentially society's most powerful force to recapture millions of youth adrift, and help every young person thrive during early adolescence. A volatile mismatch exists between the organization and curriculum of middle grade schools and the intellectual and emotional needs of young adolescents. Caught in the vortex of changing demands, the engagement of many youth in learning diminishes, and their rates of alienation, substance abuse, absenteeism, and dropping out of school begin to rise. (pp. 8-9)

Research supported the assertion that discrepancies may exist between the curriculum of middle level schools and the intellectual needs of young adolescents (Anrig & Lapointe, 1989; Elliott, 1990), and researchers continued to seek practical resolutions to the problem.

The Role of Action Research

During the 1980s and 1990s, teacher educators received many suggestions related to the improvement of education. Suggestions ranged from restructuring existing schools (Goodlad, 1984; National Assessment Governing Board, 2000) and increasing the variety of school curriculum (Goldberg & Harvey, 1983; Pate, 1997) to developing national standards for teachers (Carnegie Forum on Education and Economy, 1986; Jackson & Davis, 2000) and restructuring teacher education (Case, Lanier, & Miskel, 1986; Dickinson & Erb, 1997). As the new millennium began, an important variable in all of these suggestions was the role of the teacher, now mandated to become highly qualified. However, even the best advice did not result in educational improvements unless teachers in the classrooms believed that recommendations could make a difference and that they could successfully implement the changes (Harris, 1989; Noffke, 1995). Crucial to the success of teaching was teachers' sense of efficacy and motivation, a sense that they could make a difference (Ashton & Webb, 1986; Eeds & Peterson, 1991; Gambrell, 1995). Whether or not teachers believed in their own ability to make a difference in student achievement was related to the classroom environment and the learning that took place in the classroom (Wraga, 1997). In addition, in order to improve the education of students it was essential that teachers implement and maintain a supportive environment that was conducive to student learning (Ashton & Webb, 1986; Carnegie Forum on Education and Economy, 1986; Case, Lanier, & Miskel, 1986; Jackson & Davis, 2000). It was in these areas of teacher implementation and efficacy that collaborative action research techniques were especially useful.

In almost every report of an action research project, researchers claimed that action research promoted changes in teacher thinking (Noffke & Zeichner, 1987; Saurino, 1998; Saurino & Saurino, 1996, 2003). University researchers benefited as well; Duckworth (1986) emphasized that she always learned from teachers and saw the endless variations on how they used what they learned in their own teaching. Tikunoff, Ward, and Griffin (1979) reported that every teacher interviewed noted in some fashion that the process of collaborative action research had caused professional growth, greater understanding of important issues, a more powerful level of reflection, and a sharper attention to the complexities of classroom interaction. Henry (1986) quoted a teacher from an Australian project, "Using action research in your teaching gives you a different outlook on teaching and yourself ... you move beyond thinking about content to be taught, to how children learn" (p. 4).

The Importance of Reflection

Because of their involvement in CTAR, teachers began to reflect critically on their own actions and beliefs, and teacher research became teacher development. Through the process of self-conscious scrutiny, teachers theorized their practice, revised their theories in light of reflective practice, and transformed their practice into reflectively informed changes in their behavior (Carr & Kemmis, 1983). An important goal of this type of reflection was for teachers to develop a rational understanding of their practice and how it applied to the transfer of knowledge to students. The increase in understanding was achieved through systematic reflection on both the unconscious and deliberate acts, which constituted the process (Oberg, 1986). Another goal of the reflective process was for the participants to understand a model of team inquiry, that is, how the reflective process increased teachers' awareness of their own practice and eventually their capacity to direct it more fruitfully. Through critical reflection, participants examined the content, process, or premises on which meaning was based. Once identified and tested, previous assumptions may be modified. Cranton (1994) and Knowles (1984) assumed all adult learners have a preference for being self-directed. Self-directedness, as described by Candy (1991), included personal autonomy, the disposition toward thinking and acting autonomously in all situations; self-management, the willingness and capacity to conduct one's own education, which were important attributes of effective middle school teachers.

Current Trends

Trends in some action research have researchers including students as researchers in their methodology (McLaughlin, Earle, Hall, Miller, & Wheeler, 1995; Saurino, Saurino, Jack, Jack, & Craft, 2004) and noting their beneficial effect. Teacher researchers actively engaged in asking questions about their practice, collaboratively implementing actions, and reflecting on their results, are also creating better learning environments for their students. Much of what is involved in action research is directed toward the improved learning, higher motivation, and better socialization of students and of teachers. It is evident that teachers participating in collaborative action research become agents of their own change, and the results of their labor should be better educated students (Oja & Pine, 1983). As a result, teachers can use action research to grow professionally and to develop skills and competencies that empower them to solve problems and improve their own educational practices. When the mystical aura surrounding the practical application of teachers as researchers is removed, they generally discover that not only is it something they can do, but also something they like to do and find professionally and personally rewarding (Glesne, 1991).

In recent years action research continues to become an ever expanding arena, including student tutoring and mentoring (Powell & Mills, 1994;

Saurino et al., 2004), interdisciplinary teaching (Whinery & Faircloth, 1994), integrated curriculum (Burnaford, Beane, & Brodhagen, 1994; Gatewood, 1998), and has been used for a variety of purposes, such as learning more about how students learn (Allen, Michalove, & Shockley, 1993), understanding the cultural milieu of the classroom (Ballenger, 1992), examining innovative ways of teaching (Atwell, 1987), and teacher development (Mills & Pollak, 1993; Oja & Pine, 1987). This increasing body of evidence makes it clear that the process of action research does not simply inform teachers, but also redefines how teachers gain knowledge and their relationship to knowledge generation in the field (Lytle & Cochran-Smith, 1991).

The use of collaborative action research with middle grades educational teams has escalated in recent years (McEwin, 1997; McLaughlin, 1993; McLaughlin & Allen, 1993, 1996; McLaughlin, Anderson, Bennet, Pratt, & Stripling, 1994; McLaughlin, Earle, Hall, Miller, & Wheeler, 1995; McLaughlin & Stripling, 1995; Oldfather & McLaughlin, 1993; Saurino, 1996, 1997; Saurino & Saurino, 2002, 2004), as it has in conjunction with technology (Saurino, Bentley, Glasson, & Casey, 2000; Saurino & Saurino, 2003), and the application of CTAR as a professional development tool (Saurino, Crawford et al, 1996; Saurino, 1997; Saurino & Rice, 1999; Saurino & Saurino, 1998, 1999, 2000, 2001). The positive results from the latter studies of Saurino and his colleagues above concerning CTAR as a tool for professional development led to a desire to return to the topic for a more in-depth look at how the process of conducting CTAR might have affected the professional growth of the teachers involved. The authors interviewed eight middle school teachers and three administrators who participated in at least one of the CTAR research studies since 1996. They were asked to reflect on the CTAR model as it related to professional development and any affects it had on their teaching. What follows is a discussion of the methodology of conducting CTAR and then the reflections of the interviewed participants concerning professional development.

METHODOLOGY

The Middle School Teams

The research teams in the studies (Saurino, Crawford et al., 1996; Saurino, 1997; Saurino & Rice, 1999; Saurino & Saurino, 1998, 1999, 2000, 2001) began primarily with four content area team teachers and a university collaborator. Some teams added specialized teachers such as those from special education, and school administrators attended group meetings even if only part of the time. Throughout the study, teams met about every other week for periods of an hour or more, and an informal atmosphere was maintained. The teams meetings were where plans could be made, questions asked and answered, problems discussed, and reflections expressed. But it was the interactions of the team that were most valuable. The group setting of the teams was very conducive to the generation of new ideas, strategies, and techniques used to initiate actions, direct the research, solve problems, and ultimately answer the research questions. Collaborative action research is of little use if it does not accomplish a goal. A major justification for educational research is the extent to which it helps transform educational practice in schools (Kemmis, 1984).

The Cycles of CTAR

The research process completed in the studies involved four chronological phases and a planning phase for future cycles. The four chronological phases developed from the recursive CTAR cycle are outlined in Table 11.1 as a typical timeline. Phase 1 through 4 comprise the first research sequence of Cycle 1, and Phase 5, and any following phases, might repeat the cycle to gain more information. After the first cycle, the team could modify or replace research questions based on what they learned. One complete cycle consisted of the sequence of steps outlined in Figure 11.1.

As illustrated in Figure 11.2, Phase 1 (Planning Phase) of a typical cycle began in August 2003 with an initial meeting of the teachers, administrator if present, and university researcher(s). The general plan of creating a research question, taking actions, collecting data, and reflecting was discussed and a basic time line for the cycle of research was established. The planning phase ended with the writing of the research question. Teachers generated the research question from their interests, but it was of interest to all. Some typical questions developed by the teams include:

Table 11.1.   Typical Time Frame for One Cycle of CTAR

Phase 1: August 2003	Planning phase of the project and of Cycle 1
Phase 2: September 2003	Baseline data collection for Cycle 1
Phase 3: October-November 2003	Interactive strategies/reflection & adjustments
Phase 4: December 2003	Repeat baseline data/reflection for Cycle 1
Phase 5: January 2004	Return to planning phase for future Cycles

- What are some strategies and techniques that might help prepare our middle grades students for our standards-based state testing?
- What is the impact of tutoring on middle level content area achievement and overall success?
- How might we develop a school-wide discipline plan?
- How might we expand the use of CTAR to distance sites through video teleconferencing technology?
- What are some strategies and techniques using graphing calculators to enhance the learning of our mathematics students in the gifted classroom?
- How can we make effective use of our middle school mentoring teacher programs?
- How might we utilize visual/spatial techniques and strategies to develop an integrated curriculum?
- What are multiple literacies and how might they be added to our middle school curriculum?
- Can distance technology help motivate our underachieving students?

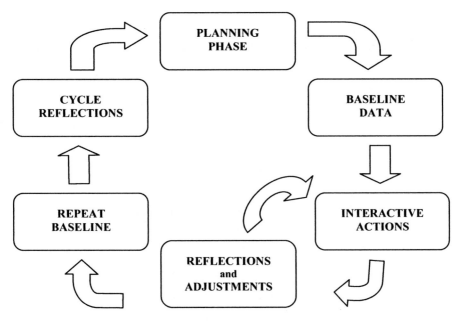

Figure 11.2.   Illustration of one cycle of CTAR.

The second phase of the research was the gathering of baseline data. Baseline data answered the question, "What is the current situation in relation to our research question?" The participants spent about a week interviewing and collecting artifacts relative to the current situation. The information was discussed at the next meeting and summarized in writing.

The next phase was the most time consuming, typically starting in September and ending in early December. It consisted of a minicycle of implementing an action in an attempt to answer the research question, reflecting on the results of the action, adjustments to the action if necessary, and then implementing a different action. The teams always had more actions they wanted to try than time to try them. Often four or five actions would be tried in a cycle, enough to answer the research question without taking so much time that the participants lost interest.

The final phases began a repeat of the baseline data collection, usually collected the first week of December. Participants repeated the same steps collecting the data as they had used at the beginning of the project. The baseline data were summarized in writing and compared/contrasted to the original baseline data at the beginning of the final phase of the cycle, the cycle reflection meeting. The two baseline data summaries were very useful in helping the participants discuss what was accomplished during the research project and led to reflections on the other data collected during the cycle. The meeting ended with a decision whether or not to continue the research with another cycle. Fall cycles typically were continued in spring, often with a modified research question based on what we had learned to date.

Data Analysis

During the research projects, meetings were audiotaped and field notes created from observations and interviews with administrators, parents, students, and other teachers. In addition, everyone in the group kept a personal journal. These data were the source for the written reports that followed. Teachers were included in all phases of the project and some even helped with the writing of the research reports. Data were coded, categories and subcategories established, and analyses utilized case study qualitative techniques (Bogdan & Biklen, 1992; Merriam, 1988). All participants were asked to read the final manuscripts and comment on the reports accuracy in narrating the details of the project. Reflections based on the analyses and the interviews follow.

REFLECTIONS

Reflections from Administrators

Instead of an interview, one of the middle school principals who joined two of our research projects offered to write about CTAR as a form of professional development:

* *Linda:* (All names are pseudonyms except the authors.) When teachers are lifelong learners, students are the beneficiaries. Administrators can help ensure teacher renewal and growth through professional development. Since professional development competes with many other demands on teachers and administrators, it is important to know which of the available models of professional development ensure maximum growth. One such program is collaborative team action research.

   The design of the collaborative team action research model lends itself to professional development of teachers. Teachers are allowed to work in small groups or teams, thus reducing or eliminating their professional isolation. When possible, administrators are involved with teachers, not only to learn, but also to build trust and become a member of their community of learners.

   Effective professional development is a faculty-directed process that encourages the modification of behaviors based on critical self-reflection and evaluation of one's assumptions and beliefs about the targeted area of development (Licklider, 1997). Single-session activities have little effect on educator behavior. Effective staff development should include multiple sessions over an extended period of time (Butler, 1989; Joyce & Showers, 1988; Sparks, 1983). Transformative learning, self-directedness, and multiple sessions underlie the model of CTAR.

   Supporting the preference for self-directedness among adults, the model includes provisions to promote and take advantage of participants' predispositions for all aspects of self-directedness; thinking and acting independently; willingness and capacity to conduct their own education; decision making about goals, strategies, and evaluation of their own development; and pursuit of learning in their own setting. Because adult learners need time to identify, challenge, and modify their beliefs and assumptions as well as their behaviors, the model provides regular sessions over a period of time to give participants ample opportunity to complete the processes of cognitive and behavior changes. Journal keeping and periodic rereading helps team members make sense out of

what in the moment may seem a confusing array of complex interactions.

Professional development is a topic that could well dictate the
success of schools in the twenty-first century. The vital role teacher
development plays in building new knowledge and skills is well
documented, but not often accepted by teachers and administrators who have spent endless hours enduring development experiences. The most common approach to teacher development, one-
shot lectures delivered to everyone in the school, are squeezed in
after school or tucked into half-day sessions once a year. A better
model of continuous professional growth would allow individual
teachers to critically examine their own situations and discover
ways in which to improve.

True professional development is a self-motivated, collegial, and
voluntary process of learning relevant knowledge, skills, and attitudes. Professional development programs cannot succeed if they
are something done to teachers, if teachers are passive recipients
instead of active participants. Teachers need to be able to see that
what they learn produces results in their classrooms and that it
enables them to improve the lives of students. Development programs where teachers are conducting school-based inquiry, evaluating programs, and studying their own practices with one another
and with university-based colleagues to facilitate the program result
in continuous professional growth.

Other administrators also responded to interview questions pertaining to
CTAR as staff development. Transcribed audiotaped responses included:

- *Susan:* I think the thing that affected me most was to see how well
  they learn from each other. The socialization of these teachers was
  great. Communication is such a crucial issue in the schools. In
  terms of staff development it is wonderful to listen to Johnny, it has
  raised some issues in his mind that are personally important and he
  is really doing individual learning. The training ground for his
  development is in his classroom and he has had to evaluate what is
  going on with the kids and what is going on with them personally.
  The reflection aspect of staff development is extremely important
  and one that is not often exercised by many staff development programs. I think this makes a great staff development [tool] because
  they have the theory, and they are actually putting it into practice.
- *Andrew:* It is professional development in its truest form. These
  teachers are beginning to look at things more deeply not only in
  terms of how it relates to their classroom, but [how it relates] to the

whole school. [The purpose of] staff development is to bring about change. Every one of them, and I as well, are going to begin to change things because of this process.

Reflections From Teachers

Responses to the interview questions from the teachers were more consistent than expected and reflected how CTAR had faired as a professional development course. The most enlightening question was, "Would you reflect on changes in your teaching, or your thoughts about the [CTAR] research process as it relates to professional development?" Transcribed audiotaped responses included:

- *Betty:* I guess I changed my mind about the research process we were using. I really doubted the validity of what we were doing initially. Then I realized we were not out to impress anyone else but were here to answer questions for ourselves as a team. I learned that this is a valid process for a team. The team works together to investigate an area that concerns us. We became a team more aware of our students, of ourselves, and have become more unified. We took something we had already knocked around and zeroed in on it, looked at it like under a microscope. I think it has been a very worthy staff development project.
- *Clark:* I really believe that communication is the key to any team project and it has helped us this year having a unifying question to discuss. It has created an open forum for our team to express ideas and realize there are a lot of different opinions about things we have done. I think we have worked with these differences and become closer as a team. I have learned about myself as a teacher and others as well.
- *John:* Over all this is the best thing I've ever done. We used to think we were teaming. I think we did a good job in the past but now we really know how to work together. This by far is the best thing I've ever done as far as actually being practical. Something I'll use and reuse. I'm embarrassed to say that in 10 years this has been the first time I ever sat down with a student and said, "What do you think about what I'm doing?" It is something I never thought to do before. Now even outside this project I ask, "How did that go? Did you like that? How can we change that?" It is like you have a customer and never asked what they wanted. I will look at children more as individuals now, and next year I will individualize more and try earlier to find out which buttons to push on different kids.

- *Fred:* As staff development I thought it worked real well to open up communication channels between teachers. I think we, like students, will do more if we are interested in a subject too. It helps us remember what we learned.

- *Lisa:* The communication between teachers and students has increased too. I feel that I learned a lot about my students.

- *Marilyn:* I've changed my mind about this type of research. At first I thought it was kind of hokey. Even though I really wanted to know the answer to these questions, I thought this was kind of a goofy way of going about doing it. I changed my mind. I think this is the best way of going about finding answers because the only thing we are really concerned with is our situation and us.

- *Joan:* The collaborative team action research model has been beneficial because it has allowed me to answer a question that has relevance to my everyday teaching life without encumbering me with unnecessary requirements in how to go about it. This method has allowed me to gather data without absorbing a huge amount of time. Also, it has allowed me insight into student and teacher opinions and attitudes about the research topic. Thirdly, I think this research will enable me to make better teaching decisions in the future.

One teacher wrote the following, which summarizes the general responses from the teacher interviews in reference to CTAR as professional development:

- *Penny:* My former experiences with professional development were after-school events or work-day events established by my principal or curriculum coordinator to fulfill some school wide purpose. Many of the events were very interesting, and since I had an excellent goal-oriented principal, they often related to something of benefit to the faculty. Workshops usually lasted from 3 hours to one or 2 consecutive days. Of these workshops, the best ones had some type of follow-up that occurred later in the year. Regardless of how interesting they were, most of the workshops did not fulfill an immediate goal in my classroom, or the techniques were forgotten by the time the need arose.

  In contrast, my experience with CTAR was very different. I appreciated the extra time with them conducting the research since recent pressure to maintain the tenants of No Child Left Behind Act has reduced our common planning time to once a week. We decided on our research question together and it was one of interest to all of us. Keeping a journal seemed like a daunting task at first, but I found that if I did not keep it updated, things or ideas I wanted to remember were soon forgotten. I noticed an almost immediate change in my students. They were aware that I was more interested in how they were processing new information and completing tasks during their lessons.

However, it wasn't always easy. At most professional development workshops I could hide in the back, and if the speaker shared something of interest to me, I might try it when I returned to my classroom. If the new idea failed, nobody knew the difference and I returned to my old methods. CTAR was very different. When I came to team meetings I was expected to share the results of my actions, so everyone noticed if I was unprepared. I was really nervous at first when Dan kept asking my opinion about how the new actions were going. I wanted to tell him that everything was fine, but the other teachers were trying them also, and we became accountable to see if we could really make them work, and even improve them. By the time the project was over we really owned the things that worked for us. One time, I tried a new action that fell on its face. I used graphing calculators for the first time, and I really didnot know them well nor see their benefit. I thought they were too complicated for my kids. I was wrong. My students really liked working with them. I learned that I did not need to know everything about graphing calculators, and I even learned from my students. It was incredible. When I thought the lesson failed, it turned out to be a good learning experience for everyone. Because of the experience, I became much more comfortable with technology.

Several years have passed since our team first conducted CTAR. Every year since then we start the school year with a new action research question. The process keeps us trying new strategies and techniques we find by reading research journals and attending conferences. We reflect in our journals and compare notes at our weekly team meetings. Our process is not formal and we do not write research reports, but I believe we continue to grow professional. We have seen achievement gains steadily rise for students who come through our classes. Finally and most important of all, I believe that we understand our students needs better, and are more effective team members and mentors for new teachers who join our team. It is the students who benefit the most.

CONCLUSIONS

Evidently, CTAR can enhance professional development, classroom instruction, and student learning. The process of the CTAR model facilitates communication among teachers, administrators, and university personnel. It is a process that allows educators to take control of their own professional development. Teachers actively learning from experiences, making observations about processes that worked well or did not work, recording data, thoughts, feelings, attitudes, and decisions, and making inferences from their reflections bring about true professional growth.

Final Thoughts

CTAR develops teachers and administrators in schools who know a research process and can continue to use it because of it cyclical structure. It can be one tool in a comprehensive program for professional development. It can be used with a significant percentage of teachers and although it takes more time than most currently used methods, it offers many benefits. More research is needed to fully understand the implications of the CTAR model as a professional development tool, but initial indications are that it can be an interesting and effective way for teachers, administrators, and university researchers to learn more about the inspiring field of middle level education.

REFERENCES

Allen, J., Michalove, B., & Shockley, B. (1993). *Engaging children.* Portsmouth, NH: Heineman.

Allington, R. L. (2001). *What really matters for struggling readers: Designing research-based programs.* New York: Addison-Wesley.

Allington, R. L. (2002). *Big brother and the national reading curriculum: How ideology trumped evidence.* Portsmouth, NH: Heinemann.

Anrig, G. R., & Lapointe, A. E. (1989). What we know about what students don't know. *Educational Leadership, 47*(3), 4-9.

Ashton, P. T., & Webb, R. B. (1986). *Making a difference: Teachers' sense of efficacy and student achievement.* New York: Longman.

Atwell, N. (1987). *In the middle: Writing, reading, and learning with adolescents.* Portsmouth, NH: Heinemann.

Ballenger, C. (1992). Because you like us: The language of control. *Harvard Educational Review, 62*(2), 199-207.

Blumer, H. (1969). *Symbolic interactionism: Perspective and method.* Englewood Cliffs, NJ: Prentice Hall.

Blumer, H. (1980). Comment, Mead, & Blumer: The convergent methodological perspectives of social behaviorism and symbolic interaction. *American Sociological Review, 45*, 409-419.

Bogdan, R., & Biklen, S. (1992). *Qualitative research for education: An introduction to theory and methods* (2nd ed.). Boston: Allyn & Bacon.

Burnaford, G., Beane, J., & Brodhagen, B. (1994). Teacher action research: Inside an integrative curriculum. *Middle School Journal, 26*(2), 5-13.

Butler, J. A. (1989). *A review of adult learning theory and staff development research.* Washington, DC: Office of Educational Research and Improvement.

Candy, P. (1991). *Self-direction for lifelong learning.* San Francisco: Jossey-Bass.

Carnegie Council on Adolescent Development. (1989). *Turning points: Preparing American youth for the 21st century.* New York: Carnegie Corporation of New York.

Carnegie Forum on Education and Economy. (1986). *A nation prepared: Teachers for the 21st century.* New York: Author.

Carr, W., & Kemmis, S. (1983). *Becoming critical: Knowing through action research.* Geelong, Australia: Deakin University Press.

Case, C. W., Lanier, J. E., & Miskel, C. G. (1986). The Holmes group report: Impetus for gaining professional status for teachers. *Journal of Teacher Education, 37*(3), 36-43.

Cochran-Smith, M. (2002). What a difference a definition makes: Highly qualified teachers, scientific research and teacher education. *Journal of Teacher Education, 53*(3), 187-189.

Coles, G. (2000). *Misreading reading: The bad science that hurts children.* Portsmouth, NH: Heinemann.

Cranton, P. (1994). Self-directed and transformative instructional development. *Journal of Higher Education, 6*, 726-44.

Dickinson, T. J., & Erb, T. O. (Eds.). (1997). *Teaming in the middle schools.* Columbus, OH: National Middle School Association.

Douglas, J. (1976). *Investigative social research.* Beverly Hills, CA: Sage.

Duckworth, E. (1986). Teaching as research. *Harvard Educational Review, 56*(4), 481-495.

Eeds, M., & Peterson, R. (1991). Teacher as curator: Learning to talk about literature. *The Reading Teacher, 45*(2), 118-126.

Elliott, J. (1990). Teachers as researchers: Implications for supervision and for teacher education. *Teaching and Teacher Education, 6*(1), 1-26.

Gatewood, T. (1998). How valid is integrated curriculum in today's middle schools? *Middle School Journal, 29*(4), 38-41.

Gambrell, L. B. (1995). Motivation matters. In W. M. Linek & E. G. Sturtevant (Eds.), *Generations of literacy: Seventeenth yearbook of the college reading associations* (pp. 2-24). Harrisonburg, VA: College Reading Association.

Garan, E. M. (2002). *Resisting reading mandates: How to triumph with the truth.* Portsmouth, NH: Heinemann.

Geertz, C. (1975). On the nature of anthropological understanding. *American Scientist, 63*(1), 47-53.

George, P. (2002). *No child left behind: Implications for middle level leaders.* Westerville, OH: National Middle School Association.

Glesne, C. E. (1991). Yet another role? The teacher as researcher. *Action in Teacher Education, 13*(1), 7-13.

Glickman, C. D. (1992, September). The essence of school renewal: The prose has begun. *Educational Leadership, 50*(1), 7-24.

Goldberg, M., & Harvey, J. (1983). A nation at risk: The report of the national commission on excellence in education. *Phi Delta Kappan, 64*(1), 73-77.

Goodlad, J. I. (1984). *A place called school: Prospects for the future.* New York: McGraw-Hill.

Gubrium, J. (1988). *Analyzing field reality.* Beverly Hills, CA: Sage.

Harris, B. (1989). *Inservice education for staff development.* Boston: Allyn & Bacon.

Henry, J. (1986). *Transitions in action research projects at Deakin, 1979-85.* Paper presented at the 4th Generation Action Research Conference, Geelong, Australia.

Institute for Educational Leadership. (1986). *School dropouts: Everybody's problem.* Washington, DC: Author.

Jackson, A. W., & Davis, G. A. (2000). *Turning points 2000: Educating adolescents in the 21st century.* New York: Teachers College Press.

Joyce, B. R., & Showers, B. (1988). *Power in staff development through research on training.* Alexandria, VA: Association for Supervision and Curriculum Development.

Kemmis, S. (1984). Educational research is research for education. *Australian Educational Researcher, 11*(1), 28-38.

Knowles, M. (1984). *Andragogy in action: Applying modern principles of adult learning.* San Francisco: Jossey-Bass.

Lewin, K. (1947). Frontiers in group dynamics. *Human Relations, 1*, 5-41, 143-153.

Licklider, B. L. (1997). Breaking ranks: Changing the inservice institution. *NASSP Bulletin, 81*(585), 9-21.

Lytle, S. L., & Cochran-Smith, M. (1991, March). Teacher research as a way of knowing. *National Writing Project Quarterly, 13*, 22-37.

McEwin, C. K. (1997). Trends in the utilization of interdisciplinary team organization in the middle schools. In T. S. Dickinson & T. O. Erb (Eds.), *Teaming in middle schools* (pp. 313-324). Columbus, OH: National Middle School Association.

McLaughlin, H. J. (1993, April). *Connections and directions: The difficulties of entry into a team action research project about student learning.* Paper presented at the International Conference on Teacher Research, Athens, GA.

McLaughlin, H. J., & Allen, J. (1996, February). *Action research collaborations as zones of proximal development.* Paper presented at the Vygotsky Centennial Conference, a meeting of the Research Special Interest Group, National Council of Teachers of English, Chicago.

McLaughlin, H. J., & Allen, M. (1993, April). *How can we hear from our students? A team action research project about student learning.* Paper presented at the annual meeting of the American Educational Research Association, Portland, OR.

McLaughlin, H. J., Anderson, J., Bennett, P., Pratt, C., & Stripling, B. (1994). Different ages and learning stages: Evaluating learning in a multiage team. *The MAGnet Newsletter, 3*(1), 3-4.

McLaughlin, H. J., Earle, K., Hall, M., Miller, V., & Wheeler, M. (1995). Hearing from our students: Team action research in a middle school. *Middle School Journal, 26*(3), 7-13.

McLaughlin, H. J., & Stripling, B. (1995, April). *Learning across the ages: A study of middle school students' achievement and attitudes in a multiage team.* Paper presented at the annual meeting of the American Educational Research Association, San Francisco.

McTaggart, R. (1991). Principles for participatory action research. *Adult Education Quarterly, 41*(3), 168-187.

Merriam, S. B. (1988). *Case study research in education: A qualitative approach.* San Francisco: Jossey-Bass.

Mills, R. F., & Pollak, J. P. (1993). Collaboration and teacher change in the middle school. *Clearing House, 66*(5), 302-304.

Moore, D. W., Bean, T. W., Birdyshaw, D., & Rycik, J. A. (1999). Reinventing adolescent literacy: A position statement. *Journal of Adolescent and Adult Literacy, 43*(5), 97-112.

National Assessment Governing Board. (2000). *Reading framework for the National Assessment of Educational Progress: 1992–2000.* Washington, DC: Author.

National Middle School Association. (1995). *This we believe: Developmentally responsive middle level schools.* Columbus, OH: Author.

National Middle School Association. (2003). *This we believe: Successful schools for young adolescents.* Westerville, OH: Author.

Noffke, S. E. (1995). Action research and democratic schooling: Problematics and potentials. In S. E. Noffke & R. B. Stevenson (Eds.), *Educational action research: Becoming practically critical* (pp. 1-10). New York: Teachers College Press.

Noffke, S. E., & Zeichner, K. W. (1987, April). *Action research and teacher thinking.* Paper presented at the annual meeting of the American Educational Research Association, Washington, DC.

Oberg, A. (1986). Using construct theory as a basis for research into professional development. *Journal of Curriculum Studies, 19*(1), 55-65.

Oja, S. N., & Pine, G. J. (1983). *A two year study of teachers' stages of development in relationship to collaborative action research in schools: Final report.* Rockridge, NH: University of New Hampshire.

Oja, S. N., & Pine, G. J. (1987). Collaborative action research: Teachers' stages of development and school contexts. *Peabody Journal of Education, 64*(1), 96-115.

Oldfather, P., & McLaughlin, H. J. (1993, Fall). Gaining and losing voice: A longitudinal study of students' continuing impulse to learn across elementary and middle school contexts. *Research in Middle Level Education, 14*(3), 47-63.

Pate, P. E. (1997). Teaming and decision making. In T. S. Dickinson, & T. O. Erb (Eds.), *Teaming in middle schools* (pp. 425-442). Columbus, OH: National Middle School Association.

Powell, R. R., & Mills, R. (1994). Five types of mentoring build knowledge on interdisciplinary teams. *Middle School Journal, 26*(2), 24-30.

Psathas, G. (1973). *Phenomenological sociology.* New York: Wiley.

Rando, W. C., & Menges, R. J. (1991). How practice is shaped by personal theories. In R. J. Menges & M. D. Svenicki (Eds.), *College Teaching: From Theory to*

Practice. New Directions for Teaching and Learning (pp. 178-192). San Francisco: Jossey-Bass.

Saurino, D. R. (1996, April). *Teacher team collaborative action research.* Paper presented at the annual meeting of the American Educational Research Association, New York.

Saurino, D. R. (1997, March). *Collaborative team action research: A model for staff development.* Paper presented at the annual meeting of the American Educational Research Association, Chicago.

Saurino, D. R. (1998). A qualitative study of middle school collaborative team action research Unpublished doctoral dissertation, University of Georgia.

Saurino, D. R., Bentley, M. L., Glasson, G., & Casey, D. (2000). Urban and rural students collaborate: Video teleconferencing technology in science teacher preparation. *Science Education International, 11*(3), 19-25.

Saurino, D. R., Crawford, L., Cornelius, C., Dillard, V., French, J., McSwain, M., Murray, M., Saurino, P. L., Upton, J. R., & Walraven, J. (1996, November). *Teacher team collaborative action research as staff development.* Paper presented at the annual meeting of the National Middle School Association, Baltimore.

Saurino, D. R., & Rice, W. R. (1999, March). *Preparing middle grades mathematics students for SOL testing: A collaborative team action research approach.* Paper presented at the annual meeting of the Virginia Middle School Association, Norfolk.

Saurino, D. R., & Saurino, P. L. (1996). Collaborative teacher research: An investigation of alternative assessment. *Current Issues in Middle Level Education, 5*(2), 50-72.

Saurino, D. R., & Saurino, P. L. (1998, November). *Developing a School-wide Discipline Plan: A collaborative team action research approach.* Paper presented at the annual meeting of the National Middle School Association, Denver.

Saurino, D. R., & Saurino, P. L. (1999, March). *Making effective use of mentoring teacher programs: A collaborative group action research approach.* Paper presented at the annual meeting of the National Association for Research in Science Teaching, Boston.

Saurino, D. R., & Saurino, P. L. (2000, April). *Strategies and techniques using graphing calculators to enhance the learning of mathematics applications in the gifted classroom: A collaborative group action research approach.* Paper presented at the annual meeting of the American Educational Research Association, New Orleans.

Saurino, D. R., & Saurino, P. L. (2002, April). *Utilizing visual/spatial techniques and strategies to develop an integrated curriculum: A collaborative interactive group action research approach.* Paper presented at the annual conference of the American Educational Research Association, New Orleans.

Saurino, D. R., & Saurino, P. L. (2003, April). *Motivating our underachieving students: Collaborative interactive group action research through distance technology.* Paper presented at the annual conference of the American Educational Research Association, Chicago.

Saurino, D. R., & Saurino, P. L. (2004, April). *The addition of multiple literacies to the middle school curriculum.* Paper presented at the annual conference of the American Educational Research Association, San Diego.

Saurino, P. L., & Saurino, D. R. (2001, April). *A constructivist approach to gifted and talented curriculum strategies and techniques: A collaborative group action research approach.* Paper presented at the annual conference of the American Educational Research Association, Seattle.

Saurino, P. L., Saurino, D. R., Jack, D. C., Jack, T. E., & Craft, J. W. (2004, April). *The impact of tutoring on middle level content area achievement and overall success.* Paper presented at the annual conference of the American Educational Research Association, San Diego.

Sparks, G. M. (1983). Synthesis of research on staff development for effective teaching. *Educational Leadership, 3*(2), 65-72.

Tikunoff, W. J., Ward, B. A., & Griffin, G. A. (1979). *Interactive research and development on teaching study: Final report.* San Francisco: Far West Laboratory for Educational Research and Development.

Whinery, B. L., & Faircloth, C. V. (1994). The change process and interdisciplinary teaching. *Middle School Journal, 26*(2), 31-34.

Wraga, W. G. (1997). Interdisciplinary team teaching: Sampling the literature. In T. S. Dickinson & T. O. Erb (Eds.), *Teaming in middle schools* (pp. 325-344). Columbus, OH: National Middle School Association.

CHAPTER 12

FRAMING AN URBAN SCHOOL-UNIVERSITY PARTNERSHIP

A Critical Analysis

Kathleen F. Malu

ABSTRACT

This chapter reports on a 5-year urban school-university partnership. This report begins with background information on the setting for this partnership and the participants. Next, the author presents the visions and activities of five principle participants: the university dean, the school principal, one eighth grade teacher, one student teacher, and the teacher educator/ university liaison (the author). The outcomes of this partnership compared with the National Council for Accreditation of Teacher Education (NCATE) standards for professional development schools (PDS) frame the analysis. The chapter concludes with recommendations for those who may seek to engage in school-university partnerships at the middle level.

The American public continues to call for higher educational standards and greater student achievement. State and local middle level educational

Making a Difference: Action Research in Middle Level Education, 239–260

leaders seek support and guidance from a variety of sources including faculty and administrators in teacher education programs at universities. At the same time, these faculty and administrators must respond to the federal call to prepare highly qualified teachers. University faculty and administrators frequently look to local schools to serve as clinical sites where student teachers may receive effective, hands-on preparation.

In this chapter, I present the setting, participants, and the methods I used to analyze a variety of data that I gathered during a 5-year school-university partnership. I report on the visions and activities at the middle level of five principle participants in this partnership. These participants include a university dean,[1] a school principal, an eighth grade teacher, one student teacher, and me, the teacher educator/university liaison for this partnership. I highlight the outcomes of this partnership and compare them with the NCATE PDS standards. Recommendations for future partnerships conclude the chapter.

THE SETTING

This partnership was created at a public K-8 school in the city of Paterson, New Jersey. One of the first industrial centers in the United States, Paterson was founded in 1791 and named after William Paterson (1745-1896), a New Jersey governor and associate justice of the Supreme Court of the United States. By the nineteeth century, Paterson, nicknamed the *Silk City*, was a major center for the production of textiles, including silk goods. It was also an important industrial center, manufacturing Colt revolvers, Roger steam locomotives, Holland submarines, and railroad cars. During World War II, Paterson produced aircraft engines.

Today, this third largest city in New Jersey with an approximate population of 150,000 (United States Census, 2000) has a high mobility and unemployment rate. Much of the middle class has left. Nicknamed an *entry-level city*, Paterson has immigrants from Central America, the Caribbean, and the Middle East who speak a variety of languages including Spanish and Arabic.

In 1991, the New Jersey State Department of Education assumed responsibility and control of the Paterson school district because this district did not meet state-established goals in student performance and management. The elected nine-member school board had limited responsibilities and no decision-making responsibilities in terms of budget or personnel. These areas were, and continue to be today, the purview of the state-appointed superintendent. This school district has approximately 25,000 students of which 82% qualify for federally funded free and reduced lunch programs.

The school in this report is a Paterson public K-8 school with a yearly average of 65 school staff members including 35 classroom teachers. The school staff was 57% European American, 27% African American, 13% Hispanic/Latino, and 3% Arab American.

Throughout the partnership, the school had approximately 700 children and a class size that remained constant at approximately 24 children. The Hispanic/Latino population was 57%. The African American population was 30% and 13% of the children were European American. Approximately 85% of the children qualified for the federal free lunch program and there was a 25% mobility rate. Language statistics reveal further diversity. In 38% of the homes, children spoke English. Children spoke Spanish in 47% of the homes; Arabic, in 9% of the homes and Turkish in 2%. In 4% of the homes, children spoke other languages such as Bengali, Greek, and Russian.

The school building has three floors with wings that give the school an H shaped floor plan. One wing houses three sixth, fifth, and fourth grade classes. In another wing, three classes at each of the seventh and eighth grade levels comprise the middle level, the focus of this report. Teaching at this level was departmentalized with content teachers responsible for instruction in both grades. There was one teacher each for reading, language arts, social studies, mathematics, science, and computer instruction. Children changed classes at 45-minute intervals.

William Paterson University of New Jersey (WPUNJ), the university involved in this partnership, also takes its name from the state's famous citizen, William Paterson. WPUNJ, originally called the Paterson Normal School, began training teachers in 1855. The campus is located approximately five miles from Paterson and 20 miles from New York City. It has approximately 11,000 undergraduate and graduate students. The College of Education, one of five colleges that comprise WPUNJ, is accredited by NCATE.

THE METHODS

The analysis of this qualitative action research project draws upon the following data sources: Official and informal meeting minutes, notes, and reports; teacher and student artifacts including lesson plans, student teaching reports, student essays, and anthologies; my personal-professional journal entries, calendar, and teaching artifacts; and the self-reported narratives of the five principle partnership participants (Agard-Jones, Jenkins, Malu, & Windley, 2003).

To analyze these data, I used discourse analysis (Coulthard, 1985; McCarthy, 1991) and identified patterns within and across the data sources. I compared these patterns with larger pieces of data and then refined and changed them as they matched or mismatched larger data pools until I could account for all pieces of data within the patterns (Brause, 1991; Guba & Lincoln, 1987). Such cyclical and on-going analysis to identify patterns within and across data is typical of qualitative, action research (Arhar, Holly, & Kasten, 2001; Hubbard & Powers, 1999).

Three patterns emerged within and across the data sources. These patterns included the visions of the participants, the activities of the participants and the outcomes of the partnership. An explanation of each of these patterns follows.

THE VISIONS

The five participants expressed visions for this partnership and their visions reflected the roles and responsibilities that they held in their professional settings. Similar among all participants was a vision for improved student achievement. The university participants wanted to improve student learning. The school participants sought to improve test scores. Participants' visions follow.

The dean conceived the idea of a partnership. He believed that in traditional school-university relationships, university faculty often entered school settings and instructed the school faculty and administration in what they needed to do. Or, in the case of WPUNJ, individual faculty created informal contacts with individual schools. With the recent state control of the Paterson school district, the dean reasoned that WPUNJ was in a unique position to offer assistance since it, too, was a state institution and within close proximity to Paterson.

The dean's vision called for changing the way WPUNJ and the Paterson school district supported excellence in the preparation of teachers and the teaching and learning of Paterson's children. The dean wanted the schools to articulate their needs, not the university. At an initial meeting with the Paterson superintendent, the dean asked, "What do you need from us?" With such an approach, the dean reasoned, the schools might be able to identify their needs. The superintendent identified a number of schools that he wanted the university to work with, one of which was this K-8 school.

A second component of the dean's vision was to prepare teachers who had knowledge of diversity and the ability to work successfully in urban schools. The school, an extremely diverse community, offered student teachers such experiences.

Recently appointed, the school principal was a doctoral student in a program where a newly hired WPUNJ faculty member was an adjunct instructor. This faculty member would eventually serve on the principal's dissertation committee. The Paterson superintendent chose the principal because he wanted someone "who could turn the school around." In the previous 3 years, the school had three principals and the school community experienced the pressures that came with poor test scores and unstable leadership. Many children were disrespectful, disruptive, and underachieving and many parents brought their complaints to school board meetings. The principal's vision followed the superintendent's lead and focused on turning the school around.

The WPUNJ faculty member introduced the principal to the notion of the school-university partnership. It was the principal's understanding that participation in this partnership would require meetings to create committees to identify school goals, involve training of the school faculty and opportunities for school faculty to receive technical assistance from the university, and include an invitation for the school to enter into a PDS relationship with WPUNJ.

The principal reported that her staff wanted whatever assistance WPUNJ might provide and they believed that access to university professors would greatly help them. The principal also expressed the need for help to improve student test scores. This focus on test scores became heightened when the No Child Left Behind Act (NCLB) began to impact on education and the curriculum in Paterson.

The eighth grade teacher was a graduate student at WPUNJ and attended two of my graduate courses during the first 2 years of the partnership. She reported her vision within the context of her master's thesis work. The eighth grade teacher wanted to "bring back the enjoyment of learning and reading...and improve the children's reading scores, one of the priorities in the district."

The student teacher, who was a student in my undergraduate reading methods class, recognized her unique position as a native of Paterson:

> As a Patersonian, I am well aware of the social and economic issues that challenge our Paterson students.... The children of Paterson are vested with many talents and are destined to do great things. It is my responsibility as a teacher to ... bring out those talents in my students.

The student teacher wanted to become the best teacher she could be for the children of Paterson.

In my role as teacher educator/university liaison, I hoped to prepare student teachers who would eventually make their careers in Paterson. I envisioned collaborating with school faculty and children to improve and enhance the children's learning. I wanted to be a facilitator, guide, resource, and kindred spirit. I hoped to help teachers and WPUNJ student teachers explore more deeply the meaning of teaching and learning. I wanted to guide and support them in their work. I wanted to use my knowledge and expertise to assist in puzzling through classroom challenges and dilemmas. I expected to be able to share my expertise in inquiry-based, hands-on learning so that together we could improve children's learning.

THE ACTIVITIES

The five participants engaged in numerous varied activities that reflected the roles of dean, principal, teacher, and student. I have grouped the activities for each participant based on the similarities I found within the activities. Examples of each participant's activities follow.

To support this partnership, the dean undertook leadership-type activities including conceiving of ideas, facilitating changes, selecting and directing personnel, and plans for actions. He undertook such activities within the university and through a federally funded grant. The dean facilitated the creation of WPUNJ's Teaching-Learning Collaborative (TLC) Program (Strasser, 2000). This program offered students a full year placement in an urban school, the first semester as a 1-day-a-week placement and the second semester as a fulltime student teacher.

The dean decided to reinstate the college's educational administration program and seek federal funding for school partnerships. To help in these areas, he hired and appointed a WPUNJ faculty member who redesigned and coordinated the administration program and developed partnerships with Paterson and other school districts. As the number of these partnerships grew, the dean supported faculty members' efforts in applying for federal grants to consolidate and formalize these partnerships. The dean selected faculty to lead each partnership, encouraged school-university meetings where participants shared problems and brainstormed solutions, and he reported on the progress of this partnership (Agard-Jones, Jenkins, Malu, & Windley, 2001; Agard-Jones et al., 2003).

At the end of the second year of the partnership at the school, the dean linked the school with the Professional Development Title I Grant that WPUNJ received. This link was significant because it converted the school's partnership into a PDS, allowing the university to offer more resources to the school, including, on average, five professional development workshops, symposia, retreats, and/or conferences per year, six student teachers and/or practicum students per year, and site visits from university mathematics, science, political science, technology, music, and library faculty.

Over the course of the partnership, the principal's activities in the partnership focused on facilitating meetings, giving directions and encouragement, and accepting and communicating information. The partnership began with the principal's accepting the dean's invitation to join the partnership. For the first 3 years, the principal communicated information to her school faculty regarding this partnership and the WPUNJ professional development programs available to them. In years 4 and 5, she chose two teachers to serve as school liaisons for the partnership.

The principal encouraged me to team-teach with the school's faculty. She asked me to mentor and support three new teachers, WPUNJ graduates, and she welcomed WPUNJ's music, library, and political science faculty to work with the appropriate schoolteachers. The principal gave permission for the seventh graders to participate in WPUNJ's Model United Nations program sponsored by WPUNJ's political science department.

The principal was often accessible to speak with me, formally and informally. She arranged for me to lead one in-service faculty workshop and one school faculty and staff overnight retreat. She completed the administrative and financial paperwork for that retreat. The principal directed me to (1) work with the computer teachers to prepare four editions of the school newsletter; (2) recruit university students to tutor children who the school identified as potentially able to pass the state tests with additional tutoring; and (3) attend workshops for the whole school reform program at the school. She encouraged teachers to give guest presentations in one of my undergraduate methods classes. She coauthored an interim report on the partnership (Agard-Jones et al., 2003).

The activities of the eighth grade teacher focused on showing, teaching, learning, participating, and asking. While completing her graduate work, she frequently showed me the work she did with her children and the student teacher from WPUNJ's TLC program. Upon graduation, when our relationship changed from teacher-student to that of professional friends, the eighth grade teacher asked me for help, suggestions, funds, and encouragement. Several of her activities intertwined with mine. Examples of these follow.

Initially, the eighth grade teacher assumed a student stance as she completed her graduate degree at WPUNJ, attending two of my graduate courses and later working on her master's thesis with a WPUNJ colleague. She eagerly shared with me her student successes with literature circles (Daniels, 1994), her thesis topic. The eighth grade teacher introduced me to one of her students, Elvin. She reported:

> I was particularly proud of Elvin [and his response to literature circles]. He began the year by telling me he did not like to read. Shortly after we began the circles, he read *Fallen Angels* (Myers, 1989). He became so excited...that he went to the library and checked out four more novels by Walter Dean Myers. Imagine the joy Elvin and I felt!

After the eighth grade teacher's graduation from the master's program, we became professional friends. She proudly showed me her annual collection of eighth grade student writings. When I realized that she only made one copy of these collections, she accepted my suggestion that we make 80 copies, one for each graduate. Together we developed a portfolio type of project. Fortunately, she saved many of the children's writings throughout the year and could invite them to select their favorite piece for publication in the anthology. The eighth grade teacher presented me with one complete copy of the anthology, which the WPUNJ print shop, with grant funds, duplicated, and the eighth grade teacher presented to each of the eighth graders.

The eighth grade teacher asked for my assistance to find funding to purchase graduation gifts for her eighth graders. She wanted to give them each a book of their own choosing, based upon the literature circles concept. When I noticed a grant announcement in a professional publication, *The New Advocate*, I passed the information along with my encouragement to the eighth grade teacher. She completed the application and subsequently received *The New Advocate's* Teacher-Librarian Grant Award, sponsored by Christopher-Gordon Publishers (Teacher/librarian grant winners, 2002). The eighth grade teacher used this award to purchase the gift books for the eighth graders. Because of her success with this grant, the eighth grade teacher applied for a larger grant, the Chase Active Learning Grant. She hoped to use this funding to continue publishing the eighth grade anthology.

The eighth grade teacher participated in the TLC program and assumed responsibility for the student teacher. As part of this TLC program, the eighth grade teacher attended a 2-day workshop on mentoring and worked with the student teacher in her eighth grade classroom for the academic year. The eighth grade teacher helped the student teacher learn and grow in her teaching abilities and she permitted the student teacher to experiment with the teaching strategies she learned in her WPUNJ preservice program.

With my encouragement, the eighth grade teacher applied for and received an adjunct position in the Department of Middle and Secondary Education at WPUNJ. She has taught a postbaccalaureate class in secondary reading and study skills for four semesters. She contributed to the interim partnership report (Agard-Jones et al., 2001) and publication

(Agard-Jones et al., 2003). Through the grant, she joined the International Reading Association and shared several journal articles with her colleagues.

An analysis of the student teacher's activities reveals that she developed a wide array of teaching strategies and worked to "combine theory and practice in her teaching," developing literacy projects with multicultural sensitivities. She practiced incorporating Bloom's taxonomy, assertive discipline techniques, and Gardner's multiple intelligences into her teaching. She learned to lead parent-teacher conferences and she developed an understanding of a teacher's administrative responsibilities. She was a copanelist and coauthor for the interim partnership report (Agard-Jones et al., 2001; Agard-Jones et al., 2003).

As the university liaison for this partnership with the school and in my role as a teacher educator, I engaged in four types of activities: administering, teaching, creating, and researching. My administrative activities focused on such tasks as (1) completing grant reports and student teaching observation reports; (2) preparing for conferences and the school's *First Annual Interdisciplinary Science and Language Arts Retreat*; (3) maintaining mentoring progress reports; (4) coordinating visits of WPUNJ faculty and grant personnel to the school; (5) submitting budget forms for professional memberships, materials, and videotapes to support and inform teachers' development; and (6) preparing, printing, and distributing the numerous anthologies that the children and teachers produced throughout the course of the grant.

In the early years of the grant, I spent time observing and listening to children and school faculty and this helped me in my teaching and professional development activities at the school. I planned, presented, and debriefed demonstration lessons and team teaching activities for new teachers, experienced teachers, and student teachers. My lessons typically focused on language arts and literacy and principally involved my use of children's picture storybooks. My teaching during the school's retreat focused on leading collaborative workshops with WPUNJ science faculty and consultants, and modeling interdisciplinary lessons. In these inquiry-based lessons, I supported literacy development by using children's picture storybooks and informational trade books. I presented information about middle level research, specifically block scheduling and alternative curriculum models (Carnegie Council on Adolescent Development, 1989; National Middle School Association, 1995), that I thought might move the school beyond departmentalized instruction and help improve test scores.

My third activity focused on creating, supporting, and celebrating student and teacher work. I created a grassroots network within the school that led me to work directly with the teachers, team teaching, and/or supervising student teachers. To ensure the success of this network, I set up a predictable, consistent schedule of school visits on Tuesday and Thursday mornings so that the teachers knew my availability. In the beginning, I worked with the eighth grade teacher and two other teachers. By the end of the fifth year of the grant, I worked with the entire faculty at the middle level. I created informal study groups by purchasing professional memberships and videotapes for teachers at the middle level. My expectation was that we would meet periodically to discuss the professional literature and view and discuss the tapes. Unfortunately, we met only occasionally due to scheduling conflicts.

With each publication of a class anthology came a celebration. When we distributed the anthologies, the children were transformed into authors: smiling, laughing, sharing, and reading their stories aloud to each other. As these new authors presented their work, the teachers and I took photographs, occasionally shared cookies and punch, and always reveled in their joy.

Over the course of the partnership, I identified three areas of research. I was curious about the impact of the partnership on the professional development of novice teachers and the children's literacy growth. After the horrific tragedy of September 11th, I found myself drawn to the Arab American teachers and staff in the school and I wanted to learn more about their professional experiences. I led two research collaborations that studied the development of the partnership, the children's literacy growth, and the student teacher's professional development (Agard-Jones et al., 2001; Agard-Jones et al., 2003). When time permits, I analyze additional data and expect to publish further findings.

THE STANDARDIZED TESTS

A reality of education in New Jersey is the power of standardized tests. Although an outcry is growing regarding these tests (Faulk, 2001), test preparation drives an overwhelming part of the eighth grade curriculum in the Paterson schools. The state of New Jersey administers standardized tests at the eighth grade level to assess student learning and score reports are used to evaluate teacher and administrator performance. The state reports these test results to the public through the NCLB and at the New Jersey Report Cards Web site. In the last 3 years of the partnership, the entire school community constantly felt the impact of these test scores, as did I.

The principal sent word to the eighth grade teachers that they strictly adhere to the district's test preparation curriculum until spring when the children completed the state exams. The district's curriculum had these children spend almost all of their instructional time learning only information that would appear on the test and reviewing test-taking skills. One day each month children took practice exams.

At the beginning of the third year of the partnership, I was pleased when the principal emailed me:

> I know that some of the work that you have been doing has had an impact on these test scores. Test scores in literacy rose this year and I believe the outcome of the grant directly affected those test scores.

Yet, at the end of year 5 of the grant on my last day in the school, the principal informed me of a 20% drop in test scores and noted:

> If I continue working with a university, I need for them to work with my staff on ways to improve our test scores. That is the help we need. Universities need to understand that people's livelihoods depend on these scores. At the very least teachers can be transferred. People will lose their jobs. People have mortgages and other bills that they won't be able to pay. Administrators will lose their jobs. These test scores have this type of direct impact on our lives and university support needs to recognize this and deal with it. Under the NCLB, scores need to improve each year. When these scores drop even just once, there are severe repercussions.

The test scores (New Jersey Department of Education, n.d.a; New Jersey Department of Education, n.d.c) reveal the roller coaster rise and fall of the Paterson district's and the school's Grade Eighth Proficiency Assessment language arts literacy scores. In each of the first 2 years of the partnership, the school's scores rose above the district average. Scores at the school and on average across the district fell in the third year. In the fourth year, the school's scores rose once again and were well above the district average. In year five, scores across the district fell once again, as did the school's scores.

THE OUTCOMES:
NCATE PROFESSIONAL DEVELOPMENT SCHOOL STANDARDS

Over the course of this partnership, WPUNJ changed this school-university partnership into a PDS relationship. Just by saying this partnership changed into a PDS did not make it happen as will become evident below. In fact, the principal does not refer to the school's PDS status when she reports:

> A partnership with William Paterson University has brought many more college students into the classrooms to support students and to encourage them to aspire to college. (New Jersey Department of Education, n.d.b)

These two different understandings of this school-university relationship may be at the core of the conflicted outcomes.

NCATE, the nationally recognized professional accreditation agency for teacher education programs, created a mission statement and standards for PDS relationships (National Council for Accreditation of Teacher Education, NCATE, 2001). I used the mission statement and standards as a framework to evaluate the outcomes of this partnership.

The mission of a PDS relationship should be "professional preparation of candidates, faculty development, and inquiry directed at the improvement of practice and enhanced student learning." Partners are "guided by a common vision of teaching and learning, which is grounded in research and practitioner knowledge." PDS partnerships "influence policies and practices at the district, state, and national levels" (NCATE, 2001, p. 1).

This mission statement highlights a major challenge in this partnership. From the beginning, the school and the university had different visions regarding the ways in which children learn and the ways in which teachers can help children succeed. The school followed the district's mandated test preparation curriculum that was designed to improve test scores. The university focused on quality preparation of teachers, particularly in diverse settings, and sought to introduce an inquiry-based, hands-on approach to teaching and learning.

At the classroom level, the teachers and I shared a similar vision. Teachers who worked to create the anthologies recognized the value in this inquiry-based project for their children. These teachers asked for extra copies of the anthologies to share with their subsequent classes. Each year, I gave the librarian copies of anthologies from the various classes. She showed me the dog-eared copies from the previous years as children from all the other classes using the library enjoyed reading through them.

In addition to NCATE's mission statement, I organized my evaluation of the partnership around the five standards that NCATE established for PDS partnerships. These standards include learning community, accountability and quality assurance, collaboration, diversity and equity, and structures, resources, and roles. Following a description of each standard, I discuss the partnership's outcomes for that standard. Subsequently, I use NCATE's evaluative standard scale to appraise the partnership.

Standard I: Learning Community

The learning community standards call for a learning community that supports inquiry-based practice grounded in research and practitioner knowledge. On many separate occasions, I proposed to the principal that the teachers and I create learning communities such as study groups, a book club, and/or a lunch and a videotape gathering. I purchased six sets of professional development videotapes and gave professional memberships for the International Reading Association to six teachers, hopeful that access to these materials could spark professional gatherings. Some occurred but not as many as I would have liked due to scheduling conflicts.

Besides the team teaching, anthology projects, and professional gatherings, the school retreat that I led helped create a partnership learning community. Out of 65 teachers and staff, 35 attended. This one weekend retreat was not enough. When I sought to organize a second retreat, the principal informed me that the district was experiencing budget cuts.

At the district's direction, the school focused on test preparation. I wanted to introduce many more hands-on, inquiry-based projects and practices to the school faculty, in addition to creating learning communities that might build on the teachers' professional knowledge. I did not fully understand the concerns that NCLB and test scores engendered in the school faculty and administration. Nor was it possible for me to change this test preparation focus to an inquiry-based approach.

Standard II: Accountability and Quality Assurance

The accountability and quality assurance standard requires an ongoing evaluation process based on local, state, and national standards with an examination of the congruence between the work of the PDS partnership and local, state, and national education policies. Although the local and state standardized test scores were used to measure student learning, I am unaware of anyone in this partnership who used these scores in a systematic, research-based manner to challenge, question, or modify district mandated teaching, learning, and testing practices. The university-based evaluative work conducted as a part of the Professional Development Title I Grant did not appear to have any impact on the school's practices or at the district level, specifically with reference to the test preparation curriculum. I was unaware of any efforts to inform the school's families or the surrounding community of this work.

Standard III: Collaboration

The third standard, collaboration, focus on "blurring of the boundaries" between the partner institutions as participants engage in jointly shared work. As a WPUNJ faculty, I worked actively in the school classrooms. With the team teaching activities, I remained close to the teachers and children. Two members of the school faculty contributed to university teaching, one as an adjunct instructor and both as guest speakers. Additionally, the joint panel presentation at the national conference with the dean, the eighth grade teacher, the student teacher, and me reflected our collaborative efforts (Agard-Jones et al., 2001).

Standard IV: Diversity and Equity

The diversity and equity standard calls upon all members of the partnership to develop and demonstrate knowledge, skills, and dispositions resulting in learning for all students with equitable learning outcomes for all participants. In addition, participants needed to include diverse learners. In this school, there were children and teachers from diverse ethnic and racial groups. Over the course of the grant, the Paterson school district offered positions to five of the WPUNJ teacher candidates who had been student teachers at the school. These candidates included one European American and four African Americans; they all accepted these positions.

I was disappointed that this partnership did not prompt the systematic examination of the curricula and assessment strategies that might positively affect outcomes for diverse children. Rarely did the student teachers or the school faculty use multiple and varied assessment approaches to measure learning. Although I encouraged the use of such assessments and demonstrated to the student teachers ways in which such assessments could be used to individualize instruction, I was not able to document any evidence of systematic, institutional changes in the school's use of individualized assessments to measure student progress.

Standard V: Structures, Resources, and Roles

This fifth standard, structure, resources, and roles, targets the establishment of governing structures that support the PDS at the school and university. The enhancement of and changes in traditional structures at both institutions should receive adequate resources to facilitate such changes. A rewards system should recognize the importance of this work.

The partnership should communicate effectively to inform the public, policy makers, and professional audiences of their work.

Despite the lack of a critical mass of participants at the school or university to support changes that a PDS relationship might prompt, those individuals who actively engaged in the partnership appeared to be dedicated and committed to this work. The partnership opened the door for the WPUNJ political science faculty and political science college student majors to work at the school with the model United Nations project. WPUNJ music faculty worked with the school music teacher and the WPUNJ education librarian worked with the school librarian.

The university recognized the eighth grade teacher's excellent teaching and active contributions to the partnership with an invitation to join the WPUNJ faculty, and she eagerly accepted. WPUNJ recognized, valued, and rewarded my PDS work as evidenced by awarding me with tenure and promotion. I am unaware of any data suggesting that this partnership created communication links at the district level beyond the traditional student teacher placement issues.

To conclude, I used the NCATE evaluative standards scale for a PDS—beginning, developing, at standard, and leading (beyond standard). This PDS was at the beginning level for standards I (learning community), II (accountability and quality assurance), and III (collaboration) and the developing level for standards IV (diversity and equity) and V (structures, resources, and roles). Much of the PDS work at the school evolved through personal relationships rather than through formal partnership activities. The challenges faced by this partnership were not just those at the two institutions but they involved larger, systemic challenges at the district, state, and national levels.

RECOMMENDATIONS

There is much to learn from this 5-year experience. I present these recommendations through the lenses of partnership participants, the outcomes, the NCATE standards, and the NCLB.

It is critically important that all members of the partnership take time to create a clear, shared vision of the goals they seek to meet. This vision needs to be reviewed on a periodic basis to ensure that it continues to match the changing and fluid politics at the local, state, and national levels. Participants may have more success when they approach this effort with a shared trust and commitment to children's learning.

The interim report (Agard-Jones et al., 2003) on this partnership noted a shared trust and commitment to children's learning by all the participants. Examples of evidence cited included: The eighth grade teacher's firsthand knowledge of my classroom and her willingness to invite me into hers with a welcoming stance, even when I appeared unannounced. The principal's open door policy to WPUNJ faculty suggested a level of shared trust.

In year 3, the change from the informal partnership to a PDS relationship and the power of test scores in NCLB should have prompted a review of our visions and expectations. This analysis reveals clearly that the partners expressed a vision to improve student achievement. However, the lack of shared, clearly articulated best practices in teaching and learning resulted in a lack of understanding for each partner's concerns—the school's for improved test scores and the university's for quality teacher preparation.

Research suggests that major problems with PDS work include fighting between constituents (Metcalf-Turner & Fischetti, 1996) and conflicts (Campoy, 2000). Although there is no explicit or implicit evidence of this phenomena in the data, lack of a mutually shared vision may also create difficult challenges.

School and university participants should engage in action research beginning with the first day of the partnership. School participants engaged in such research should include teachers, administrators, and children. University researchers should include the university liaison and other interested university members, including university students within and outside of the field of education. Such a wide variety of individuals may offer multiple perspectives on the partnership activities. By engaging in action research, participants may have opportunities to understand the impact of their activities and be in positions to change and challenge school and university practices. Examining partnership activities from the start of the grant may help participants more quickly understand the challenges they face. Partners may more quickly modify activities in ways that may be more effective for them.

The school and WPUNJ hoped that this partnership would affect student learning. The school, following the district's direction, needed to improve test scores. WPUNJ wanted a site with a diverse school community in which to train teachers. As an educational researcher and the university liaison, I wanted to help the school community understand the dangers of their testing-focus and begin to try hands-on, inquiry-based projects.

Herein was the dilemma: current research points to the positive influence that inquiry-based learning and balanced literacy activities (Moore, Bean, Birdyshaw, & Rycik, 1999; National Middle School Association, 1997; Wise & Levine, 2002) have on children's learning, but this is not what the school reported that it needed. Mindful of the question, "What do you need from me?" I wondered if it was right to promote such activities. What was my responsibility to the school, the children, and my university? Was it possible to document connections between the anthology projects and children's test scores? Were there links among the information shared at the school retreat, changes in teaching practices and children's test scores?

As Fine (1996) documents, action research that includes participant evaluation provides spaces for participants to reflect on and implement changes that they believe will improve children's learning. These reflections provide participants with insights into the strengths and weaknesses of programs and/or activities as well as new ideas and actions to improve student learning. Action research projects might have helped more of the school's teachers reflect deeply on their teaching and their children's learning.

The university's role in a partnership must include exposing to the fallacies of standardized tests and the injustices perpetrated when such tests are used to make high stakes decisions regarding student placement, and teachers' and administrators' employment status. The principal's final comments to me suggested how powerful the test scores had become and how powerless the school faculty and administration felt. Such tests may make school professionals more vulnerable to intimidation and much less aggressive in using teaching practices that they believe and know from experience will improve and enhance their children's learning.

University faculty should use the power and respect that comes with the title of professor to raise public challenges to these tests and test-centered curricula. Faculty can introduce schools and communities to position papers from a wide variety of professional organizations that challenge the power of these tests (Board of Directors, International Reading Association, 1999; Fairtest, n.d.; National Forum to Accelerate Middle Grades Reform, 2002). University faculty may become advocates for children's and teachers' educational and professional rights. They may be in a position to educate school and district leaders, teachers, parents, and politicians regarding best educational practices to improve and enhance learning for children and professional development for teachers.

I concur with Gordon's (2003) recommendation that universities work intensively with the school leadership team, including the principal, assistant principals, and selected faculty. I recommend that such work begin at least 1 year prior to entering into a PDS partnership. Just as a student teacher has a university supervisor and cooperating teacher, and a novice teacher may have a mentor, school principals should also have such support. The first year of this partnership was the principal's first year as a principal. In that year as she completed her doctorate, she needed to respond to the superintendent's call to turn the school around, the district's and parents' cries for improved test scores, the teachers' fears of disruptive children, WPUNJ's invitation to partner, and undoubtedly other issues as well. There were times when I left the principal's office wondering who she turned to for help and advice. Did she have a mentor? As far as I knew, she relied only upon herself.

This analysis indicates that there were numerous challenges that the school leadership team faced. If universities provided school leaders with mentors and worked with only the leadership team for the first year, they might experience more successes when they begin working with the school faculty in subsequent years. In addition to mentors, school principals and other school leaders might find it useful to have access to a 24 hour a day online chat room where they share problems and seek advice from retired, successful former principals and/or superintendents.

I recommend that universities find ways to respond quickly and creatively to changing circumstances. On average, six WPUNJ student teachers and/or practicum students worked each semester at the school. I wanted more WPUNJ student support at the school. I proposed using the meeting time of my methods course to bring the university students into the school to give the children tutoring and practice lessons. I suggested using the university's online delivery system to teach the course asynchronously to make up for the lost class time traveling to and from the school. At the time, I could not sign up to teach this course a semester in advance—the university scheduling committee needed a year's advanced notice.

I continue to recommend that partnerships be given time to grow at their own unique pace (Malu, 1997). Just as Miller and Silvernail (1994) assert that ideas for action maybe local, the speed at which a PDS develops, grows and meets the NCATE standards may be unique to the circumstances of the PDS and each of the participants. For instance, Trubowitz and Longo (1997) report on a middle school-college partnership that has lasted 2 decades. Further, Quatroche, Woolridge, and Dobbins (2000) note that changes at PDSs move at a very slow pace.

Time was important for this partnership as well. As a faculty member new to WPUNJ and the local community, my decision to take a grassroots approach, encouraging teachers to reach out to me as word of my work spread, gave me time to learn more about the school and community. This approach took time and enabled me to identify the needs of the teachers rather than impose my understanding of their needs on them.

Now, our grant-funded partnership has ended. Through this analysis and with the distance of time, I believe that with more time we would have seen the seeds of the reciprocal nature of the partnership take root. With more time, work, support, and mutual partner understandings, the NCATE standards were within reach.

CONCLUSION

As the College of Education at WPUNJ continues to pursue the development of PDSs, this action research project makes it clear that such collaborations can be extremely rewarding for all individuals involved. With a clear vision and necessary supports from school and university constituencies, the unique nature of each school and university partnership has the potential to improve and enhance children's learning, offer rich professional development activities for classroom teachers, and prepare highly qualified new teachers to work successfully in twenty first century classrooms. University faculties have opportunities to guide and support learning for children, teachers, and college students.

Faculty at all levels must become advocates for all learners by conducting and publishing qualitative, action research projects grounded in the rich, complex, natural settings of K-16 classrooms. The dissemination of such projects needs to reach all educational constituencies including teachers, parents, educational leaders, and policy makers at local, state, and national levels.

AUTHOR'S NOTE

Address correspondence to: Kathleen F. Malu, Department of Secondary and Middle School Education, William Paterson University of New Jersey, P.O. Box 920, Wayne, NJ 07470-0920. E-mail:maluk@wpunj.edu

ACKNOWLEDGMENT

The author wishes to acknowledge the helpful comments and feedback of Marie Grace Mutino, PhD, and Elizabeth Ann Figlear on an earlier draft of this chapter.

NOTE

1. Recent discussions suggest the need for researchers to use the real names of participants, particularly when reporting qualitative research (Brause, Feola & Malu, 2003). Further rich, complex dimensions of participants may be revealed in their real names. The use of real names may add further accuracy to qualitative reports. In this report, however, I have chosen to refer to the participants and the setting using generic names. I call WPUNJ's dean, the dean. The Paterson public school principal is the principal; the eighth grade teacher is the eighth grade teacher; the student

teacher is the student teacher. The Paterson public school setting is the school. I have chosen to use these labels to offer a shroud of privacy for the participants and the particular school in Paterson, New Jersey. My use of these generic names does not detract from the accuracy of this report and the facts that the institutions are public and the partnership was federally funded make it impossible to assure privacy, even with the use of pseudonyms.

REFERENCES

Arhar, J. M., Holly, M. L., & Kasten, W. C. (2001). *Action research for teachers: Traveling the yellow brick road.* Upper Saddle River, NJ: Merrill Prentice Hall.

Agard-Jones, L., Jenkins, C., Malu, K., & Windley, T. (2001, November). *Multiple perspectives on a school university partnership: Focus 25-21, William Paterson University and Paterson Public School #25.* Panel presentation at the annual meeting of the National Middle School Association, Washington, DC.

Agard-Jones, L., Jenkins, C., Malu, K., & Windley, T. (2003). Diverse perspectives on a school-university partnership: Seeking excellence at the middle level. In R. M. Duhon-Sells, H. C. Sells, A. Duhon-Ross, G. M. Duhon, & D. G. Jean-Louis (Eds.), *International perspectives on methods of improving education: Focusing on the quality of diversity* (pp. 91-112). Lewiston, NY: Edwin Mellen Press.

Board of Directors, International Reading Association. (1999). High stakes assessments in reading: A position statement of the International Reading Association. *Journal of Adolescent and Adult Literacy, 43*(3), 305-312.

Brause, R. S. (1991). Hypothesis generating studies in your classroom. In R. S. Brause & J. S. Mayher (Eds.), *Search and research: What the inquiring teacher needs to know* (pp. 181-206). London: Falmer Press.

Brause, R., Feola, D., & Malu, K. F. (2003, June). *Theoretical and practical concerns in naming research study participants: A collaborative conversation.* Paper presented at the annual conference of Ethnographic and Qualitative Research in Education, Albany, NY.

Campoy, R. (2000). *A professional development school partnership: Conflict and collaboration.* Oxford, England: Greenwood.

Carnegie Council on Adolescent Development. (1989). *Turning points: Preparing American youth for the 21st century.* New York: Carnegie Corporation.

Coulthard, M. (1985). *An introduction to discourse analysis: New edition.* New York: Longman.

Daniels, H. (1994). *Literature circles: Voice and choice in the student-centered classroom.* York, ME: Stenhouse.

Fairtest: National Center for Fair and Open Testing. (n.d.). *The dangerous consequences of high-stakes standardized testing.* Retrieved August 30, 2004, from http://www.fairtest.org/facts/Dangerous%20Consequences.html

Faulk, N. (2001). A national perspective: Standardized testing for fostering cultural diversity of educational opportunity enlightenment. In R. M. Duhon-Sells, A. M. Duhon-Ross, & G. M. Duhon (Eds.), *Scholars teaming to alleviate racism in society (STARS)* (pp. 105-108). Lewiston, NY: Edwin Mellen Press.

Fine, M. (Ed.). (1996). *Talking across boundaries: Participatory evaluation research in an urban middle school*. New York: Bruner Foundation.

Gordon, S. (2003). *Professional development for school improvement: Empowering learning communities*. New York: Allyn & Bacon.

Guba, E. G., & Lincoln, Y. S. (1987). Naturalistic inquiry. In M. J. Dunkin (Ed.), *The international encyclopedia of teaching and teacher education* (pp.147-151). Oxford, England: Pergamon Press.

Hubbard, R., & Powers, B. (1999). *Living the questions: A guide for teacher-researchers*. York, ME: Stenhouse.

McCarthy, M. (1991). *Discourse analysis for language teachers*. New York: Cambridge University Press.

Malu, K. F. (1997). Middle school administrator and university faculty member in partnership: A collaboration in progress. *The North Carolina Middle School Association Journal, 19*(1), 5-8.

Metcalf-Turner, P., & Fischetti, J. (1996). Professional development schools: Persisting questions and lessons learned. *The Journal of Teacher Education, 47*(4), 292-299.

Miller, L., & Silvernail, D. (1994). Wells Junior High School: Evolution of a professional development school. In L. Darling-Hammond (Ed.), *Professional development schools: Schools for developing a profession* (pp 28-49). New York: Teachers College Press.

Moore, D., Bean, T., Birdyshaw, D., & Rycik, J. (1999). *Adolescent literacy: A position statement for the commission on adolescent literacy of the International Reading Association*. Retrieved from the November 20, 2004, from http://www.reading.org/downloads/positions/ps1036_adolescent.pdf

Myers, W. D. (1989). *Fallen angels*. New York: Scholastic.

National Council for Accreditation of Teacher Education. (2001). *Standards for professional development schools*. Washington, DC: Author.

National Forum to Accelerate Middle Grades Reform. (2002). *Position statement: High stakes testing*. Retrieved September 3, 2004, from http://www.mgforum.org/Policy/highstakes/page1.htm

National Middle School Association. (1995). *This we believe: Developmentally responsive middle level schools*. Columbus, OH: Author.

National Middle School Association. (1997). *A 21st century research agenda: Issues, topics & questions guiding inquiry into middle level theory and practice*. Columbus, OH: Author.

New Jersey Department of Education. (n.d.a). 2002 NCLB school report card. *New Jersey's report cards: Meeting requirements of state law and the No Child Left Behind (NCLB) Act*. Retrieved September 4, 2004, from http://education.state.nj.us/rc/nclb/31-4010-280.html

New Jersey Department of Education. (n.d.b). 2002-2003 NCLB school report card: School profile. *New Jersey's report cards: Meeting requirements of state law and the No Child Left Behind (NCLB) Act*. Retrieved September 4, 2004, from http://education.state.nj.us/rc/narrative/static/2003/31/4010/31-4010-280.html?c=31,d=4010,s=280,name=NUMBER%2025

New Jersey Department of Education. (n.d.c). 2003 New Jersey school report cards. *New Jersey's report cards: Meeting requirements of state law and the No Child*

Left Behind (NCLB) Act. Retrieved September 4, 2004, from ttp://
    education.state.nj.us/rc/narrative/static/2003/31/4010/31-4010-
    280.html?c=31,d=4010,s=280,name=NUMBER%2025

Quatroche, D., Woolridge, D., & Dobbins, J. (2000). Developing a seamless web
    through professional development schools: K-16 partnerships. In C. Grant
    (Ed.), *Creative partnerships: Gateway to embracing diversity: Multiculturalism and
    multicultural education: Crossing borders for equity and justice* (pp. 217-230). New
    York: National Association for Multicultural Education.

Strasser, J. (2000, November). *The teaching/learning collaborative (TLC): A model for a
    one-year, urban, preservice field experience*. Paper presented at the annual confer-
    ence of the National Association of Early Childhood Teacher Educators,
    Atlanta, Georgia.

Teacher/librarian grant winners. (2002). *The New Advocate, 1*(15), 48.

Trubowitz, S., & Longo, P. (1997). *How it works—Inside a school-college collaboration*.
    New York: Teachers College Press.

United States Census. (2000). *Table DP-1. Profile of general demographic characteris-
    tics: 2000*. Retrieved May 29, 2002, from http://www.census.gov

Wise, A., & Levine, M. (2002, February 27). The 10-step solution: Helping urban
    districts boost achievement in low-performing schools. *Education Week*, pp. 56,
    38.

CHAPTER 13

USING RESEARCH TO REFINE SCHOOL IMPROVEMENT IN THE MIDDLE GRADES

Perspectives from Middle Start

Pritha Gopalan, Teri West, Patrick Montesano, and Steve Hoelscher

ABSTRACT

Learning communities are an important vehicle for the continuous improvement of teaching and learning (DuFour & Eaker, 1998; Lieberman & Miller, 2001; Sykes, 1999). Through action research on a comprehensive school reform model, we show that learning communities supporting middle grades educational improvement include school communities, as well as reform partners at the regional and national level. We conclude that multi-level learning communities are important to the ongoing improvement and growth of educational initiatives, as they together form an infrastructure for middle grades educational reform.

Learning communities traditionally refer to communities of teachers and administrators engaged in the improvement of teaching and learning

Making a Difference: Action Research in Middle Level Education, 261–284
Copyright © 2005 by Information Age Publishing
All rights of reproduction in any form reserved.

261

(Little, 1999; McLaughlin & Zarrow, 2001). The importance of these communities lies in their habits of reflection, review, and self-assessment, which drive the professional work of schools. In this chapter, we, a team composed of researchers and model developers engaged in middle grades comprehensive school reform, extend the definition of learning communities to include the external partners who provide specific educational services to schools. DuFour and Eaker (1998) identify six characteristics of learning communities: (1) collective mission, vision and goals, (2) collective inquiry, (3) collaborative teams, (4) action orientation and experimentation, (5) continuous improvement, and (6) results orientation. They hold that collective inquiry is the *engine* (p. 25) that drives the cycle of inquiry and improvement undertaken by collaborative teams, and that these efforts always result in *purposeful improvement* because of the ongoing assessment that such communities subject themselves to (p. 28).

We discuss how Middle Start, a comprehensive school improvement program designed for the middle grades, developed learning communities that embedded a culture of inquiry at all three levels of the initiative—national, regional, and school-based—in order to ensure that the development of the initiative at the national and regional levels draws from and in turn informs school level implementation of the comprehensive school improvement program. We describe how action research conducted on Middle Start at each of the three levels informs and refines an educational infrastructure that supports school improvement efforts, is of a unified piece, and draws from the needs identified and promising practices developed at each of the three levels.

The Middle Start Approach

Action research strengthens the design of the Middle Start model and its implementation in schools. The first level is the national level, where the research and development process drives the ongoing refinement and scale-up of the Middle Start model. At this level, the Middle Start research and development team, composed of researchers and model designers at the Academy for Educational Development (AED), conducts systematic research to refine and strengthen the principles and practices of the program. Research strategies include reviews of relevant research and literature; interviews with Middle Start technical assistance and service providers; and site visits to schools. The second level is the regional coaches' networks. At this level, the coaches, who provide technical assistance to schools on implementation of the Middle Start comprehensive school improvement model, serve as the interface between developers at the national level and the school. They participate in a series of seminars that provide them the opportunity to broaden their repertoire and share strategies to address difficult situations in schools. Coaches learn about and engage in various modes of inquiry in these seminars, including using texts to drive discussion and asking questions that foster reflection. The third level is that of the school itself. The staff in Middle Start schools learns about and practices a variety of reflective review and self-assessment strategies, including surveys, reviews of student work, analysis of achievement data, and classroom *walk throughs*. These practices help staff monitor, assess, and continuously improve school improvement activities and improve academic and developmental outcomes for all students.

Throughout this chapter, we apply DuFour and Eaker's (1998) definition of learning communities to describe how Middle Start practitioners—national design team members, regional coaches, and school staff—use reflection, data collection, and other forms of inquiry to inform school improvement activities carried out in their respective learning communities. Drawing on research that embeds action research in learning communities, we extend the definition of such communities to include a multilevel infrastructure for educational improvement, including national, regional, and school level stakeholders.

We expand the traditional definition of action research, wherein reflection and inquiry usually take place within the context of an individual school or classroom, and apply it to comprehensive school improvement. As a team, we conduct action research on the Middle Start comprehensive school improvement model to address needs identified in schools, such as consistent literacy practices that improve student learning at the school level or improved coaching practices that better support school improvement teams at the regional level. Such research and development is ongoing to ensure that the developers of Middle Start at the national level, the coaches at the regional level, and the teachers and staff at the school level engage continually in inquiry, related action, and continuous assessment to ensure that the strategies being implemented are helping middle grades schools become academically excellent, developmentally responsive, and socially equitable.[1]

We conclude that multilevel learning communities working together create a nested infrastructure for the continuous and sustainable improvement of teaching and learning. We believe that such an educational infrastructure that practices ongoing action research is essential for improving educational reform, as well as expanding and sustaining it in the long run.

BACKGROUND

Multilevel learning communities have contributed to Middle Start's success in building school capacity to foster improved student outcomes and have supported its endorsement by national educational laboratories specializing in school improvement. Nationally, Middle Start is among the 25 most implemented school improvement models (Southwest Educational Development Laboratory, 2003) and is featured in the prestigious Catalog of School Reform Models (Northwest Regional Educational Laboratory, 2002). The Middle Start comprehensive school improvement model has been implemented in 74 schools in Michigan and the Mid South states of Arkansas, Louisiana, and Mississippi, since 1994. We carried out the activities reported in this chapter in Michigan, where Middle Start began its middle grades improvement initiative. Similar research-based improvement efforts are also underway in the Mid South under the sponsorship of the Foundation for the Mid South.

Evidence of Effectiveness

Overall, studies show that Middle Start schools demonstrated gains in student achievement compared to state averages, as well as improved teaching, learning, and school climate (Academy for Educational Development, AED, 2004). Middle Start improves student performance in the gatekeeper subjects of reading and math, according to longitudinal studies conducted in Arkansas, Louisiana, Michigan, and Mississippi. Studies of Middle Start conducted from 1994 to 2003 show that schools implementing Middle Start for 2 or more years: (1) demonstrated academic gains and behavioral improvements by students, and (2) showed improved instructional practices and school climate. Aggregate findings from survey research, conducted by the Center for Prevention Research and Development (CPRD) at the University of Illinois from 1994 to 2001, illustrated that student achievement in Middle Start schools in Michigan outpaced that of comparison schools and comparable state aggregates (Center for Prevention Research and Development, CPRD, 1998; CPRD, 2001). CPRD's (2004) analyses of test scores from Louisiana Middle Start schools demonstrated considerable progress in student achievement in reading and math between 2001 and 2003, surpassing comparable state averages.

Additionally, qualitative studies by AED researchers (AED, 1998; Gopalan, 2001; Williams, 2004; Williams & Mitchell, 2003) showed that the majority of Middle Start schools developed effective leadership, a positive climate, rigorous instructional practices, and greater student engagement in learning over the period of implementation (3 years).

THEORETICAL SIGNIFICANCE

A Broader Scope for Practitioner Research

More than a decade ago, Holly (1991) stated that action research was the missing link in teacher professional development, as teacher collaboration, a concept then gaining popularity, would only work if teachers had opportunities for participatory learning. The professional development landscape changed significantly in the ensuing period, with the focus changing from individual teacher learning-to-learning communities of educational practitioners (DuFour & Eaker, 1998; Little, 1999). Practitioner research, action research, teacher research, and teacher inquiry were among the many terms used to characterize a cycle of inquiry, reflection, and action undertaken by teachers, sometimes in collaboration with researchers, to improve teaching and learning (Anderson, Herr, & Nihlen, 1994; Ball & Cohen, 1999; Cochran-Smith & Lytle, 2001). Anderson, Herr and Nihlen (1994) stated their preference for the term "practitioner research" because it is more inclusive of the varied stakeholders interested in education than action research, which is traditionally used to describe teachers' research into their classrooms and schools. They described practitioner research as *insider research* (p. 2), which educators conduct in their own schools, districts, and/or communities. They wrote, "Most practitioner research is oriented to some action or cycle of actions that practitioners wish to take to address a particular situation" (p. 2).

Collective inquiry and action are also components of prominent whole school improvement approaches practiced in varied forms by growing numbers of schools (Stokes, 2001). In this chapter we describe how Middle Start embeds the tool of action research within the structure of three levels of learning communities, including schools, the Middle Start coaches' network, and the Middle Start National Center, linking the layers of the nested model, as well as improving reflection, inquiry, and action within each layer.

Learning Communities Enhance Internal Accountability

The concept of the learning community has influenced education research and practice since the early 1990s. Lave and Wenger's (1991) writing on communities of practice and Lieberman and Miller's (1991) emphasis on "the teacher as a learner, leader and a colleague in helping shape a professional community" (p. vii) were influential in removing the focus from the teacher as an individual needing or seeking professional development to ongoing teacher collaboration as the vehicle for school improvement.

There was considerable agreement in the literature on learning communities' capacity for building internal accountability or shared responsibility for student learning. Ancess (1996), Sykes (1999), and Little (1999) linked the development of a culture of inquiry with growing internal accountability for the improvement of teaching and learning. Little, for instance, emphasized teacher learning and a collective focus on students as critical for teachers to "assume shared responsibility for students" (p. 239).

Multilevel Learning Communities Build an Infrastructure for Educational Improvement

Stokes (2001) comments on the trend to integrate inquiry approaches with whole-school reform models, stating,

> A professional community of practice and of inquiry has become a fundamental principle of progressive education reform. Many prominent school reform networks ... try to foster a professional culture of inquiry as an integral condition of and contributor to a high-quality environment for teaching and learning. (pp. 141-142)

Middle Start's approach and experiences bring a fresh perspective on nesting schools within a multilevel infrastructure to enhance improvement within schools. We believe this multilevel educational infrastructure is essential for improving school reform as well as expanding and sustaining it in the long run.

LEVEL ONE: RESEARCH AND DEVELOPMENT AT THE MIDDLE START NATIONAL CENTER

The model development team at the Middle Start National Center at AED conducted a collaborative and exhaustive review of research at the national, regional, and school levels to craft the four principles that form the pillars of the Middle Start comprehensive school improvement design. The culture of inquiry that we intentionally developed through professional learning communities at all three levels of the initiative ensured that varied stakeholders engaged in Middle Start were involved in and contributed to the development of the four core principles and practices. By engaging is such action research, we ensured that all levels of the initiative remained connected and that work on the development of the school improvement model was informed by school level implementation.

Using a Team Approach

The model development team consisted of researchers and developers from the Middle Start National Center, regional coordinators from Michigan and the Mid South, technical assistance coaches, and independent researchers conducting studies of Middle Start. This team developed the principles through a process of collaborative design based on an exhaustive review of qualitative and quantitative research that lasted over a year. Team members shared information about the schools and their assistance to the schools, disseminated and discussed articles about school improvement and professional development, reflected on the progress of their work, considered the implications of their experiences with the schools on the development of the school improvement model, developed materials and approaches together that were then brought to the coaches for review, and finally, implementation in schools. Coaches, in turn, provided feedback to this team on specific design components and their implementation at the school level. Formative researchers from AED and independent evaluators also provided qualitative and quantitative analyses of trends at the school level that completed the cycle of research, reflection, and action.

Principle I: Reflective Review and Self-Assessment

The model development team used a variety of data sources to guide the development of the principle on *Reflective Review and Self-Study*. Drawing from research on teacher inquiry and internal accountability, this principle calls for ongoing and sustained inquiry into teaching and learning; using data to make decisions; and developing a culture of inquiry and reflection among all members of the school for the purpose of continuous improvement. One key source the team used was a formative study (Gopalan & Jessup, 2001) of the first year of implementation in a cohort of Middle Start schools. The study design included extensive interviews in 22 schools as well as participant observation in 10 schools. The report indicated that building the capacity of the staff to engage in reflective review and inquiry created a foundation for substantive changes in curriculum and instruction as well as the development of a positive school climate and recommended instituting self-assessment approaches and practices to promote goal oriented and results-driven implementation.

Principle II: Effective Small Learning Communities

The model development team wrote the principle on *Effective Small Learning Communities* to capture the composition and functions of interdisciplinary teams at each grade level. Specific practices accompanying the principle emphasize teams meeting to set instructional priorities, develop interdisciplinary units, review student work, and engage families in the learning of students.

One of the key sources of data used to inform this principle was quantitative research conducted by independent researchers. CPRD administered biannual surveys to Middle Start schools. CPRD provided the model development group with aggregate reports and analyses of key findings and longitudinal trends. The model development group paid special attention to CPRD's finding that high levels of interdisciplinary teaming in Middle Start schools were positively correlated with improved student achievement, reports of lower substance abuse, higher levels of student self-esteem, improved discipline, and school safety (CPRD, 1998). The model development team also reviewed other research (Flowers, Mertens, & Mulhall, 2000; Jackson & Davis, 2000; Kruse & Louis, 1997; National Forum to Accelerate Middle Grades Reform, 1999) and concluded that the evidence pointed toward making teaming a central principle of Middle Start.

Principle III: Rigorous Curriculum, Instruction, and Assessment

Lipsitz, Mizell, Jackson, and Austin (1997) critiqued the middle grades reform movement for over emphasizing developmental responsiveness and underplaying academic rigor in middle grades schools, reporting that schools made gains in developing small learning communities but were struggling to integrate age-appropriate teaching practices such as project-based learning and thematic instruction in their teams and classrooms. Additionally, feedback collected by the model development team from Middle Start coaches showed that schools needed better guidance on aligning Middle Start's instructional emphasis with state standards; as well as improved frameworks for integrating curriculum, instruction, and assessment. The model development team developed the principle of

Rigorous Curriculum, Instruction and Assessment to emphasize student learning and achievement by matching rich curriculum with best instructional practices and varied forms of assessment to address the learning needs of students of varying abilities, backgrounds, and interests.

Principle IV: Distributed Leadership and Sustainable Partnerships

Middle Start's fourth and final principle, *Distributed Leadership and Sustainable Partnerships*, focuses on engaging families and community members in student learning and developing a culture of shared leadership within schools. The model development team envisioned that Middle Start coaches would work with democratically elected school leadership teams to build the capacity of teachers, family members, and community representatives to play leadership roles in schools. Model developers based this principle on the growing body of research showing that distributed leadership that includes varied school stakeholders such as principals, teachers, district representatives, family and community representatives have success in fostering instructional leadership, rather than focusing solely on school administration (Elmore, 2000; Spillane, Halverson, & Diamond, 1999). AED's own research also showed a need to build organizational capacity and diverse school leadership in order for Middle Start to foster continuous improvement (Gopalan & Jessup, 2001).

In addition to the literature in the field, almost all Middle Start schools reported that family engagement was one of their top three goals for school improvement and asked Middle Start coaches for assistance in how to engage families in schools. In turn, coaches began asking the model development team members for guidelines on what constitutes an effective family engagement approach. As a result, the model development team read the research, engaged in multiple text-based discussions, and consulted an expert in the field to develop the principle on distributed leadership and sustainable partnerships.

Putting It All Together

In 2001, the model development team invited a national panel of researchers, advocates and implementers of middle grades educational reform to examine a near final draft of the four principles and suggest improvements based on their experience with middle grades schools, as well as their knowledge of national research on middle grades school improvement. The team incorporated changes resulting from this panel's review and finalized the four principles.

The model development team exemplified the definition of a learning community as they systematically and intentionally consulted Middle Start's own research and other national research, incorporated the knowledge and feedback of coaches working at the school level, and finally integrated the feedback of a national panel of reviewers. Throughout the process, team members engaged in continuous learning and held one another accountable for completing various pieces of the work, served as reviewers for the drafted principles, and kept the work focused on the continuous improvement of teaching and learning.

Revisiting DuFour and Eaker's (1998) definition of a learning community, the model development team employed several strategies of such a community as team members addressed the goal of strengthening the Middle Start principles and practices. The team consulted several pieces of research, internal as well as national, in crafting and refining the four principles, worked collaboratively with team members, coaches, and national experts in ensuring that different perspectives were represented and varied aspects addressed. They reviewed training strategies for coaches and school teams to ensure that the revised principles informed the structure and content of training programs. They continued to monitor closely ongoing research on school level implementation and coaching to ensure that the concepts and materials they were designing reflected patterns and findings uncovered by recent research. Finally, the team continued to work on model refinement by addressing new areas that research on the model and its implementation had identified as needing attention. The following section provides an example of new work in progress at the Middle Start National Center under the leadership of the model development team.

Next Steps: Developing a Family Engagement Strategy

The following example highlights new work in progress at the Middle Start National Center under the leadership of the model development team. This example shows how a community of model developers continuously use modes of inquiry to inform their actions in refining the model and ensure that promising practices developed at the school level are integrated into the model and vice versa.

The majority of Middle Start schools identified family engagement as a goal of their implementation. Several experts emphasized that meaningful family engagement in schools is critical for student achievement, particularly for low-income students and students with high risk factors

(Henderson & Mapp, 2002). The National Center based its design of a family engagement component of *Principle IV: Distributed Leadership and Sustainable Partnerships* on the advice of a leading researcher and advocate for family engagement in schools and on a case study of a Middle Start school's literacy initiative that brings together families, teachers, and students to jointly address its literacy as well as family engagement objectives. The following description characterizes our efforts to design the family engagement component and illustrates Middle Start's ongoing efforts to inquire into and act on areas of priority.

The case study, conducted by an AED research consultant in Michigan, documents a Middle Start school's pilot involving 25 parents and teachers in a literacy development initiative who met one night a week over a six-week period to share their experiences about parenting and schooling through reading, writing, and discussion. The Middle Start coach who designed the project draws upon *The Parent Project* developed by Vopat (1998), a nationally acclaimed model. The study includes detailed interviews, review of documents produced during the pilot, and one instance of participant observation to document parents' participation in and continuing support of the program. In this case study (Jessup, in press), the consultant delineates the project's process and preliminary impact on parent-teacher relationships, parent attitudes about becoming more engaged in the school's academic program, and parent-child interactions about reading and writing.

The model development team is currently considering the findings of the case study as well as consulting with experts on family engagement in the middle grades to determine the design elements of a sound and doable family engagement strategy for Middle Start. Additionally, members of the group reviewed the literature on family engagement, and consulted with other national comprehensive school reform models to learn about effective strategies that they have adopted to promote family engagement as part of comprehensive school improvement. Once the design is completed and reviewed by coaches and school leadership teams, the group will develop workshops, materials, and other elements to help schools and coaches undertake this component.

LEVEL TWO: PROFESSIONAL DEVELOPMENT IN THE REGIONAL NETWORK OF COACHES

A core group of Middle Start coaches supports schools in putting the Middle Start principles in practice. Researchers state that coaches are the vital link that bridge design with implementation, and research and practice (Neufeld & Roper, 2003). Middle Start coaches typically spend about 3 to

4 days a month in each school, working with school leadership teams and grade level teams. Their role is to help leadership teams develop their capacity to lead the school in goal setting, implementation, self-assessment, and the ongoing improvement of teaching and learning. Middle Start coaches work with grade level teams to improve their capacity to become small learning communities focused on improving instruction and climate within their teams. In addition, coaches participate in and help plan monthly school leadership team seminars, a professional network of leadership teams from Middle Start schools. The seminars help teams develop a consistent understanding of the Middle Start principles, and guide their implementation by networking schools, providing them with opportunities for inquiry (e.g., review of student work), and teaching facilitation, data analysis, and other leadership skills.

As former building principals, central office administrators, or teacher leaders who have demonstrated outstanding leadership in their previous work in schools, Middle Start coaches have experience in developing learning communities. Coaches also meet monthly with the Middle Start regional director to enhance their own knowledge and skills of effective coaching. Thus, every Middle Start coach is a participant in a professional learning community of Middle Start coaches, who learn and deepen their knowledge of the Middle Start principles, explore their own practice, and engage in reflection and dialogue on developing school's capacity for improving teaching and learning.

Deepening Coaches' Understanding of Middle Start Principle Two: An Example

We offer a description, from documentation of a coaches' meeting (AED, 2003a), to illustrate how coaches' learned more about the Middle Start principle of *Effective Small Learning Communities* at their monthly meeting. At this particular meeting, the facilitator's goal was to help coaches develop a clear vision of a high-performing grade-level team and to use consistent practices as they guided schools in establishing and improving such teams. The facilitator randomly organized the group into smaller groups of three or four. The first step of the process was to ask coaches to define a high-performing team. The facilitator gave prompts to guide their thinking about what a high-performing team looks like. The prompts included such things as "What do you see at this team meeting? How is it being conducted? What structures are in place? What are the roles of the participants?" The groups were given time to think, discuss, and record their ideas. Then, they responded to another series of prompts that delved deeper into the specific issues under discussion:

What did the high-performing team *sound like*? What kind of language do you hear coming from the team, and what is the depth of the discussion? Groups were given time to think, discuss, and record before being asked to respond to another series of prompts around what the team *feels like*. Again, there was time for thinking, discussing, and recording. The facilitator brought everyone back together, asked groups to share their ideas, and recorded the ideas on a chart for everyone to see. After reviewing the chart, participants discussed common themes evident across all lists, the most common of which included the development of a shared vision and mission. This led to a deeper discussion about when and how coaches should work with teams on developing a shared vision and mission.

Through discussion, coaches agreed that they needed to ask questions of the school leadership teams to prompt their examination of their mission and vision and help make them more compelling. Coaches then brainstormed some questions to ask school leadership teams. Examples of the questions included: How are we exploring and tracking the values of our vision and mission? How are we translating the school vision and mission into our team vision and mission? How are we making the vision and mission meaningful and compelling throughout the school? How will our students be different 3 years from now when they leave middle school? How will we know? Another idea that emerged from this work was that coaches should work specifically to help team leaders become high-performing leaders. The Middle Start regional coordinator suggested that one of the goals for coaches should be to help every school have a high-performing team leader. The coaches discussed this and shared several questions and comments related to this suggestion and ultimately came up with some recommendations and strategies for incorporating this goal into the work that they do.

At the end of this activity, the facilitator debriefed the process by explaining what he had asked the coaches to do, the purpose of doing it, what the intended result was, what results the coaches came up with, how they were going to take that back to the schools they were working with, and how to use this kind of activity with their school leadership teams. The facilitator also asked coaches to consider the impact on their own work of helping schools develop high-performing team leaders. The discussion that followed clarified that coaches agreed to work with team leaders. Then, coaches engaged in writing and role-playing activity to help them think about how they might go about doing this in their schools.

This example illustrates how coaches' meetings emphasize ongoing collaboration, reflection, and inquiry to build knowledge and understanding of coaching and effective school level implementation. In this meeting, coaches addressed the facilitator's question in small group discussions, explored their own thinking on the topic, shared their knowledge, skills, beliefs, and experiences with one another, and devised strategies to use in their schools. Applying DuFour and Eaker's (1998) criteria, the coaches' network addressed the collective goal of improving coaching and making it consistent in Middle Start schools through studying their practices in a collaborative manner, and planning actions that they would employ in their schools that would spur continuous improvement of school-based Middle Start implementation. Coaches focused, in this particular instance, of strengthening the effectiveness of leadership teams. They improved their own understanding of high-performing teams in order to assist school leadership teams in achieving their goals for students in a timely and efficient manner.

LEVEL THREE: LEARNING COMMUNITIES IN MIDDLE START SCHOOLS

Learning communities take three main forms in Middle Start schools. The school leadership team is a learning community in each school and includes the principal, teachers from each grade level, special education, and electives, and, increasingly, parents and community members. Interdisciplinary grade-level teams are another form of learning community, which include subject area teachers and, in some cases, special education teachers and a counselor. Special committees are a third kind of learning community and are convened on an ad hoc or continuing basis (this depends on the school's needs and preferences), and are concerned with specific professional development initiatives such as literacy, differentiated instruction, cooperative learning, parent engagement, or school self-assessment.

The Middle Start coach is an active guide and partner for all three kinds of learning communities emphasizing an intentional focus, inquiry-based decision-making, collaborative process, and results-oriented efforts for every community. The coach and leadership team also ensure that grade-level teams and special interest committees adhere to the Middle Start principles and are working toward the school's overarching goals.

In the following section, we apply DuFour and Eaker's (1998) definition of learning community to discuss examples from four Middle Start schools that used varied forms of inquiry to improve their learning environment. The four examples include: (1) a school leadership team's collaboration with grade level teams to conduct walk throughs[2] and analyze data aimed at improving teaming practices; (2) a grade-level team's review of varied student assessments to inform instructional approaches that would better address the varied academic interests and needs of their students; and (3) a literacy committee's data-gathering effort to select the most appropriate professional development to boost the school's literacy-across-the-curriculum initiative; and (4) a principal's effort to engage students in ongoing dialogue as part of an effort to improve school climate. We illustrate how each learning community used different types of data as they made decisions about the best course of action to take, and/or assessed their progress.[3]

Walk Throughs Aid Reflection and Improvement

School leadership teams (composed of administrators and teacher leaders representing every grade level) attend a series of Middle Start leadership development seminars fostering their capacity to implement the Middle Start principles. The principal's walk through, a data collection strategy aimed at building the principal's understanding of instructional and organizational changes in the schools, is one of several strategies promoted in the seminars to develop instructional leadership.

The leadership team of a rural Middle Start school, eager to learn more about the workings of newly formed grade-level teams, shared its knowledge of walk throughs with the entire staff and suggested that the principal conduct regular walk throughs to observe how teams were serving their students' academic and developmental needs. Initially, concerned that they would be evaluated during a walk through, teachers in the school resisted the plan. Teachers on the leadership team assured them that walk throughs were not a form of teacher evaluation but rather an information gathering approach to help the principal offer constructive feedback to improve teaming.

During her first walk through, the principal spent a few hours observing the eighth grade team during its common planning time; shadowing students from class to class; and looking at student work from different classes. Using a walk through protocol, she noted the key activities and discussions of teachers and students and used these notes to compile her feedback to the team on the areas in which it was serving students, as well as areas needing attention.

The principal completed similar walk throughs of the sixth and seventh grade teams and met with the Middle Start coach and leadership team to identify the kinds of support that teams needed to address the academic and developmental needs of all their students. With the coach's help, the leadership team conducted a *gap analysis* of student assessment data to determine which students needed additional help and studied the information from the walk throughs to better understand the unique needs of each team. The findings of the gap analysis indicated that teams needed better strategies for reaching out to parents of struggling students as well as additional professional development in middle grades-appropriate teaching strategies, e.g., interdisciplinary thematic instruction and cooperative learning.

The grade-level teams responded well to the feedback they received and agreed that the time the principal spent with them gave her a *slice of our reality*. Each team also had a representative on the leadership team who participated in the review and decision-making process, so that team members were reassured that their team's perspectives were presented. As a result, teachers viewed the suggestions for professional development as valid, and with the help of the Middle Start coach, started to pilot a cooperative learning approach as a first step.

In this example, the leadership team was intentional in its data collection activities and focused on better understanding the functioning of grade-level teams in order to inform their ongoing development. The process used by the team was collaborative, as teachers on the leadership team clarified the aims and scope of the walk through project to the grade-level teams; and the principal provided constructive, rather than critical, feedback to the teams, based on her observations during the walk through. The exercise was results oriented, and teams agreed with the findings of the walk through and the leadership team's gap analysis and participated in the design of a cooperative learning pilot. The success of the walk through rested with the leadership team's intentional focus, collaborative approach, and attention to results. It is likely that the walk through would have felt like an evaluation to teachers, had any of these three elements been missing. This example emphasizes the importance of these three elements in any school-level data-gathering activity.

Realizing All Students Can Learn

A midsized urban Middle Start school procured district consent for regular common planning time for teachers on grade level teams in the early stages of its participation in Middle Start. The principal, in order to ensure that the time was not spent on *housekeeping details* began brainstorming protocols for the use of common planning time with the staff. He urged teams to disaggregate their student performance data and discuss students' behavior and engagement with each other during their planning period as a first step, as the data would provide a baseline and inform goal setting and action plans.

The principal circulated among the teams as they began to compile student data, including performance on class assignments, final exams, and state assessments (where available). Several teachers, as they began to discuss student performance, also found themselves discussing students' interactions with them during classes. They reported being surprised that students who were doing poorly in their class were very engaged and doing better in another teacher's class, and vice versa. When they looked at the number of completed assignments that students turned in, they found that some students with several incompletes in one subject had turned in all their work in another subject. Teachers reported that reviewing varied types of student assessment data greatly altered their perceptions of individual students and gave the principal's *mantra* of *all students can learn* greater credibility.

This first step of looking at student data helped the principal build teacher support for the goal of the equitable improvement of teaching and learning. The school housed a diverse student body representing varied racial/ethnic, and ability groups. The staff began discussions about the need to adopt instructional practices to support struggling students, as well as provide stronger learners with opportunities for enrichment. The leadership team, with the assistance of the Middle Start coach, investigated diverse approaches and decided that mastery learning, an approach requiring students to redo assignments until they produce work that is satisfactory, best fit the needs of their school. The majority of staff agreed with this assessment after an introduction to mastery learning. The school adopted a system of grading that ran from A good, B satisfactory, and, I incomplete. Thus, any student who did not complete an assignment or pass a test received an I, and had additional chances to redo or complete the assignment until s/he attained a B on the task.

Grade-level teams realized they would need to work several additional hours each term, as they trained to implement the new system. However, the principal encouraged them to try it and provided opportunities for several teachers to become instructional guides to teams. Some strategies tried by teams included tutoring small groups of students over lunch, during the after school program, and even during pizza parties and other after school study events where students could prepare together for important tests. Teachers spent their common planning period reviewing assignments to identify the students with the greatest number of incompletes and assisting them during and after the school day. Several teachers stated that mastery learning was demanding but also successful in proving that all students can learn. "It's very satisfying," a teacher said, "to look at my assignment log and see that all my students are finally caught up and at least made a B!" The example below describes mastery learning at work.

During a visit to the school, an eighth grade language arts class is deeply engaged in a discussion of capital punishment. Students read a series of newspaper and magazine articles representing views for and against capital punishment, and after the class discussion, begin to write an essay supporting their views on the topic. A few students complete their essays and submit them to the teacher, who asks them to act as peer reviewers and read each other's essays. Other students struggle with spelling and expression and raise their hand for assistance. A few students are reading the articles and are not yet ready to write. The teacher walks around, talking with students about the assignment and assuring them that she will be available to help them during lunch and after school. Instructional methods are consistent throughout the school: teachers allow students multiple opportunities to master the content at their own pace.

In this example, grade-level teams developed a constructive and consistent approach to supporting the varied learning needs of their students through clarifying their understanding of the gaps in learning as well as variations in student-teacher interactions. The principal paved the way for improved instructional strategies encouraging teams to look at student data. The intentional focus on understanding learning gaps, as well as the collaborative manner in which teachers analyzed their team's ability to meet students' needs resulted in the school wide adoption of an improved instructional approach.

Data-Based Decisions Build Buy-In

Teachers and administrators in all Middle Start schools work regularly with a Middle Start coach during the first 3 years of implementation of the Middle Start model. At the beginning of the first year, a Middle Start coach asked the staff of a large urban middle school, "What is the first priority that we should attend to this year?" The answer was unanimous: literacy. Several teachers expressed concern that several of their students were struggling readers, reading well below grade level. Others described the problems that slower readers had when they could not keep up with other students and became distracted and sometimes disruptive. Several teachers stated that they needed strategies that would help them teach heterogeneous groups. The coach asked teachers to think of the strategies that they used to help students read better and keep up with stronger readers in their class. Again, almost unanimously teachers said that they tried varied strategies but felt that they still needed help. As a next step, the coach helped the school select a reading committee representing staff from all grade levels, electives, and special education. The committee brainstormed ways of helping teachers connect with the most appropriate professional development in literacy and sought the input of the entire staff to select the right approaches. To gather such input, the committee designed a survey asking teachers to check off strategies they already used and strategies they wanted to learn more about. The committee then compiled the survey results and presented them to the school. The findings were that teachers were leaning in the direction of a supplementary reading program for use with heterogeneous groups of students.

The Middle Start coach presented the committee with a potential list of professional development programs in reading. The list, in keeping with Middle Start's standards of professional development, included high quality, research-based programs combining offsite and onsite support. The committee invited representatives of three programs on the list to present the strategies, materials, and evidence of effectiveness of their approach. The committee reviewed each approach and presented their strengths and weaknesses to the entire staff. The staff used the reviews to decide and voted for a novel-based method of teaching reading to heterogeneous groups of students.

A core group of teachers attended off-site workshops to learn the program. The entire staff also participated in on-site professional development offered by a local representative of the reading program. The reading committee continued to work with administrators to develop a daily reading period, during which teachers could begin to implement the novel-based reading approach and decided to pilot it during the enrichment period.

In this school, the careful use of data in decision making led the school to the use of a reading program that matched the needs of the majority of teachers and students and had the support of the entire staff, which participated in several stages of the decision-making process. We see the powerful role played by the reading committee in matching the school with a professional development program in literacy to foster literacy across the curriculum and address the needs of struggling as well as strong readers. The intentional and collaborative approach resulted in the adoption of an instructional approach that teachers were excited about and that engaged readers of varied abilities and interests.

Distributed Leadership Should Include the Student Voice

A rural school provided students with several opportunities to share their perspectives on the school with the principal as one strategy of an initiative to improve school climate and build better within school communication. The principal began a series of breakfast conversations with small groups of students to "get to know the students in a positive context" and not just when students come to the office because of "a behavior issue." She selected students by their birthdays and took them to breakfast at a local café in order to talk with them about their goals, their families, and what they liked and did not like about the school. She described these conversations as powerful, given that students rarely have the opportunity to talk to their principal in an informal context and she rarely had the opportunity to see the school from the perspective of students. The conversations continued for several years and fostered an open school climate in which students feel welcome to share their perspectives with school leaders without fear or hesitation.

The principal's sustained focus on gaining student feedback through personal conversations with small groups of students communicated a powerful message to students about the importance of their opinions about school. The ongoing dialogue resulted in an improved school climate and demonstrates potential for greater student engagement in decision making and activities regarding school improvement in Middle Start schools.

IMPLICATIONS FOR LEARNING COMMUNITIES SERVING MIDDLE GRADES STUDENTS

In this chapter, we focused on examples of learning communities that were successful in using inquiry and research to enable school improvement that is academically rigorous, developmentally responsive, and socially equitable in order to show that multilevel communities within the nested Middle Start infrastructure were all focused on the same goals for students. In summary, we discuss two main implications of Middle Start's approach for school improvement in the middle grades: (1) Middle Start's educational infrastructure promotes and sustains collective responsibility for improving teaching and learning; and (2) model developers must be considered members of an extended learning community including school stakeholders, coaches and national designers, if designs are to keep abreast of knowledge in two important fields: research on school improvement and school-level implementation.

Collective Responsibility for Middle Grades Education

The structure and knowledge of the learning community have the potential to outlast individual members, providing a stable foundation for continuing the work at every level in meaningful and sustainable ways. This is important, as there is tremendous transience at all levels of the educational infrastructure; individual teachers may transfer, coaches may retire, and national level staff may move. Middle Start has developed a strong program for schools because of the investment in an infrastructure to support the continuous and collaborative learning of adults throughout all levels of the initiative. Each of the nested layers of the Middle Start design is linked to the other so that knowledge and information flow in both directions. While each layer functions as its own learning community, the infrastructure, as a whole, is also an active learning community. While the members of each community have their unique and particular role to play in the improvement of teaching and learning, they are continuously learning about what is happening at the other levels. The shared understandings and practices of such learning communities allow new members to quickly learn about and contribute to their joint work.

The important outcome of such consistent and sustainable communities is that they streamline their goals through the process of inquiry and self-correction. The collective strength that multilevel learning communities bring to addressing the academic, developmental and equity goals for middle grades students enhances the likelihood that students will learn and develop in better, more equitable schools.

Partnerships between Model Developers and Schools

We believe that Middle Start's approach expands on current understandings of learning communities. Through the case of the learning community that leads model development, we make the argument that educational partners need to adopt the practices that they preach to schools in order to remain relevant to their shifting contexts. By unifying the three levels of Middle Start's infrastructure in its work toward shared goals, we make the case for two-way communication between model developers and schools. Middle Start's collaboration with national as well as school-level experts in its model refinement activities illustrates the value that the model places on the contributions of teachers, administrators, and students.

As we continue to refine the Middle Start model, we hope that students will come to play a key role in the activities of school-level and other learning communities. We believe that students need to share and contribute to the collective vision for their education that the Middle Start infrastructure supports. Middle grades advocates have often remarked on the unique developmental stage of students entering early adolescence whose energy, curiosity and intellect are a largely untapped source (Anfara, 2001). We end this chapter with a charge to middle grades school reformers, including ourselves, to invite students into our learning communities in meaningful ways. Middle grades students are at a stage in their lives when they can take responsibility for their own learning, envision their future, and develop goals. Through engaging students in our learning communities, we can encourage them to seek and share knowledge, and engage in reflection that enhances their learning and development.

NOTES

1. Goals of the National Forum to Accelerate Middle Grades Reform and have been adopted by Middle Start.
2. Walk throughs are a data collection strategy by which school observers, including principals, teachers and parents, use systematic methods of observation, interview and data analysis to answer specific instructional questions that they develop in advance of a walk through. Observers then analyze their data to develop a school wide picture and present it in a collaborative mode to individual teachers, teacher teams or the entire staff; ask clarifying questions, and provide feedback (Richardson, 2001).
3. The examples from this section are drawn from *Voices from Middle Start Schools* (AED, 2003b), a document summarizing findings from AED's qualitative studies of Middle Start. The examples accompany Middle Start's Rubrics for School Improvement, and illustrate pathways that schools adopted as they implemented particular Middle Start principles.

REFERENCES

Academy for Educational Development. (1998). *Working paper #4: Progress of the Middle Start comprehensive school improvement schools.* New York: Author.

Academy for Educational Development. (2003a). *Notes from the November, 2003 coaches' seminar.* New York: Author.

Academy for Educational Development. (2003b). *Voices from Middle Start schools.* New York: Author.

Academy for Educational Development. (2004). *Middle Start: Evidence of effectiveness.* New York: Author.

Ancess, J. (1996). *Outside/inside, inside/outside.* New York: National Center for Restructuring Education, Schools and Teaching.

Anderson, G. L., Herr, K., & Nihlen, A. (1994). *Studying your own school: An educator's guide to qualitative practitioner research.* Thousand Oaks, CA: Corwin Press.

Anfara., V. A., Jr. (2001). Setting the stage: An introduction to middle level education. In V. A. Anfara, Jr. (Ed.), *The handbook of research in middle level education* (pp. vii–xix). Greenwich, CT: Information Age.

Ball, D. L., & Cohen, D. K. (1999). Developing practice, developing practitioners: Toward a practice-based theory of professional education. In L. Darling-Hammond & G. Sykes (Eds.), *Teaching as the learning profession: Handbook of policy and practice* (pp. 3-32). San Francisco: Jossey-Bass.

Center for Prevention Research and Development. (1998). *The status of Middle Start grantee schools: An analysis of the Middle Start self-study assessment data.* Urbana, IL: University of Illinois.

Center for Prevention Research and Development. (2004). *Analysis of 2001-02 and 2002-03 Louisiana Achievement Data (LEAP21) for Mid South Middle Start and the Foundation for the Mid South.* University of Illinois, Institute of Government and Public Affairs. Unpublished raw data.

Center for Prevention Research and Development. (2001). *An evaluation of Michigan Middle Start schools from 1994 to 2001.* Unpublished manuscript. Champaign, IL: University of Illinois.

Cochran-Smith, M., & Lytle, S. (2001). Beyond certainty: Taking an inquiry stance on practice. In A. Lieberman & L. Miller (Eds.), *Teachers caught in the action: Professional development that matters* (pp. 45-60). New York: Teachers College Press.

DuFour, R., & Eaker, R. (1998). *Professional learning communities at work: Best practices for enhancing student achievement.* Bloomington, IN: National Educational Service.

Elmore, R. F. (2000). *Building a new structure for school leadership.* Washington, DC: Albert Shanker Institute.

Flowers, N., Mertens, S. B., & Mulhall, P. (2000). How teaming influences classroom practices: Five research-based outcomes. *Middle School Journal, 31*(2), 57-60.

Gopalan, P., & Jessup, P. (2001). *Reaching for goals: Key areas of Michigan Middle Start comprehensive school reform implementation in 1999-2000.* New York: Academy for Educational Development.

Gopalan, P. (2001). *Lake Middle School: A case study.* New York: Academy for Educational Development.

Henderson, A. T., & Mapp, K. L. (2002). A new wave of evidence: the impact of school, family and community connections on student achievement. Austin, TX: Southwest Educational Development Laboratory.

Holly, P. (1991). Action research: The missing link in the creation of schools as centers of inquiry. In A. Lieberman & L. Miller (Eds.), *Staff development for education in the '90s: New demands, new realities, new perspectives* (pp. 133-157). New York: Teachers College Press.

Jackson, A. W., & Davis, G. A. (2000). *Turning points 2000: Educating adolescents in the 21st century.* New York: Teachers College Press.

Jessup, P. (in press). *Report from the parent project.* New York: Academy for Educational Development.

Kruse, S. D., & Louis, K. S. (1997). Teacher teaming in middle schools: Dilemmas for a schoolwide community. *Educational Administration Quarterly, 33*(3), 261-289.

Lave, J., & Wenger, E. (1991). *Situated learning: Legitimate peripheral participation.* Cambridge, England: Cambridge University Press.

Lieberman, A., & Miller, L. (1991). Preface. In A. Lieberman & L. Miller (Eds.), *Staff development for education in the '90s: New demands, new realities, new perspectives* (pp. vi – x). New York: Teachers College Press.

Lipsitz, J., Mizell, M. H., Jackson, A. W., & Austin, L. M. (1997). Speaking with one voice: A manifesto for middle grades reform. *Phi Delta Kappan*, *78*(7), 533-540.

Little, J. W. (1999). Organizing schools for teacher learning. In L. Darling-Hammond & G. Sykes (Eds.), *Teaching as the learning profession: Handbook of policy and practice* (pp. 233-262). San Francisco: Jossey-Bass.

McLaughlin, M. W., & Zarrow, J. (2001). Teachers engaged in evidence-based reform: Trajectories of teacher's inquiry, analysis and action. In A. Lieberman & L. Miller (Eds.), *Teachers caught in the action: Professional development that matters* (pp. 79–101). New York: Teachers College Press.

National Forum to Accelerate Middle Grades Reform. (1999). *Our vision statement.* Retrieved January 15, 2004, from http://www.mgforum.org/about/vision.asp

Neufeld, B., & Roper, D. (2003). *Coaching: A strategy for developing instructional capacity.* Washington, DC: Aspen Institute Program on Education and Providence, RI: Annenberg Institute for School Reform.

Northwest Regional Educational Laboratory. (2002). *Catalog of school reform models: User's guide.* Retrieved January 15, 2004, from http://www.nwrel.org/scpd/catalog/guide/faq.shtml

Richardson, J. (2001). Seeing through new eyes: Walk throughs offer new way to view schools. *Tools for Schools Oct./Nov. 2001.* Oxford, OH: National Staff Development Council.

Southwest Educational Development Laboratory. (2003). *Comprehensive school reform awards database.* Retrieved January 15, 2004, from http://www.sedl.org/csr/awards.html

Spillane, J. P., Halverson, R., & Diamond, J. B. (1999, April). *Distributed leadership: Toward a theory of school leadership practice.* Paper presented at the American Educational Research Association Annual Meeting, Montreal, Canada.

Stokes, L. (2001). Lessons from an inquiring school: Forms of inquiry and conditions for teacher learning. In A. Lieberman & L. Miller, (Eds.), *Teachers caught in the action: Professional development that matters* (pp. 141-158). New York: Teachers College Press.

Sykes, G. (1999). Teaching as the learning profession. In L. Darling-Hammond & G. Sykes (Eds.), *Teaching as the learning profession: Handbook of policy and practice* (pp. xv-xxiv). San Francisco: Jossey-Bass.

Vopat, J. (1998). *More than bake sales: The resource guide for family involvement in education.* York, ME: Stenhouse.

Williams, L., & Mitchell V. (2003). *Voices from Mid South Middle Start: Developing learning communities.* New York: Academy for Educational Development.

Williams, L. (2004, February). *Rural middle-grades schools in the Mid South Delta.* Paper presented at the meeting of the National Middle School Association: Middle Level Essentials conference, Chicago.

CHAPTER 14

RECOMMENDATIONS AND RESOURCES FOR ACTION RESEARCH

Micki M. Caskey

ABSTRACT

To make a difference in middle grades education, teachers, administrators, college and university faculty, researchers, and policy makers explore many pathways. One compelling approach is the action research project. Educators often look to colleagues, higher education institutions, or school districts for information to support their action research ventures. To guide action researchers with their journey into action research, this chapter reviews briefly the exemplars of action research, outlines a series of recommendations, and provides a useful set of resources.

How do you make a difference in middle level education with action research? A well-reasoned approach is to become acquainted with the work of others. For instance, *Making a Difference: Action Research in Middle Level Education* offers an overview and twelve exemplars of action research in middle grades education. A brief review of these examples begins this chapter. After this introduction to action research in the middle grades,

Making a Difference: Action Research in Middle Level Education, 285–298
Copyright © 2005 by Information Age Publishing
All rights of reproduction in any form reserved.

you can explore scores of books, various journal articles, and numerous electronic information sources.

To facilitate your exploration of theoretical and practical resources, a modest selection of books, journals, and Web sites spans the final pages of the chapter. Between the exemplars and the resources are a series of recommendations for aspiring and practicing action researchers.

REVIEW OF EXEMPLARS

Action research in middle grades education is alive and well. Numerous exemplars of action research fill the pages of this volume of *The Handbook of Research in Middle Level Education*. To begin, Arhar provides a brief history, defines action research, and details a model of action research. She explains the entire process from problem identification to publicly sharing the results by describing the experiences of a middle school science teacher. Arhar's example characterizes a classroom teacher's journey with action research.

Cases of inquiry conducted by three middle grades classroom teachers reveal the power of action research. These teachers grapple with the same types of issues facing other middle grades teachers. Sanguras shares that her young adolescent learners welcomed specific praise and their vocabulary test scores improved with its use. She is not convinced that grades were an effective motivator for her students and remains unclear about the value of incentives. Similarly, Shrum weighs thoughtfully the results of using manipulatives in seventh grade mathematics. While she finds that manipulatives improved students' performance in some concept areas (measurement, geometry, probability, and statistics), the use of manipulatives did not necessarily help to advance their attitudes toward learning mathematics. The third middle school teacher, Stanton, witnesses the tangible benefits of inclusive teaching for both special education and general education students. Her special education students demonstrate academic growth (preparedness, on-task behavior, completion of class and homework assignments), yet this achievement is not evidenced by standardized test scores. In each of these studies, the teachers reflect, pose additional questions, and consider future courses of action.

The use of action research in teacher and administrator preparation programs is noteworthy. Stacki discloses how preservice teachers' observations and interviews result in a deeper understanding and appreciation of the professional life of teachers. Beyond enculturation into the teaching profession, this collaborative field-based inquiry affords students with authentic experience with action research methodology to use in their prospective classrooms and schools. Likewise, Wilder, Combs, and Resor note that action research is a good match for alternative teacher education programs. They convey how action research engages their graduate students in purposeful research that cultivates lifelong learning and reflective teaching ability. Future administrators also benefit from experiencing action research during their preparation program. Thompson, Gregg, and Caruthers show how aspiring administrators use a cycle of inquiry and their emergent leadership skills to enact meaningful changes in their middle level schools. Undoubtedly, these cases highlight the importance of action research in professional preparation programs.

Professional development schools (PDS) are logical sites for implementing action research studies. Thornton exemplifies how university faculty and teachers collaborate to resolve a local concern, an equitable way to select master teachers. Through their collaborative inquiry, teachers assume ownership of the teaching standards for their school. Barker and Basile's four cases highlight the evolutionary nature of action research in the PDS. They disclose that inquiry plays a central role in creating and developing effective middle schools and advocate a posture of inquiry among middle grades educators.

Collaboration continues to surface as a critical element in action research conducted in middle level education. Bishop, Boke, Pflaum, and Kirsh display how collaborative endeavors can result in a school-wide emphasis on reading instruction that helps young adolescents to become strategic readers. Though their action research study on reading is contextual, the interest in effective literacy practices is universal. Another collaborative inquiry model holds promise as well. Saurino, Saurino, and Crawford advance the Collaborative Team Action Research (CTAR) for professional development in middle schools. They relate how interdisciplinary teams use the CTAR cycle to bring about genuine professional growth. These examples highlight the importance of reflective processes and communication among teachers.

Researchers are also using action research to analyze university-school partnerships and school reform models. Malu reveals the rollercoaster nature of one university-school relationship and recommends ways to develop and sustain viable partnerships. Importantly, she calls upon school and university partners to use action research to scaffold their collaborative work and to understand the effects of their actions. Gopalan, West, Montesano, and Hoelscher employ action research to study systematically a comprehensive school improvement model. They reveal how multilevel learning communities interact and help to shape an infrastructure for middle grades educational reform.

Examples of action research span middle grades education. From individual classroom teachers to prospective teachers and administrators to university researchers and collaborative teams of researchers, cases of action research continue to emerge. The initiative of individuals and groups is making a difference in middle grades education.

RECOMMENDATIONS

Action Research Rationale

Action research allows classroom teachers to examine systematically their practice and its effect on student performance. Researchers (Wilson, Floden, & Ferrini-Mundy, 2001) report that new teachers learned the most from field experiences when required to do action research in their classrooms. Similarly, a set of model standards for beginning teachers (Interstate New Teacher Assessment & Support Consortium, 1992) highlight the importance of reflection—an integral part of the action research process—in Principle 9. This principle calls for teachers to be reflective practitioners who continually evaluate the effects of their choices and actions on others (students, parents, and members of the learning community) and who seek actively opportunities to grow professionally. In fact, action research holds a prominent position in teacher education, professional development, and school reform (Cochran-Smith & Lytle, 1999). Teachers' professional growth is essential for student growth. What teachers know and can do is the most important influence on what students learn (National Commission on Teaching and America's Future, 1996, p. 10).

Why should classroom teachers engage in action research? McNiff (1992) suggests three benefits for teachers: political, professional, and personal. Politically, the teacher is the central figure in education. Teachers' influence views and attitudes of students, parents, and others through their teaching practice. As professionals, teachers use methods based on theoretical research and knowledge. Action research allows teachers to design context-specific research, construct meaning, and grow professionally. In addition, action research provides opportunities for self-discovery and personal growth. When teachers engage in systematic inquiry and reflection, they learn about themselves.

Why should teacher education institutions incorporate action research into their programs? Action research affords preservice teachers with a coherent process to improve their own practices, understand these practice, and the situations where these practices occur. Through a reflective process, preservice teachers gain more than an understanding of their specific action research project. Potentially, they develop their capacity for critical analysis. Liston and Zeichner (1987) suggest that action research is one instructional strategy associated with the development of critical pedagogy. Additionally, the reflective nature of the action research process may illuminate for preservice teachers the divide between their practices and beliefs. When engaged in such inquiry, preservice teachers gain new insights and deeper understanding into their developing practice. Furthermore, when teacher educators also use action research to examine their practice, they contribute to a supportive climate of preservice teacher inquiry in their professional preparation programs (Liston & Zeichner, 1990).

Research in Middle Grades

Research findings have the potential to shape attitudes toward middle level practices (Anfara et al., 2003). Teachers, administrators, parents, community members, and other stakeholders often form their beliefs based upon their own understanding of research. Practitioners also may apply knowledge gleaned from research to their daily practice. More and more, educators are implementing action research. Indeed, action research accounts for 19.2% of the middle grades research studies published from 1991 to 2001 (Hough, 2003). Potentially, action research can capitalize on the strengths of quantitative and qualitative research. Reasons for this mixed methods approach for action research are two-fold (1) better triangulation of data sources, and (2) the contextual nature of qualitative data can help to clarify quantitative results. Furthermore, middle level researchers (Anfara et al., 2003) endorse mixed-methods studies in their recommendations for future research.

Starting and Sustaining Action Research

Educational action research is a dynamic process that takes place in the social and cultural contexts of schools. As teachers face issues related to their effectiveness in the classroom, they need to develop the ability to recognize and resolve identified issues. An action research cycle of planning, action, observation, and reflection facilitates teachers' capacity to improve their own practice. Importantly, teachers need to see themselves as the primary researchers of their action research investigations. Arguably, the emphasis on teacher ownership is among the most significant ways that teacher-based action research differs from traditional research (Reagan, Case, & Brubacher, 2000). In summary, teachers need to retain ownership of their action research study throughout the entire inquiry cycle.

Schools need to provide teachers with professional development, support, and tools to do their classroom research. This includes time for individual teacher researchers to plan, act, and reflect upon their actions. Collaborative teams need time for regular meetings to collaborate on action research projects and share their classroom research. In addition to time, teachers benefit from common work areas where they can work on curriculum, instructional strategies, and assessment techniques. Beyond time and space, teacher researchers may need funds or other resources to support their efforts. As administrators of the schools, principals must encourage and support inquiry within their schools to examine systematically how students are doing and develop strategies for improvement (National Commission on Teaching and America's Future, 1996).

Another avenue for action research in middle grades education is the partnership between schools and higher education. A school-university partnership can offer forums for research groups and site-based research on issues of immediate concern to the school. Additionally, schools can make professional development an ongoing part of teachers' work through collaborative planning, research, curriculum and assessment work, study groups, and peer coaching (National Commission on Teaching and America's Future, 1996). In this manner, action research becomes a natural and integral part of the partnership.

An area of inquiry, lesson study, is gaining attention in the United States and holds promise for middle grades education. Teachers in Japan and China give teach demonstration lessons to each other and discuss the nuances of specific concepts, lesson presentation, possible student questions, and the kinds of questions teacher should pose to garner student interest. In fact, teachers in countries such as Germany, France, and Japan gather in a shared workroom for breaks and for regular meetings to work on issues of curriculum, assessment, and school management together. (National Commission on Teaching and America's Future, 1996). Middle grades educators need to consider how lesson study could support instruction and curriculum in their schools. As an action research method, lesson study warrants further attention in middle grades education.

To facilitate discourse and action, a set of action research resources are presented in the final section of this chapter. The resource list includes an annotated books (1990-2004), recommended titles (1980-2004), print and electronic journals, databases, Web sites, networks, and professional organizations. Ideally, your explorations of these resources and this volume will empower you to make a difference through action research.

RESOURCES

Annotated Books: 2000-2004

Burnaford, G. E., Fischer, J., & Hobson, D. (Eds.). (2001). *Teachers doing research: The power of action through inquiry* (2nd ed.). Mahwah, NJ: Erlbaum.
Very accessible text describes the process of conducting teacher action research and provides specific examples of teacher research projects. The book includes three sections: Part I details methods of doing action research; Part II addresses school and professional contexts; and Part III examines broader issues of teacher research and school reform.

Holly, M. L., Arhar, J. M., & Kasten, W. (2004). *Action research for teachers: Traveling the yellow brick road* (2nd ed.). Columbus, OH: Prentice Hall.
Unique approach details the journey of becoming an action researcher. This book guides teachers through the action research process using metaphors from the *Wizard of Oz*. Provides both systematic instruction in conducting action research and authentic examples to illuminate the process.

Kincheloe, J. L. (2003). *Teachers as researchers: Qualitative inquiry as a path to empowerment* (2nd ed.). New York: RoutledgeFalmer.
A scholarly text challenges experienced teachers to address the educational debate by conducting their own meaningful research. The author contends that only through critical research of their own teaching practice will educators be positioned to reclaim their profession, regain power in their classrooms, and improve student learning.

Mills, G. E. (2003) *Action research: A guide for the teacher researcher* (2nd ed.). Upper Saddle River, NJ: Merrill Prentice Hall.
An excellent handbook provides systematic instruction for teachers who wish conduct action research. Very practical and user-friendly text describes the process of action research, provides concrete examples and an extensive companion Web site. The Web site (http://www.sou.edu/ education/action_research.htm) includes summaries, PowerPoint presentations to accompany each chapter, video clips, samples, and numerous resources.

Reason, P., & Bradbury, H. (Eds.). (2000). *Handbook of action research: Participative inquiry and practice*. Thousand Oaks, CA: Sage.
A significant volume in action research articulates an array of approaches and applications of action research. The handbook serves as a reference for scholars, advocates, and practitioners. The well-known contributing authors address action research theories, traditions, and methodologies in a variety of contexts.

Sagor, R. (2000). *Guiding school improvement with action research*. Alexandria, VA: Association for Supervision and Curriculum Development.

A succinct text provides information about how teachers can research their own practice. The text outlines a quasi-experimental research process for teachers to follow. A companion video is available, which includes examples of teacher's action research and the author's explanation of the action research process.

RECOMMENDED TITLES: 2000-2004

Arhar, J. M., Holly, M. L., & Kasten, W. C. (2001). *Action research for teachers: Traveling the yellow brick road.* Columbus, OH: Merrill Prentice Hall.

Bray, J. N., Lee, J., Smith, L. L., & Yorks, L. (Eds.). (2000). *Collaborative inquiry in practice: Action, reflection, and making meaning.* Thousand Oaks, CA: Sage.

Cole, A. L., & Knowles, J. G. (2000). *Researching teaching: Exploring teacher development through reflexive inquiry.* Boston: Allyn & Bacon.

Hopkins, D. (2002). *A teacher's guide to classroom research* (3rd ed.). Buckingham, England: Open University Press.

Johnson, A. P. (2002). *A short guide to action research* (2nd ed.). Boston: Pearson Allyn & Bacon.

Kember, D. (2000). *Action learning and action research: Improving the quality of teaching and learning.* London: Kogan Page.

Lieberman, A., & Miller, L. (Eds.). (2001). *Teachers caught in the action: Professional development that matters.* New York: Teachers College Press.

MacIntyre, C. (2000). *The art of action research in the classroom.* London: David Fulton.

McNiff, J. (2002). *Action research: Principles and practice* (2nd ed.). London: Routledge.

McNiff, J. (2002). *Action research for professional development: Concise advice for new action researchers* (3rd ed.). [Electronic publication]. http://www.jeanmcniff.com/booklet1.php

Meyers, E., & Rust, F. (Eds.). (2003). *Taking action with teacher research.* Portsmouth, NH: Heinemann.

Parsons, R. D., & Brown, K. S. (2002). *Teacher as reflective practitioner and action researcher.* Belmont, CA: Wadsworth.

Stringer, E. (2004). *Action research in education.* Columbus, OH: Merrill Prentice Hall.

Annotated Books: 1990-1999

Hollingsworth, S. (Ed.). (1997). *International action research: A casebook for educational reform.* London: Falmer Press.

Foremost practitioners and advocates of action research contributed to this collection of international papers. Authors represent the United Kingdom, United States, Australia, Canada, South Africa, Malaysia, Mexico, Italy, Israel, and Austria.

Hollingsworth, S., & Sockett, H. (Eds.). (1994). *Teacher research and education reform. Ninety-third yearbook of the National Society for the Study of Education.* Chicago: The University of Chicago Press.
    Collection of essays highlights the contemporary teacher research movement. Among the contributors to the volume are D. Jean Clandinin, F. Michael Connelly, Marilyn Cochran-Smith, Ann Lieberman, Susan L. Lytle, Susan Noffke, Jonas Soltis, and Kenneth Zeichner.

Hubbard, R. S., & Power, B. M. (1999). *Living the questions: A guide for teacher-researchers.* York, ME: Stenhouse.
    An outstanding resource for novice and experienced action researchers is both informative and passionate. The book describes teacher research, provides practical advice and models, and offers numerous written samples from teacher-researchers.

McKernan, J. (1996). *Curriculum action research: A handbook of methods and measures for the reflective practitioner* (2nd ed.). London: Kogan Page.
    A useful guide for teachers and administrators conducting action research focused on the classroom or school curriculum. The text describes the context of curriculum action research, details research methods and resources, and addresses issues in action research.

McLean, J. E. (1995). *Improving education through action research: a guide for administrators and teachers.* Thousand Oaks, CA: Corwin.
    A brief and practical text describes a quantitative approach to educational action research. Details how practioners can use statistical procedures to analyze data.

Noffke, S. E., & Stevenson, R. B. (Eds.). (1995). *Educational action research: Becoming practically critical.* New York: Teachers College Press.
    This text presents a collection of cases on action research for teacher education, school improvement, and schools. Teachers, administrators, academics, and staff developers contribute case studies to exemplify the value of action research in their diverse settings.

RECOMMENDED TITLES: 1990-1999

Atweh, B., Kemmis, S., & Weeks, P. (Eds.). (1998). *Action research in practice: Partnerships for social justice in education.* London: Routledge.
Brooks, A., & Watkins, K. E. (Eds.). (1994). *The emerging power of action inquiry technologies.* San Francisco: Jossey-Bass.
Calhoun, E. F. (1994). *How to use action research in the self-renewing school.* Alexandria, VA: Association of Supervision and Curriculum Development.
Carson, T. R., & Sumara, D. J. (Eds.). (1997). *Action research as a living practice.* New York: Peter Lang.

Cochran-Smith, M., & Lytle, S. L. (1993). *Inside/outside: Teacher research and knowledge*. New York: Teachers College Press.

Elliott, J. (1991). *Action research for educational change*. London: Allen & Unwin.

Glanz, J. (1998). *Action research: An educational leader's guide to school improvement*. Norwood, MA: Christopher Gordon.

Grady, M. P. (1998). *Qualitative and action research: A practitioner handbook*. Bloomington, Indiana: Phi Delta Kappa Educational Foundation.

Greenwood, D. J., & Levin, M. (1998). *Introduction to action research: Social research for social change*. Thousand Oaks, CA: Sage.

Hubbard, R. S., & Power, B. M. (1993). *The art of classroom inquiry: A handbook for teacher-researchers*. Portsmouth, NH: Heinemann.

Jarvis, P. (1999). *The practitioner-researcher: Developing theory from practice*. San Francisco: Jossey-Bass, 1999.

MacLean, M. S., & Mohr, M. M. (1999). *Teacher-researchers at work*. Berkeley, CA: The National Writing Project.

McNiff, J., Lomax, P., & Whitehead, J. (1996). *You and your action research project*. New York: Hyde Publications.

McTaggart, R. (Ed.). (1997). *Participatory action research: International contexts and consequences*. Albany, NY: State University of New York Press.

Patterson, L., Santa, C. M., Short, K. G., & Smith, K. (Eds.). (1993). *Teachers are researchers: Reflection and action*. Newark, DE: International Reading Association.

Schmuck, R. A. (1997). *Practical action research for change*. Arlington Heights, IL: IRI/Skylight Training and Publishing.

Selener, D. (1998). *Participatory action research and social change* (3rd ed.). Ithaca, NY: Cornell Participatory Action Research Network, Cornell University.

Stake, R. E. (1995). *The art of case study research: Perspectives on practice*. Thousand Oaks, CA: Sage.

Stringer, E. T. (1999). *Action research* (2nd ed.). Thousand Oaks, CA: Sage.

Wallace, M. J. (1998). *Action research for language teachers*. Cambridge, England: Cambridge University Press.

RECOMMENDED TITLES: 1980-1989

Atwell, N. (1987). *In the middle: Writing, reading, and learning with adolescents*. Upper Montclair, NJ: Boynton/Cook.

Carr, W., & Kemmis, S. (1986). *Becoming critical: Education, knowledge and action research*. London: Falmer.

Oja, S. N., & Smulyan, L. (1989). *Collaborative action research: A developmental process*. London: Falmer Press.

Schön, D. A. (1987). *Educating the reflective practitioner: Towards a new design for teaching and learning in the professions*. San Francisco: Jossey-Bass.

JOURNALS

Print

Action Research

An international, interdisciplinary, refereed journal provides a forum to develop the theory and practice of action research. Sage Publications (London, England) publishes four issues of the journal a year. Both print and electronic versions of the journal are available. For information about the journal including past issues, submission guidelines, and subscription rates, access Sage Publication's Web site at http://www.sagepub.co.uk

Educational Action Research

An international, peer-reviewed journal offers action research studies that examine the intersection of research and practice. The journal is a publication of CARN, the Collaborative Action Research Network, an international network for professional development. Triangle Journals (Oxford, England) distributes three issues of the journal each year. For more information about past issues, submission guidelines, related conferences and Web sites, and subscription rates, visit Triangle Journal's Web site at http://www.triangle.co.uk

Electronic

Action Research International

http://www.scu.edu.au/schools/gcm/ar/ari/arihome.html
An online, refereed journal of action research sponsored by the Southern Cross Institute of Action Research at Southern Cross University Press (Lismore, Australia).

Action Research Electronic Reader

http://www.scu.edu.au/schools/gcm/ar/arr/arow/default.html
An electronic publication edited by Ian Hughes of the University of Sidney (Sidney, Australia)

The Ontario Action Researcher

http://www.nipissingu.ca/oar
A refereed online journal invites elementary, secondary, and university educators to contribute action research reports and articles.

Practical Assessment, Research, and Evaluation (PARE)

http://pareonline.net
An online peer-reviewed journal provides education professionals access to articles on assessment, research, evaluation, and teaching practice.

DATABASES

PARchives
> http://www.parnet.org/parchives
> An interactive bibliographic database sponsored by Cornell Participatory
> Action Research Network.

WEB SITES

Action Research at Queens University
> http://educ.queensu.ca/~ar/index.html
> Queens University (Kingston, Ontario, CA) hosts a Web site, Action
> Research at Queens University, which highlights action research
> resources as well as reports by preservice teacher candidates and gradu-
> ate students.

ActionReseach.net
> http://www.bath.ac.uk/~edsajw
> An extensive action research Web site maintained by Dr. Jack Whitehead,
> Faculty in the School of Education, University of Bath (Bath, England).

Action Research Resources
> http://www.scu.edu.au/schools/gcm/ar/arhome.html
> A significant and comprehensive action research Web site at Southern
> Cross University (Lismore, Australia) is maintained by Bob Dick. The
> Web site includes links to *Action Research International*, AREOL (an online
> action research course), papers and conference abstracts, lists of recent
> action research books, electronic mail lists, and links to other action
> research Web sites.

AROW: Action Research Open Web
> http://www2.fhs.usyd.edu.au/arow
> The University of Sydney (Sydney, Australia) hosts the Action and
> Research Open Web. This expansive Web site has sections for active
> projects, research projects and resources, opening learning modules, and
> networking.

Action Research Support
> http://leo.oise.utoronto.ca/~lbencze/Action_Research_Help.html
> A comprehensive Web site for supporting action research at the Ontario
> Institute for Studies in Education at the University of Toronto (Toronto,
> Ontario, CA). Dr. Larry Bencze designed and maintains the Web site.

Center for Action Research in Professional Practice
> http://www.bath.ac.uk/carpp/carpp.htm
> The Center for Action Research in Professional Practice offers postgraduate
> programs in action research at the University of Bath (Bath, England), a lead-

ing research institution. Professor Peter Reason, a noted action researcher is director of Studies Postgraduate Programme in Action Research.

Internet Resources for Participatory Action Research
http://www.goshen.edu/soan/soan96p.htm
Goshen College provides this expansive list of Web links to participatory action research for students and practitioners.

Jean McNiff.com
http://www.jeanmcniff.com
A comprehensive action research Web site includes links her detailed booklet, *Action Research for Professional Development: Concise Advice for New Action Researchers* (3rd ed.). and numerous publications.

National Staff Development Council
http://www.nsdc.org/library/strategies/actionresearch.cfm#models
A set of articles and Web site highlights the value of action research, the process of action research, and examples of action research projects in classrooms across the U.S.

NETWORKS

Collaborative Action Research Network (CARN)
http://www.did.stu.mmu.ac.uk/carn/
A network for professional development is maintained by Institute of Education at Manchester Metropolitan University.

Cornell Participatory Action Research Network
http://www.einaudi.cornell.edu/cparn/
A network for participatory action research (PAR) is hosted by Cornell University (New York, United States). The network sponsors PARnet and PARchives.

PARnet
http://www.parnet.org
An interactive community on action research hosted by Cornell Participatory Action Research Network.

Teacher Inquiry Communities Network (TIC)
http://www.writingproject.org/cs/nwpp/print/nwpn/4
A national network that links sites interested in promoting teacher research. The network emerged from the National Writing Project
(http://www.writingproject.org/index.html).

PROFESSIONAL ORGANIZATIONS

American Educational Research Association: Special Interest Groups

Action Research Special Interest Group (SIG)
http://coe.westga.edu/arsig
This SIG involves teachers, administrators, researchers, and community members in dialog about action research to examine educational practice, encourage educational reform, and advance professional development.

Teacher as Researcher Special Interest Group
http://www.teacherasresearcher.org
This group supports the research and participation of classroom teachers in American Educational Research Association.

Self-Study Special Interest Group
http://www.ku.edu/~sstep
Teacher educators who work on the problems of education through the study of their own practices.

REFERENCES

Anfara, V. A., Jr., Andrews, P. G., Hough, D. L., Mertens, S. B., Mizelle, N. B., & White, G. P. (2003). *Research and resources in support of This We Believe*. Westerville, OH: National Middle School Association.

Cochran-Smith, M., & Lytle, S. L. (1999). The teacher research movement: A decade later. *Educational Researcher, 28*(7), 15-25.

Hough, D. L. (2003). *R3 = Research, rhetoric, and reality: A study of studies*. Westerville, OH: National Middle School Association.

Interstate New Teacher Assessment & Support Consortium. (1992). *Model standards for beginning teacher licensing, assessment and development: A resource for state dialogue*. Washington, DC: Council of Chief State School Officers.

Liston, D. P., & Zeichner, K. M. (1987). Critical pedagogy and teacher education. *Journal of Education, 169*(3), 117-137.

Liston, D. P., & Zeichner, K. M. (1990). Reflective teaching and action research in preservice teacher education. *Journal of Education for Teaching, 16*(1), 235-255.

McNiff, J. (1992). *Action research: Principles and practice*. London: Routledge.

National Commission on Teaching and America's Future. (1996). *What matters most: Teaching for America's future*. New York: Author.

Reagan, T. G., Case, C. W., & Brubacher, J. W. (2000). *Becoming a reflective educator: How to build a culture of inquiry in the schools* (2nd ed.). Thousand Oaks, CA: Corwin.

Wilson, S. M., Floden, R. E., & Ferrini-Mundy, J. (2001). *Teacher preparation research: Current knowledge, gaps, and recommendations*. Washington, DC: Office of Educational Research and Improvement, U.S. Department of Education.

ABOUT THE AUTHORS

Joanne M. Arhar is a professor of curriculum and instruction, associate dean of student services, and director of Teacher Education at Kent State University. Joanne has been teacher, administrator, staff development specialist, and consultant to numerous schools and corporations. *Action Research for Teachers: Traveling the Yellow Book Road,* written with Holly and Kasten (2004) is in its second edition. Her dissertation on interdisciplinary teaming in the middle grades won two national dissertation awards.

Heidi Bulmahn Barker, PhD, is an assistant professor of education at Regis University in Denver, Colorado. Her research interests include teacher education, teachers' impact on school reform, personal aspects of school change, and relationships between and among teachers, children, and content in the context of school reform. She was previously on the faculty at the University of Colorado at Denver.

Carole G. Basile, EdD is the associate dean of teacher education and professional leadership in the School of Education at the University of Colorado at Denver. Her research topics have included impact of context on learning, environmental education, popular culture, school culture and humanity, and teacher education.

Penny A. Bishop directs the Middle Level Teacher Education Program at the University of Vermont. She teaches in the areas of middle level school organization, pedagogy, and early adolescence. Her dissertation research received the Distinguished Dissertation Award by the National Association of Secondary School Principals. Her current research includes a qualitative analysis of student perceptions' of academic engagement, and a quantitative examination of current issues in initial teacher preparation.

Nicholas Boke served as director of programs for the Vermont Center for the book developing family literacy programs. As codirector of the Vermont Strategic Reading Initiative, he oversaw a statewide adolescent literacy program and wrote *A Classroom Guide to Reading in the Content Areas.* He currently works for the Education Development Center's literacy programs in Sudan. He has published in *Education Week, Principal Leadership, The Washington Post, The Boston Globe,* and *The Christian Science Monitor.*

Loyce Caruthers is an assistant professor in urban leadership and policy studies at the University of Missouri, Kansas City where she facilitates the development of prospective school administrators and has been involved in a study of a multiyear urban reform initiative. She has over 25 years of experience in urban education and has held many positions from classroom teacher to assistant superintendent for curriculum and instruction.

Micki M. Caskey is an associate professor in the Department of Curriculum and Instruction at Portland State University. She holds a PhD in Curriculum and Instruction from the University of South Florida. She draws on more than 20 years of public school teaching experience as she guides the development of preservice and inservice educators in Portland State's Graduate School of Education. Her areas of specialization include middle grades education, teacher preparation, literacy, and action research.

Dorie Combs is an associate professor in the College of Education at Eastern Kentucky University where she teaches undergraduate and graduate courses in middle and secondary reading and language arts as well as the courses for the Master of Arts in Teaching Program. She taught middle school language arts for 15 years and serves as the Undergraduate Program Coordinator for the Department of Curriculum and Instruction.

Linda Crawford is currently the principal at Sonoraville East Middle School, and was assistant principal at the time of the research project. She was a middle school teacher for many years and has been involved in several collaborative team action research projects. She continues to utilize collaborative interactive group action research in her school as a form of professional development for her teachers. She is involved with a variety of middle school and professional associations.

Pritha Gopalan conducts qualitative and formative research on comprehensive school reform and inquiry-based school improvement at the Center for School and Community Services at the Academy for Educational Development. She received her doctorate in educational anthropology from the University of Pennsylvania in 1997. Recent publications include Developing Distributed Leadership in the Middle Grades: Lessons from School Self-Assessment in *Leaders for a Movement: Professional Preparation and Development of Middle Level Teachers and Administrators* (2003).

Larry Gregg has been a learner in the field of education for 37 years. Dr. Gregg is an assistant professor in urban leadership and policy studies in education at the University of Missouri, Kansas City. He previously served as director of elementary education and professional development for the Blue Valley School District in Overland Park, Kansas, following service as an elementary teacher and principal.

Steve Hoelscher coordinates technical assistance, quality assurance, and outreach to Middle Start schools in Michigan and is the chair of the Michigan Middle Start Steering Committee. He holds a masters in guidance and counseling from Western Michigan University and is a longstanding member of the National Forum to Accelerate Middle-Grades Reform. He has extensive experience as a teacher, counselor, and principal in Battle Creek Public Schools, and was recently elected to the Battle Creek school board.

Ned Kirsch was Vermont's 2003 Middle School Principal of the Year, and is principal of Essex Middle School in Essex, Vermont. Essex Middle School was recognized as a Spotlight School by The New England League of Middle Schools. Mr. Kirsch earned his JD from Vermont Law School, his CAS in educational leadership from the University of Vermont, and graduated from the Snelling Center for Educational Leadership.

Kathleen F. Malu, associate professor, teaches in the Graduate Reading Program. She taught language and literacy at the K-12 level for many years in a wide variety of settings including the Congo, Rwanda, Washington, DC, and the United Nations International School in New York City. Her research interests include teaching rhetoric and practice, educational reform, and multiculturalism at the middle level. She is the mother of two boys who attended New York City public schools.

Patrick Montesano is codirector of the Center for School and Community Services at the Academy for Educational Development and the director of the Middle Start initiative. He has extensive experience with research, development, and technical assistance in middle grades educational reform and is a founding member of the National Forum to Accelerate

Middle Grades Reform. He holds a masters in curriculum and teaching from Teachers College, Columbia University, where he also studied anthropology and education.

Susanna W. Pflaum, now retired, was a member of the faculty at the University of Illinois at Chicago, at Queens College CUNY, the University of Namibia (as a Fulbright Professor), and at Vermont College. She was dean of education at Queens College and dean of the graduate school at Bank Street College. Her publications have been in reading, language development, reading disability, progressive education, and student perception of learning.

Cynthia Resor is an assistant professor in the College of Education at Eastern Kentucky University and teaches secondary social studies methods and courses for the master of arts in teaching program. She was high school history teacher for 7 years prior to becoming a teacher educator. Dr. Resor also serves as the coordinator of the Master of Arts in Teaching Program.

Laila Sanguras is a language arts teacher at Wy'east Middle School. She earned her bachelor's degree from Western Oregon University and a master's in curriculum and instruction from Portland State University. Laila presented her action research study at the 2002 National Middle School Association Conference. She is a candidate for National Board certification and continues to examine her ability to motivate her students. She lives in Hood River, Oregon with her husband and daughter.

Dan Saurino is currently a professor at The University of West Georgia, and has previously taught at Eastern Oregon University and Virginia Tech, as well as middle and high school. His dissertation project at the University of Georgia developed a new model of collaborative interactive group action research. He has been active in action research professional associations for over a decade, and has authored more than 40 action research papers on a variety of topics.

Penelope Saurino currently teaches in the education department of The University of West Georgia. She was an elementary and middle grades teacher before her doctoral work at Boise State University, where her dissertation project developed a multiliteracy model. She has been active in action research for over a decade, and has authored more than 30 action research papers on a variety of topics. She is involved with a variety of action research and professional associations.

Theresa Shrum is a seventh grade mathematics and science teacher at The Dalles Middle School in The Dalles, Oregon. She has been a middle school teacher for 8 years. Theresa graduated from Washington State University with a B.A. in education and a minor in mathematics in June of 1981 and received a masters of science in curriculum and instruction from Portland State University in August of 2002. She lives in White Salmon, Washington.

Sandra L. Stacki is the middle level coordinator in the Department of Curriculum and Teaching at Hofstra University in New York, a board member for the New York State Association of Teacher Educators, and a member of the Middle Level Education Liaisons. She teaches courses in middle level, curriculum, educational practice, gender issues, qualitative research, and international/comparative education. Her research interests include teacher development and empowerment, gender, teaming, policy analysis, and qualitative and feminist research.

Diane Stanton has worked in special education for over 20 years, the last 8 years of which have been at Louisa County Middle School. She earned a bachelor's degree in anthropology from Temple University, a special education certification from Pennsylvania State University, and a masters in education from George Mason University. Diane currently lives with her family in Louisa County, Virginia.

Sue C. Thompson is an assistant professor in the Urban Leadership and Policy Studies in Education Division at the University of Missouri, Kansas City. She has been a middle school teacher, principal, and director of middle level education. She serves on the National Forum to Accelerate Middle Grades Reform and is past chair of the National Middle School Association's (NMSA) Urban Issues Task Force. She is a faculty member of NMSA's Middle Level Leadership Institute.

Holly Thornton is an associate professor and middle grades program coordinator at the University of North Carolina Greensboro. She is a National Board Certified Early Adolescence Generalist, an NCATE/NMSA program reviewer, and represents National Middle School Association on the NCATE Board of Examiners. Her 21 years in education includes 13 years as a middle school teacher.

Teri West leads the development of several components of the Middle Start comprehensive school reform design at the Center for School and Community Services at the Academy for Educational Development. She holds masters degrees in education from Harvard University and Boston

University. She is coauthor of *Schools-to-Watch Case Studies as Part of the National Forum to Accelerate Middle Grades Reform* and is the author of several articles on middle grades reform and a language arts curriculum for Boston Public Schools.

Melinda Wilder is an associate professor in the College of Education at Eastern Kentucky University. She teaches both undergraduate and graduate classes in middle and secondary science teaching methods, middle grades curriculum, and courses for the master of arts in teaching program. Prior to joining Eastern Kentucky University's faculty, she was a science and math teacher and national park ranger.

Printed in the United States
38771LVS00002B/155